More Praise for Reaching Boys, Teaching Boys

"*Reaching Boys, Teaching Boys* is the best, most practical book about teaching boys that I have ever read. Reading it is like visiting the classrooms of two hundred master teachers who really 'get' boys. Any teacher who has ever struggled to engage boys in the classroom—and isn't that every teacher?—will want to own this book."

—Michael Thompson, Ph.D., author, *Best Friends, Worst Enemies: Understanding the Social Lives of Children*, and coauthor of the *New York Times* best seller *Raising Cain: Protecting the Emotional Life of Boys*

"Reichert and Hawley take us beyond the grim realities of the 'boy crisis' to reveal how some schools and teachers are winning with boys. Here, at last, is the help we have all been hoping for."

—F. Washington Jarvis, director, Educational Leadership and Ministry Program, Berkeley Divinity School at Yale University, headmaster emeritus, The Roxbury Latin School

"For those who believe that the full potential of boys is a distant hope, Reichert and Hawley obliterate that assumption. The authors have pulled together a commonsense and intuitive collection of strategies that work. It is a must-read for anyone who believes that all boys can excel. *Reaching Boys, Teaching Boys* is just in time!"

—Ron Walker, executive director, Coalition of Schools Educating Boys of Color

REACHING BOYS, TEACHING BOYS

Strategies That Work—and Why

MICHAEL REICHERT
RICHARD HAWLEY

Foreword by Peg Tyre

JOSSEY-BASS
A Wiley Imprint
www.josseybass.com

Published by Jossey-Bass
A Wiley Imprint
989 Market Street, San Francisco, CA 94103-1741—www.josseybass.com

Jossey-Bass books and products are available through most bookstores. To contact Jossey-Bass directly call our Customer Care Department within the U.S. at 800-956-7739, outside the U.S. at 317-572-3986, or fax 317-572-4002.

Jossey-Bass also publishes its books in a variety of electronic formats. Some content that appears in print may not be available in electronic books.

Library of Congress Cataloging-in-Publication Data

Reichert, Michael.
  Reaching boys, teaching boys: strategies that work—and why / Michael Reichert and Richard Hawley.–1st ed.
    p. cm.
  Includes bibliographical references and index.
  ISBN 978-0-470-53278-2 (pbk.)
 1. English language–Composition and exercises–Study and teaching (Elementary) 2. English language–Composition and exercises–Study and teaching (Secondary) 3. Boys–Education (Elementary) 4. Boys–Education (Secondary) 5. Effective teaching. I. Hawley, Richard. II. Title.
  LB1576.R445 2010
  371.821–dc22

                                                                        2010007010

Printed in the United States of America
FIRST EDITION
PB Printing 10 9 8 7 6 5 4 3 2 1

CONTENTS

PART ONE:
EFFECTIVE LESSONS

PART TWO:
EFFECTIVE RELATIONSHIPS

PART THREE:
LESSONS FOR EDUCATORS

ABOUT THIS BOOK

If there is a crisis in boys' education, answers are not hard to find. Thousands of teachers around the world have found the secret to making lessons successful for boys. Despite a continuing stream of concern on the part of researchers, demographers, and cultural pundits about a crisis in boys' social development and schooling, surprisingly little attention has been paid to what is perhaps the richest pool of data: current, observable teaching practices that clearly work with boys. In schools of all types in all regions of the globe, many boys are thriving. Boys of limited, ordinary, and exceptional tested aptitude; boys of every economic strata; boys of all races and faiths—*some* of them—are appreciatively engaged and taught well every day.

A study of teachers and students conducted by a psychologist and an educator at schools in six countries—the United States, Canada, New Zealand, Great Britain, South Africa, and Australia—found profound similarities in successful lessons for boys. Using the testimony of teachers and boys themselves, this book offers a host of examples of approaches that have been honed by classroom practice to engage boys in learning.

In particular, the book also offers three key insights into boys' lives that shape successful approaches to teaching:

1. Boys are relational learners. Establishing an affective relationship is a precondition to successful teaching for boys.

2. Boys elicit the kinds of teaching they need. Teaching boys has a feedback dynamic in which ineffective practice disengages boys, which causes teachers to adjust pedagogy until responsiveness and mastery improve.

3. Lessons for boys have transitivity. Successful lessons have an element that arouses and holds students' interest.

Reaching Boys, Teaching Boys introduces concerned parents, practicing teachers, and whole schools to classroom practices that have been proved worldwide to engage boys in school work, resulting in the kind of confident mastery that leads to life-long learning.

FOREWORD

Maybe you picked up this book because you work in an all-boys' school and are wondering how to engage the kids who always sit in the back row. Or maybe you are a school administrator who has noticed that boys make up the majority of behavioral problems in your division. Perhaps you work in a mixed-gender school and have spotted the ever-present achievement gap between boys and girls, especially around reading and writing. Or maybe you are a parent who is wondering just how it came to be that while you cherished your school days, your own school-aged son barely tolerates his teachers and classrooms.

For a long time, we pretended the so-called boy problem did not exist. But experts have begun reaching a consensus on a myriad ways in which boys are falling behind. In school in the United States, for example, boys are retained at twice the rate of girls, are identified as having learning disorders and attention problem at three times the rates of girls, and get more C's and D's and do less homework than girls do. With the exception of sports, boys have all but withdrawn from extracurricular activities like class plays, the school newspaper, and the marching band. And boys are more likely to drop out of school. Right now in the United States, 2.5 million more girls than boys attend college. The underachievement of boys in the United States is echoed in nearly every industrialized country where boys and girls have equal access to education.

For a long time, we blamed the failure of boys on boys themselves. But that conversation has begun to change. The phenomenon is simply too pervasive—and in these recessionary times, too expensive—to assert once again that school-aged boys need to change to better suit our current set of educational conventions. Policymakers in the United States calculate that if 5 percent more boys completed high school and matriculated to college, the nation would save $8 billion a year in welfare and criminal justice costs. Around the world, the costs of male underachievement—lost opportunity, dampened climate for innovation, increased poverty and joblessness—grow every day. We can—indeed we must—do better.

But how do we fix our schools in order to get and keep boys engaged? And how do we do that while taking care to ensure that the boys we teach will become young men who are fit to share a workplace, and maybe a home, with our educated, high-performing young women?

In this remarkable book, *Reaching Boys, Teaching Boys*, Michael Reichert and Richard Hawley have come up with some answers. In a study sponsored by the International Boys' School Coalition, they polled nearly one thousand educators at eighteen boys' schools from Canada, England, New Zealand, South Africa, Australia, and the United States.

In answer to the researchers' question, "What works with boys?" successful teachers convey their best—and sometimes highly novel—solutions. Many of their techniques use activity and physical movement. Others stress hands-on learning. Competition is introduced in different ways again and again. Some of the most imaginative teachers take advantage of a boyish determination to show off to other boys by using drama or display to deepen learning. Some teachers take the boys on a journey of self-discovery or freight learning with raw emotion. There are some successful lessons that depend on surprise (one English teacher dresses in a costume to match a particular play). Some, like the geology teacher who begins the lesson by lighting up the lava on a model volcano, rely on pure fun. The common elements are that all take as their baseline rigor, respect, and mutual trust.

The authors also asked the boys themselves what worked best for them in the classroom and have neatly organized the fifteen hundred responses they got. And the answers Reichert and Hawley elicited are moving ones. Boys want clear rules and directions. They also want relevance—a clear line drawn from their lessons to their lives or feelings. They want to be protected from public shaming (the pedagogical equivalent of DDT on a boy's wild and sometimes disorderly appetite for learning). Boys want to be scaffolded while they try and fail so they can rebound and try again. And they want to be recognized—sometimes by a quiet gesture, sometimes with great fanfare in front of their peers—when they succeed. To be successful in school, boys want connection: mentors, guides, and, most of all, caring teachers. They want what the authors call relational teaching—the ability to know and be known beyond a seating chart, a test score, or a semester grade.

To teach boys and teach them well, educators and boys seem to agree that lessons must be taught with passion. The aggregate wisdom of the teachers' lounge tells us that ideal learning environments tend to be conventional ones—a result of careful planning, heavy-handed duty classroom management, and unbending rules of decorum. The teachers and youthful respondents to Reichert and Hawley's survey remind us that to teach boys well, both teacher and student must, from time to time, feed their appetite for innovation and sometimes even risk.

There is no silver bullet in these pages that will fix the problem. But that is because the cause of male underachievement is as variable as boys themselves. Instead, quite sensibly, Reichert and Hawley offer a host of remedies—each one wise but each as unique as the teacher or student who proposed it.

Savor these pages. Take what you can use. It is becoming clear to all of us—teachers, administrators, parents, and policymakers—that schools must evolve in order to do a better job educating young men. It will not happen overnight, but it must happen.

How to start? Turn to Chapter One. You will be taking the first step on what I promise will be a fascinating journey.

June 2010   Peg Tyre
Brooklyn, New York   author of *The Trouble with Boys*

ACKNOWLEDGMENTS

This book is drawn from the findings of an international study of effective teaching practices for boys undertaken on behalf of the International Boys' Schools Coalition for the sake of its member schools. Without the vision and support of the Coalition's trustees and staff, we would not have been able to amass and assess the data reported here. In particular, we thank Brad Adams, executive director of the coalition, who worked closely with us from the inception of this project. His guidance in selecting the participating schools, suggestions for how to shape and solicit the survey data, and his shrewd and thoughtful advice on how best to compose our findings were an invaluable help in reaching our conclusions. His executive assistant, Kathy Blaisdell, worked imaginatively and very hard to produce online surveys that were easily accessible for globally far-flung participating schools, and she was quick and responsive to our needs to view the survey data in a variety of ways.

We also thank Chris Brueningsen, headmaster of the Kiski School in Saltsburg, Pennsylvania, and David Armstrong, headmaster of the Landon School in Bethesda, Maryland, for welcoming us into their schools to conduct a year-long boys' audit, in the course of which we came to see the promise of an international study of effective teaching practices for boys.

Schools in session are always busy places, sometimes worryingly so. Gathering whole faculties and selected groups of students to address our questions cannot have been easy or convenient, and we are deeply grateful to the leaders of the eighteen participating schools, their faculties, and their boys for so thoughtfully responding to us—and thus contributing to the possibility of improving the teaching of boys everywhere.

Finally, we gratefully acknowledge the enthusiasm and unvaryingly helpful suggestions that our editor at Jossey-Bass, Marjorie McAneny, offered us.

THE AUTHORS

Michael Reichert, Ph.D., is a psychologist who has worked with children and families in a clinical and consulting practice for the past twenty-five years. He created and directed an urban youth violence prevention program for the tristate area around Philadelphia and serves as executive director of the Center for the Study of Boys' and Girls' Lives, a research collaborative comprising independent schools operating in partnership with the University of Pennsylvania. He has consulted with many organizations and schools and is on staff at the Haverford School in Pennsylvania. Reichert has spoken and published widely on the topics of boys' and girls' identity development, including strategies to make schools more responsive to developing children.

Richard Hawley, Ph.D., has worked in all-boys' schools for more than thirty years. During his tenure, he has taught English, history, economics, and philosophy, serving also in a number of administrative posts including, for seventeen years, headmaster. In 1995 he was named founding president of the International Boys' Schools Coalition. A writer of fiction, poetry, and literary nonfiction, he has published twenty books and numerous essays, articles, and poems. His work has appeared in the *New York Times*, the *Atlantic Monthly*, the *Christian Science Monitor*, *American Film*, *Commonweal*, *America*, *Orion*, and many literary anthologies. Hawley has lectured extensively at universities, schools, and conferences in the United States, Canada, Great Britain, and Australia.

INTRODUCTION

For more than a decade, there have been periodic eruptions of concerns that boys generally are not thriving in school. Newspapers and magazines herald a "crisis" in which boys lag significantly behind girls in all subjects, drop out of school earlier and in greater numbers than girls, comprise most of those in schools' remedial programs, account for most of schools' disciplinary troubles, and are far more likely than girls to be medicated for an array of learning and behavioral disorders. This gloomy picture darkens with new evidence showing a rising gap in the number of young men and women entering colleges and universities. Demographers and other social scientists are now looking at the cultural consequences of this decline in prospects for men, including their diminishing inclination to form stable relationships and marriages, their disinclination to vote and take on other civic responsibilities, and their failure to find satisfying work—or any work at all—in a challenged economy.

The public airing of these concerns has raised its share of counterclaims —some reasonable, some more strident—to the effect that the "boy crisis" reflects little more than that girls have made important and long-overdue advances in school performance and gender equity. Seen this way, any systematic attempt to improve boys' scholastic and social position can look suspiciously like a patriarchal attempt to restore male entitlements. But to have one's hackles raised by either the claim that boys are experiencing something like a crisis or that the "crisis" is no more than an admirable advance in feminine achievement is to enter the agonizing polemics of what have been called the gender wars—which is far from our intention and even further from our interest.

In a more positive spirit, we set out over the course of 2007–2008 to identify what we believed might be the most concrete and most useful data bearing on boys' success in school. We were fortified in this resolve by our career-long immersion in a variety of effective schools. The hypothesis driving the study we wanted to conduct was staggeringly simple: while boys may not be thriving overall in the educational complex, some of them are. *Some* teachers in *some* schools in *some* classrooms are conducting lessons that result in boys who are deeply engaged, retain essential material, and master new skills. In effect, we hoped to identify within a larger set of teaching approaches that are not demonstrably effective with boys a subset of those that clearly are.

We were confident we could get the kinds of data we needed from teachers; prior to undertaking our international study, we had worked intensively with a few schools doing what we called a Boys' Audit. These audits are year-long immersions in the cultures of individual schools in the course of which we collect a variety of objective data—students' grades, achievement and aptitude test scores, ethnic and demographic profiles—as well as subjective data drawn from small group meetings with students, faculty, and parents. From all of it, we can offer a school a rich, data-based picture of its "boy curriculum" and of how well boys are doing.

One of the data points we have collected from teachers in the course of this work has turned out to be particularly illuminating. We asked all of the teachers to review their current practice and describe a lesson they consider especially effective with boys. Reading through these narratives, we have been struck by the recurrence of certain elements in these reported "best lessons": lessons that require students to get up, get out, and move; lessons in which the teacher embeds desired learning outcomes in the structure of a game; lessons that require individuals or teams of students to build, design, or create something that is judged competitively against the products of classmates; lessons that make students responsible for presenting consequential material to other students; lessons that require students to assume a role, declare and defend a position, or speak persuasively; lessons that spark and hold students' attention by surprising them with some kind of novelty; and lessons that address something deep and personal in the boys' lives: their sexuality, their character, their personal prospects in the world beyond school.

These features of effective teaching have not merely recurred in the faculty narratives; they appear—in remarkably similar language—in the reports of teachers of every scholastic discipline, male and female teachers, teachers of elementary school boys and high school boys, teachers of remedial classes and Advanced Placement classes. We have been struck also by the similarity in the best lessons reported by the faculty of a highly competitive college preparatory day school in Washington, D.C., to those reported by the teachers in a small western Pennsylvania boarding school with a mission to educate boys who need special support.

If these common features of successful lessons—active learning, movement, teamwork, competition, consequential performance, risk taking, surprise—cannot be attributed to the age or gender of the teacher, the type of subject taught, or the age or ability level of the student, to what can they be attributed? It did not take us long to conclude that the success of these lessons stems from their ability to engage and energize boys. In their efforts to reveal an instance of their best work with boys, these teachers had, without intending it, provided us with tantalizing clues to what might engage boys everywhere in learning and mastery.

THE TEACHING BOYS PROJECT

We knew that if there really were teaching approaches distinctly tuned to boys' learning, we ought to be able to see them at work in a broader sample of school settings. As it happened, our interest in identifying the elements and contours of effectively teaching boys found an eager partner in the International Boys' Schools Coalition (IBSC), an organization of over two hundred schools around the world whose mission is to identify and share best practices. Happily, this organization contracted with us to conduct a study among its member schools in the hopes of offering back to them a reflection of their expertise (for a full report, see Reichert & Hawley, 2009).

Over the course of 2007–2008, we selected eighteen member schools that we felt represented a broad global sampling as well as a substantial range of student abilities, school size, and school mission. The participating schools were in the United States, United Kingdom, Canada, Australia, New Zealand, and South Africa. These schools enroll only boys, but otherwise they are far from homogeneous. Some are boarding schools, and some are day. Some are intimately small (fewer than three hundred students), and some are robustly large (a thousand or more students). Of the Southern Hemisphere schools, which represent half the sample, some require fees. Others are entirely state supported; unlike North American private schools, admission is unselective, open to all ability levels, and not all students go on to colleges and universities. Taken together, these schools represent a sample of a wide range of boys, including those representing racial minorities and lower-income families.

It was important to us in conducting this global study that we could see the teaching of boys in the clearest possible relief—that is, in schools for boys. This by no means suggests that the effective practices we might identify would be possible and replicable only in all-boys' schools. We made no such assumption and in fact maintain that the implications of our findings for coeducational schools may well be one of the study's most fruitful by-products.

What We Asked

Teachers in the participating schools were invited to consider the elements of a successful lesson: "YOUR TASK: to narrate clearly and objectively an instructional activity that is especially, perhaps unusually, effective in heightening boys' learning."

We were gratified that so large a pool of faculty from such far-flung places clearly understood what we asked of them and responded with detailed and thoughtful accounts of their lessons. In all, we received just under a thousand faculty responses. Three-quarters of the reporting teachers were male; the rest were female. Respondents were spread fairly evenly in years of teaching experience from one to forty-four years.

We also surveyed a sample of boys at each participating school, receiving over fifteen hundred responses overall that ranged neatly across grade, achievement, motivation, and demographic differences. We asked these boys to give us their name, age, school, and grade; to rate their motivation and achievement levels; and to indicate their socioeconomic status and ethnicity. Then we gave them these instructions: "In the box below, tell us the story of a class experience that stands out as being especially memorable for you."

What We Found

A thorough reading of the submissions from all of the participating schools revealed a number of clear and distinctive features—some of them unexpected. One was the remarkable convergence of similar accounts of what teachers found effective in their teaching. As in previous research we conducted in the United States, these global accounts of effective practices did not appear to vary with structural features of the schools—such as day or boarding, large or small—or with cultural differences in the regions and nationalities represented by the participating schools. Nor did teachers' gender, age, subject specialty, or years of teaching differentiate the nature of the lessons they found effective with their students.

After considerable analysis, we determined that all of the narrated lessons fell into one or more of thirteen categories, which we later distilled to eight. Although we identify the effective lessons under a single category, such as gaming, teamwork, competition, or created product, nearly every reported practice includes multiple elements—as when a teacher devises a game in which the boys form teams to create a product that will be judged competitively against the products of other teams.

Our early impression that there was a distinct for-boys cast to the accounts of successful lessons tended to deepen with subsequent readings and analysis. In the chapters that follow, we examine representative lessons from each of the categories, as well as student responses to the lessons.

THE OVERARCHING FINDINGS

The successful lessons reported in the following chapters share three essential features: (1) they include a "transitive" factor or factors that carry the lesson, (2) the effective features of the lesson tend to be elicited by the boys' responsiveness, and (3) there is an establishment of a positive relationship between teacher and boy.

The boys' and teachers' responses together made it clear that productive student-teacher relationships were essential. When that kind of reciprocity is established, students begin to make connections, respond to stimulation, and set themselves to challenges in ways that dissolve whatever resistance to schooling a particular boy may carry with him to class. Indeed for many of the reporting students, schooling at its best is continuous with their lives at their best. In their accounts of favorite lessons, boys do not report feeling caged into classroom settings until released by a bell, nor do they grudgingly acknowledge a mere overlapping of their interests with some chance offering that day in school.

In the boys' accounts of being emotionally and intellectually engaged by their teachers, they convey a sense of being transported, exploring new territory, and feeling newly effective, interested, and powerful. Experienced this way, school is not an institution or an imposition of any kind; it is instead the locus of a particular, often quite personal, learning relationship in which the boy is not so much a "student" as he is fully himself, only incidentally at school.

Finding 1: Effective Lessons Have a Transitive Factor

We identified a quality of transitivity running through all the categories of effective lessons. By *transitivity* we mean the capacity of some element in a lesson—an element perhaps not associated with the subject at hand—to arouse and hold student attention in a way that leads to understanding and mastery. That is, the motor activity or the adrenal boost of competing or the power of a dramatic surprise in the classroom does not merely engage or delight; it is *transitive to*—that is, attaches to and carries along—highly specific learning outcomes. For example, an English teacher's narrative of teaching *Romeo and Juliet* to his seventh-grade students included introducing them to the discipline of stage swordplay, to the extent that the boys trained, practiced, and mastered some of the conventions of swordsmanship. The activity is highly engaging on a number of counts: it is physically rigorous; it is dramatic, holding even the faint promise of danger; and it is novel. And as the teacher's account reveals, it is also transitive to a deeper, enlivened reading of the scenes in which Tybalt slays Mercutio and Romeo slays Tybalt—and to the play as a whole. The active exertions infuse the experience of tackling a dense, rich text with an altogether different kind of energy, enthusiasm, and appreciation.

This kind of transitivity from pedagogical approach to learning outcome is clearly in evidence in the lessons set out in this book. In fact, we maintain that these transitive factors are central to the effectiveness of the lessons reported, and some forms of this transitivity may be especially effective with boys.

Finding 2: Boys Tend to Elicit the Pedagogy They Need

Another central finding of this study is that boys tend to elicit the pedagogy they need. This point was brought into high relief in the accounts of many teachers who reported that their best lesson was conceived as a result of prior failures to engage boys productively. Boys' responses to ineffective teaching— disengagement, inattention, disruption, unsatisfactory performance—are intolerable to a conscientious teacher. Such teachers adjust course content, pedagogy, and relational style until student responses improve. Improved responses over time tend to reinforce the adjustments the teacher has made. Or to put it even more simply, resistant student behavior elicits changes in teacher behavior, and when students respond positively to those changes, the teacher retains them as standard practice. From this observation, it follows that when boys succeed in revealing their learning preferences, responsive teachers adjust in a dynamic of continuous improvement.

This, of course, sounds marvelous, but why doesn't it always happen? This question lies at the very heart of the worldwide concern about boys' scholastic progress. As it happens, there are clear reasons that boys might continue to disengage and that necessary adjustments are not made.

- Boys and girls in class together may elicit different and even contradictory teacher responses, resulting in muddy, only partially successful lessons.

- State- or school-mandated protocols may not allow teachers flexibility to adjust their teaching to more effective practices.

- There may be insufficient openness on the part of teachers or whole schools to examine actual student-teacher dynamics.

- Teachers may lack the empathy or the openness to consider the variety of student responses and instead proceed according to a prescribed method or an eccentrically established personal approach.

- Other conditions bearing on students' lives—troubled homes or a lack of physical or emotional safety—may make their engagement in scholastic activity impossible.

The good news is—or should be—that all committed teachers and school leaders can identify and address all of these deterrents. Boys and teachers able to elicit from each other the responses they need are well on their way to more productive teaching and learning.

Finding Three: Boys Are Relational Learners

Perhaps the most revealing and promising finding in our study was one that appeared without our seeking it. We had asked both boys and teachers not to discuss, mention, or name individual persons when they recounted an especially effective scholastic experience. And not a single teacher named or even profiled an individual student. By contrast, almost all of the boys named or profiled teachers. In many cases, boys veered away from discussing the nature of the lesson into deeply feeling responses to the impact a specific teacher had made. There was no single quality or even pattern of qualities singled out in the boys' responses; they appreciated especially attentive and nurturing teachers in equal measure with daunting taskmasters who displayed an impressive command of their subjects. They celebrated teachers who found ways to be genuinely funny, as well as teachers who freely disclosed their own personal experiences and struggles. Common to all of the accounts in this chorus of praise and appreciation from students was a sense that the teacher in question had somehow seen and known the writer as a distinctive individual. Especially touching were the boys who identified themselves as frustrated and unsuccessful in their studies but experienced a transformation in understanding and motivation as a result of a teacher's reaching out to him.

It is impossible to read the two thousand-plus pages of these boys' narratives and not be struck by the centrality of relationships in their school fortunes. The notion that an engaged, positive, trusting relationship to a mentor must precede specific learning outcomes is perhaps not surprising to seasoned teachers, but this notion has been notably absent from the dominant schemes for pedagogical and general school reform worldwide. The primacy of relationship building in the learning process appears to be continuous with the findings in the psychological and developmental literature that a mutually trusting and warm relationship between an individual—whether child, patient, or client—and his or her caregiver must be established before progress can be made in facilitating growth and positive adjustment.

TEACHING FITTED TO BOYS' LIVES

The teachers and boys who shared these accounts of especially effective classroom experiences have, we believe, described the common contours of teaching practice that could serve as a blueprint for any school seeking to do better by the boys in its care. Central to these lessons is the willingness and capacity of teachers to adjust their practice to the various ways boys present themselves in their classrooms. Together teachers and boys execute a reciprocal partnership that at its best can be productive and personally satisfying for both.

The fact that these lessons were forged in schools for boys and, beyond that, schools with very focused missions certainly influenced how ably teachers could respond to the boys in their classrooms. Yet we believe the results of their attention and responsiveness to their male students transcends their particular classrooms and has relevance beyond even their schools. In the lessons culled across these classrooms and schools resides a wisdom born of effort and practice that offers insights for all who hope to reach and teach boys in public as well as independent schools, urban as well as rural and suburban, coed as well as single sex.

The book is divided into three parts. The chapters in Part One focus on teachers' lessons and include a sampling of lessons from each categorical type. These narratives reveal the transitive and reciprocal elements that make the lessons work. Selected student responses to these lessons are also included. These teaching chapters are followed by a series of chapters in Part Two exploring the essential place of relationships between teachers and students for effective teaching and learning. Central to these lessons is the willingness and capacity of teachers to adjust their practice to the way the boys present themselves in the classroom through a process we call *eliciting*. We conclude in Part Three with the immediate implications of our findings for practicing teachers and school leaders.

One

Effective Lessons

Teachers from the participating schools were asked to select and narrate what they believed to be an especially effective instance of teaching boys—a specific lesson, an extended unit of study, or a particular approach to an assigned task. We formed no hypothesis about the responses we would receive, determining instead to see what, if any, patterns might emerge from each school's responses and from the submissions taken together.

As it happened, teachers' submissions as a whole revealed clear and distinctive features, some of them surprising. Perhaps the most pronounced feature was the remarkable similarity in what a wide variety of teachers found effective in their teaching.

As might be expected from a large, unselective sample of teachers representing all scholastic disciplines, some of the narratives were nuanced and eloquent, others terse. The very few teachers who announced themselves as traditional with respect to pedagogy tended then to present a notably imaginative and untraditional example of effective practice. In the parlance of educational theory, many of the submissions might be labeled "progressive" or "constructivist," although none of the submitting teachers identified themselves in this way. The language of the narratives was largely free of theoretical educational jargon, though there were a few references to "assessment rubrics" and "scaffolded sequences." Many of the submissions included frank and self-effacing admissions, including references to classes and approaches that had, with the exception of the reported practice, not gone well—classes in which teachers found their students unresponsive or difficult.

PRODUCTIVE PARTNERSHIPS

The boys' submissions strongly supported what their teachers reported. As we read through the responses of both groups, it became clear that respondents wrote in their own vernacular—teachers in the language of lesson planning and boys often in that of electronic media. In asking them to describe a school experience that had been successful, we evoked teachers' pride in their craft and boys' fondest memories of their teachers, schools, and studies.

The stories we collected suggest that teaching boys effectively can be likened to a dance, an intricate partnership: although someone leads and another follows, this is a partnership of both people united in common purpose.

ACTIVE LEARNING EMPHASIS

Taken together, the responses combine to suggest a powerful endorsement of active, project-centered learning: boys on their feet and moving about, working individually, in pairs, and in teams to solve problems, create products, compose presentations to their classmates who are held accountable for the material presented. There is no reason to suppose that the reporting teachers did not otherwise engage effectively in more traditional kinds of instruction, such as lecture presentations and Socratic question-and-answer exchanges, but virtually none of the reporting teachers selected such lessons as "especially effective" or "best."

Men and women teachers, as well as beginning and seasoned teachers, reported strikingly little difference in the kinds of teaching they found effective. Also notable was the similarity in reportedly effective approaches to students of different grade and ability levels.

EFFECTIVE LESSONS: FORMATIVE OR MERELY FUN?

Teachers were asked if the effectiveness of the practice they reported had been measured or whether it could in principle be measured. A sprawling variety of responses emerged. Many of the lessons reportedly resulted in measurably improved results on classroom exams and standardized tests. Other practices, especially those resulting in an artistic composition, lay outside standard metrical assessment. The dominant note struck in the responses to the question of measurability—struck with special fervor by teachers of analytical disciplines, such as laboratory sciences, mathematics, and social sciences—was that measurability aside, the affirming feature of the reported practice was the visibly high engagement of students in their assigned tasks and their warmth of response. Several of the reporting teachers took pains to point out that years later, students indicated the formative impact of the lesson selected.

Nevertheless, a skeptical response might fairly be made to the effect that practices felt to be engaging and energizing to teacher and boys are not necessarily educationally formative. Creating products, engaging in open-ended research, competing, game-playing, and introducing classroom novelties and surprises may be memorable and fun but perhaps not improving. This line of criticism is valid if it can be shown that engagement and enjoyment were the sole aim and ultimate result of the practice in question. As the teacher narratives in the chapters in Part One make clear, however, diversion and easy engagement are far from the aim or the result of their effective efforts.

THE UBIQUITY OF TECHNOLOGY

A word perhaps might be said at this point about information technology (IT)—computer-related school activity in particular. Information technology has been a steadily evolving and increasing presence in schools worldwide—clearly so in the schools participating in this study. Classroom PowerPoint presentations, interactive whiteboards, sophisticated information searches, global positioning applications, software specific to mathematics computations, animation, and historical simulations are not only in wide use in the schools participating in this study; in many cases, the technology itself is claimed to be central to the effectiveness of lessons. Some teachers make the further claim that ready engagement and facility in IT are specifically appealing to boys. A good deal of additional evidence and analysis are required to make a persuasive case that IT is in some way boy specific in its effects, but the prominence of technology applications is a consistent feature in the teachers' accounts of their most successful lessons.

CHAPTER

1

TRANSITIVITY AT WORK

Five Effective Lessons

Neither the reporting teachers nor the boys found it difficult to identify what they felt worked for them in the lessons they selected as especially effective. Across academic disciplines, teachers and students reported elements of instruction that carried the intended points and resulted in understanding and mastery on the boys' part. These conductive elements are what we call the *transitive* factor in a lesson's effectiveness.

To illustrate this transitivity at work, we have selected five lessons from different academic subjects to highlight in this chapter. The students in these classes range from middle schoolers to older high school boys. Although not all of these classes are tracked by ability level, the boys in them range from modest to high aptitude. The reporting teachers represent schools in both the Northern and Southern Hemispheres, and their years of teaching range from three to thirty-eight.

We selected these lessons on the basis of their variety and because they seemed representative of the tone and substance of the larger sample, many examples of which follow in the succeeding chapters. These five lessons were emphatically not selected because we thought they were exceptional or dazzling. In fact, one of our conclusions from this study is that effective teaching—even best teaching—is rarely dazzling. Moreover, "dazzling" may be something of an impediment to effective teaching, in that it calls attention to the manner and methods of the teacher rather than to the engagement in subject matter and ultimate mastery on the part of the students. So what follows here is a series of ordinary lessons, notable only for the fact that the teachers who conducted them found them to be especially effective with boys.

We believe teachers everywhere will recognize elements of their own practice—including quite ordinary ones—in the "best lessons" that follow. What makes these lessons effective and best for the teachers and boys reporting them is not that they are anomalous or, in most cases, surprising, but simply that they engaged boys' attention and energy. In short, they worked.

LESSON 1: "TWICE THE SPEED": A LESSON ON THE PRINCIPLES OF MOMENTUM

Many of the effective lessons reported in this study required building something, that is, creating a product. A variety of these lessons are included in the next chapter. A New Zealand teacher of technology reported gratifying results in conducting the following lesson with his middle school boys:

This unit of work was based on the F1 in Schools CO_2 dragster project, an international competition for school children (aged eleven to eighteen), in which groups of three to six children (in this case, individual students) have to design and manufacture a miniature car out of balsa wood. The cars are powered by carbon dioxide cartridges and are attached to a track by a thin wire. They are timed by a computer from the moment they are launched to when they pass the finish line. The cars have to follow specific guidelines (for example, the wheels of the car must be in contact with the track at all times). The cars are raced on a 20 meter long track (in the international competition, it is roughly 25 meters) with two lanes, to allow two cars to be raced simultaneously.

The lesson started with an introduction in the classroom to the project and an explanation of the processes involved. This included showing the students the balsa wood billets, carbon dioxide canister, and wheels they were going to use and an example of a completed dragster. They were then asked what main features or key factors they needed to research in order to start designing and manufacturing their own car. These included aerodynamics, friction, momentum and inertia, surface finish, and some others, and they were written on the board and copied by the boys. Then the boys were asked how fast the car would travel down the track, and a general consensus was met of about 30 to 40 kilometers per hour, again written on the board.

Next, they went into the workshop and formed two lines down each side of the track. Waiting until they had settled down and were paying attention, I explained the mechanics of the start gate, finish gate, and timing system. We use a simple set of microswitches to start and stop two timers with red LED electronic displays. I then converted a predicted speed of 36 kilometers per hour to a time of 2 seconds. Then the example dragster was placed on the track and attached to the wire. The carbon dioxide canister was placed in the back of the car, which was loaded into the start gate.

Then the students were instructed to start a countdown from 3. At the end of the countdown, the spring-loaded firing pin was released with a loud snap and a puff of carbon dioxide. In a second, the car had disappeared down the track and into the finish gate.

When the boys calmed down, the time was checked and converted into kilometers per hour. At less than 1 second, the speed was an average of about 70 kilometers per hour and the maximum was obviously higher, taking into account friction and wind resistance versus momentum.

When the boys returned to the classroom, they analyzed the dragster's performance with regard to identifying the most important factor to achieving a good race time and what they needed to research.

This introduction led into a series of theory-based research lessons that had a practical example to put them into context. The initial demonstration provided motivation to the students to produce self-motivated work and was referred to as much as possible.

In this lesson, the instructor challenges his students to design a model vehicle that will compete with other models to see which can go fastest. The learning objectives are student mastery of a number of physics principles—momentum, aerodynamics, friction—and an understanding of the competition's specifications and the applied construction skills necessary to make and modify the vehicle.

The boys are challenged to predict the speed of their vehicles given their understanding of the principles set out in the exercise. Because teams of boys will construct the dragsters, they will exercise interpersonal skills as well.

A number of factors are transitive to achieving these learning outcomes:

- The stimulus of competition

- The stimulation of interactive exchanges with team members

- Opportunities for physical movement and manipulation of materials

- The drama of the demonstration—perhaps the most transitive component of the lesson. The kind of dragster that the teacher demonstrated not only sped down the miniature raceway; it did so at twice the speed the boys had predicted. The teacher heightened the drama of the demonstration by a simulated countdown to the launch of the car. The demonstration model raced down to the finish line at 70 kilometers per hour—twice the predicted speed. The boys were stirred to the extent they had to be "calmed down" before proceeding to subsequent analysis and tasks.

The demonstration was thus clearly transitive to a variety of learning outcomes. In the narrating teacher's words, the demonstration was "referred to as much as possible" as the boys undertook their subsequent tasks, which, the teacher reported, had become "self-motivated."

LESSON 2: RISING TO POWER, RULING THE WORLD: "GAMING" THE TEACHING OF LATIN AND CLASSICAL CULTURE

The teachers participating in this study reported a variety of successes in converting all kinds of scholastic work—from mastering rudiments of foreign language to reviewing extensive sweeps of material before exams—to a game. (The various ways teachers employed games to enrich classroom business considered in Chapter Three.) In this instance, an experienced U.S. teacher of Latin recounts how he and his colleagues converted the school's eighth-grade Latin curriculum to an extended game:

Our eighth-grade Latin curriculum has been transformed over the past three years. We have attempted to help our eighth graders improve their transition into our high school Latin program. We created a new textbook that emphasized a grammatical approach while also including longer stories to translate, an introduction to questions similar to the ones the boys would see on the national Latin exam, work with derivatives to improve the students' English vocabulary, and a threefold increase in the number of vocabulary words. We have incorporated daily use of a Smart Board to emphasize the work introduced in our text and enable the students to interact with manipulative exercises. We incorporate work at the board, in partners, in every class. We use PowerPoint productions to show the relationship between what we are reading and studying as it appears in later art and literature.

Each activity has an element of competition to it on a number of levels. First, students strive to move up the Cursus Honorum [to honors course level] throughout the year. This is based on the student's average. His picture begins at the rank of "citizen," and he strives to improve his status until he reaches the position of "consul," or leader of his team. Lone perfect scores within a team enable that student to claim dictatorial power until his quiz scores are no longer the highest.

The teams are designated by color, similar to the teams that raced in the Circus Maximus. A class is divided into two teams of eight students each. There are six classes and thus twelve teams. These teams compete in a game called Bellum. Each quarter, the twelve teams (rotating each quarter) compete in a game of world domination loosely based on the game of Risk. With each new quarter comes a new map that represents roughly the time period being studied in their ancient history class.

Each day the teams strive to earn a maximum of forty denarii (points), accomplished in a number of ways. Each team's homework is placed on the board after the partners deliberate, questions are asked of individual students, and sight work is completed with the help of a partner. At the conclusion of each class, teams may then use accumulated denarii to purchase armies at a rate of ten denarii per army. These are placed on the map in an area currently controlled, and movement can then take place—often initiating a battle. Battles are resolved through a comparison of quiz scores. There are approximately two quizzes each week.

At the conclusion of the quarter, the team controlling the greatest number of territories is declared the winner, and prizes are awarded.

In this account, the scholastic aim of building a strong foundation in Latin language and Roman culture is subsumed into a continuing game in which students advance—rise in power—as they master scholastic tasks.

Several transitive factors are at work. The instructor begins with an account of information technology applications—Smart Boards and PowerPoints—that engage boys actively in the material presented.

Transitive competition, both individually and in teams, is built into the entire instructional program. Through the Cursus Honorum, gradual student achievements enable students to rise out of the ranks of humble citizenry into positions of power in the Roman hierarchy. The challenges and pleasures of negotiating this passage are transitive to learning not only the structure of Roman society but also its Latin vocabulary.

The Risk-like game Bellum, which engages all students in all sections, is similarly transitive to students' learning the geography of the classical world. The many competitive elements in these exercises are complemented by collaborative team interactions as contending teams vie to advance strategically.

LESSON 3: TACKLING—LITERALLY—AN ABSTRACT CONCEPT IN PHYSICS: THE TRANSITIVITY OF EMBODYING

This lesson, from a teacher of beginning chemistry in New Zealand, is an example of the dozens of lessons other teachers submitted to illustrate the effectiveness of active movement in helping students to grasp and retain a wide variety of highly conceptual material:

This is a lesson on reaction rate—in particular, looking at the role of activation energy on the rate of reaction. Normally this topic, although interesting, can be rather theoretical and is difficult for students who are not particularly self-motivated. Although it is possible to show increases in reaction rate using chemical reactions, it is never possible for the boys to see what the reacting particles are doing. Students often do not grasp the behavior of molecules, a concept that is absolutely essential to understanding chemistry.

This activity is best done on soft ground outside with lots of boys and space. The lesson begins by looking at the simple idea that molecules must collide to react. A reaction is modeled by a rugby tackle where the outcome could be a failed tackle (unsuccessful collision), students (reactants) still standing after collision, or a successful tackle (successful collision, that is, a reaction), where the students end up on the floor. They can play no further part because they are now products.

The students begin by walking around, and therefore most meetings do not involve a successful tackle, so the reaction rate is slow. We next introduce increasing temperature, and the students now run around. The tackles become much more frequent and more likely to be successful because more students have the required energy to tackle (react). This is generally a successful way to introduce activation energy—the minimum collision energy that results in reaction.

It is now possible to introduce the idea of a catalyst, which lowers the activation energy. Half the students are asked to hop around on one leg and are now very easily tackled by the others. We have now decreased the minimum collision energy that results in a reaction. The students will find that everyone gets successfully tackled (reacts) quickly even when the others are walking (low temp). It is even possible to get some students (catalysts) to hold the others in place so they are tackled easily, thus explaining why surface conditions are useful in "heterogeneous catalysis," the process of holding molecules in place in order to facilitate reactions.

It is now possible to go back to the classroom with motivated students who have a good visual feel for the topic.

This chemistry teacher was concerned about the theoretical and potentially unengaging nature of an important concept in molecular chemistry: the role of activation energy in chemical reaction rates. He was especially concerned that students who were not "particularly self-motivated" would fail to engage and master the concept.

Sensing perhaps an openness to sports play among his students, he devised a workable analogy between a human collision—a rugby tackle—and a completed chemical reaction. The key concept to convey was the necessary energy among chemical reactants to

[The teacher] devised a workable analogy between a human collision—a rugby tackle—and a completed chemical reaction.

complete a successful reaction. The novelty and motor stimulation of simply tackling one another may have been transitive enough to deepen students' understanding of the role of energy in reactions, but the elaborations of the analogy—how increased speed of the tacklers (running versus walking) allowed more successful tackles, how the relative ease of tackling boys who were hopping on one leg was analogous to chemical reactions aided by a catalyst—deepened, and literally embodied, the boys' understanding.

LESSON 4: THE TRIUMPH OF THE NERDS: THE TRANSITIVITY OF ENGAGING BOYS IN A CONSIDERATION OF THEIR DEEP NATURE

A number of effective—and affecting—lessons we gathered were those in which boys were engaged by their teachers in a consideration of their own nature and character. (Many of these are reviewed in Chapter Eight.) In the following lesson, a seasoned American teacher of high school English challenges his boys by advocating for outwardly unattractive underdogs in two canonical school novels:

Nothing gives me greater pleasure than playing advocate for two of contemporary literature's oddballs: Leper in John Knowles's *A Separate Peace* and Simon in William Golding's *Lord of the Flies.* To healthy-minded, optimistic, teenage boys, each of these characters, if not a candidate for the loony bin, is certainly the kind of odd-man-out adolescents dismiss as a "nerd" or "geek." For one thing, both are loners. Neither is varsity material. Leper spends his time collecting snails, drawing pictures of birds, and cross-country skiing in search of beaver dams when he should be working with his classmates shoveling snow to clear the tracks to help the war effort. Simon, another "nature freak," who also has epilepsy, has the odd habit of wandering off into the jungle, which frightens everyone else. He goes to a little hideout where he sits and—of all things—thinks! Neither of these characters is the sort of boy other boys admire. They are tolerated but consistently viewed with barely concealed irritation and suspicion. They are what Thomas Mann called wallflowers: creatures of the margin who fall down in the dance of life. What vigorous, sports-playing, outgoing, college-aspiring boys' boy would want anything to do with them?

I love playing defense lawyer for Simon and Leper, citing on their behalf evidence from the text that their creators, John Knowles and William Golding, respectively, are their secret admirers. Attracted by risk taking and daredevil acrobats, and just as compelled by an allegiance to fairness, to rendering a just verdict, boys are curious, then, to observe the intellectual gymnastics they think must be required to justify my claim that in the most important sense imaginable, Simon and Leper are the sharpest boys in their books.

The transitivity of a teaching element lies in its capacity to connect an object under study to a student's abiding concerns. Certain books, ideas, and discussion topics—in an emotional climate that is both stimulating and safe—can be inherently transitive to student engagement. Histories, biographies, and fiction that explore universal human concerns—one's true nature, worth, social place—have that transitive potential.

The transitivity of a teaching element lies in its capacity to connect an object under study to a student's abiding concerns.

In this lesson, the teacher draws on distinctive types in two classic novels: John Knowles's *A Separate Peace* and William Golding's *Lord of the Flies*. He is teaching adolescent boys texts about adolescent boys. The transitive potential of identifying with central characters, especially admirable ones, is thus considerable (and why such books become canonical in schools). But in this case, the teacher strikes an additional transitive note. He surprises and challenges his students by celebrating—"playing advocate for"—two characters, Leper and Simon, who, in their respective texts, are marginalized painfully. The teaching objective here is to invite boys to reconsider their standard, reflexive assessments of these characters and begin to appreciate them in a fresh, objective way: to see the quite real merits of these two characters once their "loser" appearance has been dissolved by the teacher's reappraisal.

It is easy to sense the transitivity the boys experience in the pleasure of seeing through earlier, easier perceptions, of the empowering feelings of recognizing and valuing an underdog, and the possible realization that one might be an underdog oneself—and therefore acceptable and valuable.

It no doubt helps to experience this gain in self-understanding in the presence of a teacher for whom "nothing gives me greater pleasure than playing advocate for two of contemporary literature's oddballs."

LESSON 5: SUFFERING SLAVES: THE TRANSITIVITY OF DRAMA, NOVELTY, AND SURPRISE

In Chapter Nine we consider a variety of ways teachers make effective use of engaging students by expanding their expectations of a typical classroom experience. In the following lesson, an experienced teacher of "extremely low-ability" New Zealand seventh-grade social studies students succeeds in engaging them in a consideration of the American slave trade through a thoughtful—and uncomfortable—variation in routine:

I had an extremely low-ability year 9 [thirteen-year-old students] social studies class a few years ago. We were studying the slave trade, and specifically the voyage from Africa to America. I sensed that the boys had gained no real understanding of the horrific nature of the voyage. The text we were using was dry, and the language was perhaps pitched a little too high, so I decided to take a different approach.

Without any real preparation or lead-in, I instructed the boys to group their desks together in a solid block. Then they had to climb under their desks. They had to make sure that their entire body fit within the boundaries of their desk. I joined them, under my desk. Once they were in place and settled, I told them to close their eyes. I told them to imagine that they were slaves, chained and stuck in this tiny space for six weeks or more. They were on the middle of the fourth deck, with hundreds of other slaves packed above, below, and beside them like human sardines. I described rough seas, forcing the sailors to keep the hatches closed; slaves vomiting, urinating, defecating as they sat chained in the dark. I talked about fellow slaves dying next to them and starting to decompose in the hot and humid conditions. The language I used was graphic, at times profane. I conjured up images of the most horrific sights, sounds, and smells. Within two to three minutes, we were all extremely uncomfortable, and the boys simply had to cope. They didn't make a sound apart from some rustling and jostling of desks even as the discomfort levels rose. All up, we were under the desks for something like only ten minutes, but everyone was greatly relieved when we finally came out.

The follow-up activity was a piece of empathy writing. The students were asked to imagine that they were sixty years old, having lived in the

United States as slaves all their adult lives, and they had to describe their slave ship experiences on the voyage to America to their grandchildren who had been born into slavery in the United States. This was arguably the best piece of empathy writing that the class produced all year.

The teacher notes at the outset the "extreme low ability" of this class, although few early adolescents are likely to appreciate the excruciating awfulness of the oceanic crossing of African slaves, especially if conveyed in dry textual print.

The teacher senses the need to close the gap between the events narrated and the boys' own experience. A number of factors were transitive to the boys' producing what their teacher thought was their most expressive, empathic writing of the year. As in several of the previous examples, this lesson involved motor activity. The boys got up and moved their desks and then confined themselves beneath. Moreover, the instruction to do so was a novelty, a surprise, dissolving the boundary between typical class work and inventive play. In addition to leading the boys to a physically new and surprising condition in the classroom, the teacher guided their imaginations with a vivid, even "profane," account of the horrors below decks on a slave ship. This was not only dramatic; the drama was embodied to the point of discomfort. The drama, novelty, and surprise of this lesson, including the element of embodiment, were transitive to the boys' engagement in the historic experience of the slaves—to the extent that these boys of extremely low ability were able to produce especially successful written accounts.

The rest of the chapters feature many more lessons, most of them transcribed in their entirety, to illustrate the range of methods and the transitive elements at work in them. Practicing teachers will undoubtedly see aspects of their own approaches at work and may perhaps view them with a heightened sense of why such approaches are especially effective with boys. Teachers may also sense the promise in approaches that they have not previously considered. Whatever the case, teachers of boys are likely to recognize the voices and intentions of these colleagues who have reported their best lessons.

CHAPTER

2

CREATING PRODUCTS

Educational theorists from John Dewey forward have proposed that a person cannot be proven to have learned something until he or she has performed some kind of operation on it. The operation may be as basic as answering a question or transcribing material from one medium to another—chalkboard to notebook—but at the heart of the theory is the notion that some active imposition of a learner on the subject under review is essential to effective learning.

Possibly no scholastic task requires a more thoroughgoing imposition of the learner's resources on the subject at hand as does making the thing under study or creating a product that demonstrates the concept under study. Thus, it is perhaps unsurprising—although no less instructive—that so many teachers reported that their most effective practices involved student-created products. Moreover, many of them felt that vigorous creation of products was especially effective with boys.

PRODUCTS THAT GO

In Chapter One, we used the construction of a model dragster to illustrate how designing and building moving vehicles was transitive to boys' learning certain principles of physics. This Australian teacher of general science reported similar high engagement on the part of his eighth-grade boys assigned to create a "land yacht." In addition to the design and construction elements of this lesson, the teacher introduced elements of teamwork and competition:

Eighth-grade boys attempted to build land yachts as part of their junior science energy unit. The students enjoyed the activity immensely and were totally engaged for both classes. The activity was different and fun, and it involved groups and competition—everything the boys love!

The students see a photo of a land yacht and are then asked to design and build one using set materials. This sets up the challenge, and the ideas start to flow. As the designs take shape, groups get to see each other's ideas, and some make changes to their original designs. Paper sails need to be large but strong and light. Wheels need to turn with minimum friction. The whole yacht needs to be sturdy enough to survive the testing procedures. The final challenge is a race to see whose yacht can go the farthest distance.

The students love the races. They crowd around the desks and cheer on other groups. Those with poor results continue to modify their craft to better their distance. There is plenty of laughter and friendly banter. The race class needs to be time-tabled for before recess or lunch as they always stay overtime to race again.

The allure of propulsion, movement, speed, trajectory—"things that go"—was a godsend to this next teacher, a young American teaching physics, who confessed to "having no idea as to what I was doing" as he took up his post. His vision cleared somewhat, he writes, as he saw his students' considerable engagement in constructing catapults of highly particular function:

When I began teaching at this boys' school in the fall of 2003, I had no idea as to what I was doing, but I did know that boys needed to learn by means of doing, touching, and experiencing. Over the first few years of teaching, I developed a project that I have titled "Catapult Mini-Golf." I use this project in my physics classes to teach a number of topics, including projectiles, springs, and graphing. Since I began this project, the boys have begun to get VERY competitive with each other.

The project is introduced about three weeks into the school year, and the boys have two weeks to complete their catapult. After we have discussed projectiles and vector calculations, I introduce the project, and the boys are paired up. Each pair is given the "spring" (a bungee cord with a hook on each end) and told to build a catapult. The boys research designs and the history of the catapult, slingshot, and trebuchet to get their design ideas—they are not allowed to use plans from the Internet—and watch select scenes of different age-appropriate movies that show different uses of catapults, slingshots, and trebuchets. After researching, they begin building and testing. Two or three class periods are used for building and testing. Groups that do not use this time wisely are docked points from their final grade.

There are a few requirements for the project that have evolved over the few years that I have been doing this project. The catapult must be portable, meaning that the boys must be able to carry it themselves. The base of the catapult can be no larger than about twenty-four by thirty-six inches. The spring used must be the one supplied in class. Also, the group that spends the least amount of money on the catapult gets bonus points. This is to encourage the boys to build their catapult out of materials that they find around their houses.

As part of the project, each group must create a user's manual for their catapult. This manual must describe the function of each part, the materials and procedure used to create the catapult, and graphs that show how far, high, and the spring constant of their spring. The manual also must include a bibliography that shows where they researched catapults using MLA [Modern Language Association] format.

Toward the end of the two weeks, the boys are shown descriptions of the different tasks that their catapult must complete. This part of the project is the competitive aspect that the boys really get into. The tasks range in difficulty, just like a miniature golf course does, and a "par" is set for each "hole." Some of the holes are shooting a tennis ball into a recycling bin or through the uprights on the football field. My personal favorite task is shooting a tennis ball through a basketball hoop.

The grading of the project is done in three sections: building, golf, and user's manual. The final weight of the grade ends up to equal one and a half test grades. Also, there are bragging rights for the rest of the year on whose catapult won mini-golf, which seems to mean more to the boys than their actual grade!

PRODUCTS OF USE

Teachers reported similar success in overseeing projects in which students were asked to conceive and create something with a necessary or practical purpose. After considerable deliberation, this New Zealand Design teacher challenged her middle school boys to design a tent that would sleep four campers. Central to this lesson is a requirement that boys work in teams and that they devise assembly instructions that enable other boys to use their product successfully:

I taught a third-form [ninth-grade] technology group a lesson where I wanted to encourage them to think about the user when designing new and innovate products.

I decided to find an everyday item for the pupils to assemble and disassemble while also providing other users with a set of clear and concise instructions to enable them to complete the task with a reasonable level of success. I decided it should be an everyday item that many of them would have used.

I asked my more experienced colleagues if they could help me to think of possible items that are suited to this type of activity, and we discussed the relative merits of furniture, toys, electronic devices, vehicle engine systems, cleaning tasks, CD racks, DVD racks, changing a punctured tire, and outdoor equipment.

We then hit on the idea of looking into outdoor equipment and after a quite intense consultation process decided it should be based on an item that offered the greatest chance for pupils to excel and achieve our goals.

We stumbled on the idea to look at outdoor sleeping arrangements, that is, tents. We decided on this because it requires pupils to work as a team, encourages natural leadership, and would encourage those more comfortable with theory-based tasks to be involved. Along with this, it fit in nicely with the upcoming fourth-form camps that all the boys would be attending, so it included a practical application.

The task for the groups was to assemble a four-person tent without the use of instructions; the instruction booklet would be put together by the group explaining what tasks they are undertaking to another member of the group and then documenting the tasks using words and drawings. These drawings and words would be used to produce a comprehensive instruction booklet for the next group to use. They would use this instruction booklet to assemble the tent to establish the quality of instructions given.

Groups had to decide whether to use pictograms, pictures, illustrations, or text, or a combination of these. The first task was to investigate other instruction booklets and decide what they felt were the most successful aspects of each; this in turn enabled them to plan how they would lay out the instruction booklet.

This project encourages all members to be engaged and take ownership of the work, which inspired the group to show some passion for the task, a timed event.

In the next example, an Australian teacher of seventh-grade geography assigned her boys to research desert conditions and then design an energy-efficient house suitable for desert life. She reports that their interest and energy mounted as they began to explore the practical considerations of cooling and ventilating the actual rooms they designed—and also by the prospect of employing poisonous flora and fauna to control pests:

This task was a culminating task based on the student's work on [hot] deserts. Prior learning involved the students' understanding the climatic conditions associated with deserts, the influence of high-pressure systems, the nature of water and its availability, the adaptive characteristics of desert animals, and how people have adapted to living within an arid environment. The age of students undertaking this task was thirteen to fourteen.

This task used a three-step approach. Step 1 was to research examples of energy-efficient homes in hot deserts of the world. Their research should involve researching and making notes on the following topics: the solar power of desert homes' water storage and supplies in arid areas, ventilation in desert homes' keeping warm in a desert home; building and construction materials used to make desert homes; household waste disposal in arid areas; and native desert plants.

Step 2 involved the drawing of an annotated plan of a desert home: "YOUR home MUST have the following: three bedrooms, two bathrooms, a kitchen, a lounge [sitting room], a dining room, a family room, and a garden."

Step 3 was demonstrating the application of steps 1 and 2. For example, the students were required to use a map to show the desert in which their houses were located, applying their understanding of map scale by estimating the distance (kilometers) between the capital city and the location of the desert houses.

The most frustrating part of this work for the students was doing the research. However, once they found some specific sites, they were stimulated and enjoyed their research. This interest reached even further heights as the boys started experimenting with the size of their rooms and how to keep their house cool during the day and warm at night. Some boys became particularly imaginative and wanted to use a geodesic shape for part of their home, while others incorporated part of their house underground.

The least enjoyable aspect of this task included the design of the garden. However, when they came to realize that they could place poisonous plants and snakes within their garden to deter outsiders from entering, they thought this was "cool."

PRODUCTS THAT ILLUSTRATE

A number of teachers reported deep student immersion in creating products that illustrated the concepts under general study, as did this American English teacher who found his eleventh-grade students especially stimulated by the prospect that their created work would find an audience beyond the classroom—and thus "really mattered":

This particular lesson took place in April 2008, which is National Poetry Month as well as Diversity Month. My class is quite small, with only five boys. Because of the large amount of time I can devote to each student,

I often try to create projects that may ask a lot of each student in terms of his talents, but in turn, I am able to help guide them during the added time per student that I am able to give.

The boys were asked to write a poem modeled after one of their favorite contemporary American poets. The main guidelines asked the boys that their poems focus, somehow, on diversity. Their poems were required to be at least three stanzas of four lines per stanza. Outside of those guidelines, the boys had almost total freedom. The final instruction was for them to post their works on the class blog page, which is open for public viewing.

The energy was palpable as the boys excitedly bounced ideas, themes, and potential voices back and forth between one another. The fact that their works were going to be available for (theoretically) anyone to read registered immediately. I was very impressed by how often the boys asked me to proofread their poems. They were very concerned with staying on point and having a consistent "feel" or "flow" or "voice." This was the first time I had every single student check with me at least once before he was satisfied that his poem was as strong and creative as he could make it.

After posting their poems, most of the boys related how proud of themselves they were. One student mentioned that he felt as if he had "been published." Two of the boys said that since the posting, they had been inspired to write on their own and wanted to post more of their works on the blog page. The entire class loved at least one aspect of that project. I plan to incorporate similar lessons soon.

An American teacher of jazz history found that requiring his boys to create a radio show featuring the achievements of a distinguished jazz artist was highly effective in grounding various elements of jazz into students' understanding. Again, the reporting teacher noted his students' heightened engagement as a result of creating a product—in this case, a broadcast—that might matter to others:

A recent project/lesson I used in jazz history was to study the music of four artists of the late 1950s. The class was split into four groups, and they had to design and record radio shows for each artist. The students were all seniors and a mixed group both culturally and racially. From the start, they were intrigued by the idea, and as we started the process, they were more engaged than usual. That the boys were aware of their job as announcers encouraged them to take added responsibility for their work.

They started by listening to the music of the artists, and then they researched their lives. The next step was to write a narrative for the radio show, record it, and insert the music they selected. The students found a new appreciation for announcers, as they found, when confronted by the recordings of themselves, that it wasn't as easy as they had thought. This led to increased effort on their part and an increased level of engagement. This process acted as a mirror when they heard how they sounded on the recording. In effect they "saw" themselves, and that was an important lesson. In addition, they learned the material more deeply because they were involved personally in the project. I think the boys responded to this lesson in a profound way because of the multidimensional aspects of completing this project. It has made me reconsider the way I teach as well.

A Canadian computer science teacher wrote appreciatively about his class's collaboration to produce a documentary film that will have an audience beyond the school. Here the challenge of meeting a deadline, the stimulation of collaboration, and the pleasure experienced in mastering the task are transitive to engagement in the subject of the film—in this case, robotics:

The most successful thing I do with my media students in grades 10 and 11 is producing a ten-minute highlights video for the CRC Robotics Competition (www.robo-crc.ca) in February each year. The competition involves about 750 students from over twenty-five high schools and college engineering schools, who spend three months building a robot, and then gathering for three days of action to crown a champion. My students arrive at the competition to catch the highs and lows on and off the playing field. They work together filming hours of competition and editing hours of tape to produce a highlights video, which is shown at the CRC Robotics awards ceremony on the evening of the last day of the competition.

Several components make it memorable for my students. First and foremost is the rush of emotion generated as they show their work to an audience of nearly a thousand people. Very few students have the opportunity to showcase their work in front of such a large audience, and the response is always tremendous as the competitors relive the moments. Having an outside audience makes the students want the highest-quality product they can create. It pushes their imagination and creativity.

Having an outside audience makes the students want the highest-quality product they can create.

Another important component is the deadline. The movie has to be produced, and they have to show it. Extensions are not an option. The robots are built to play a game. As the competition progresses, schools are eventually knocked out until, in the finals, only four robots remain. The winner of the game is not known until about 5:30 on the last day. The highlights video has to be ready for 8:00. Anyone familiar with movie editing on a computer can attest to how long a process it is. Technical difficulties are inevitable, and solving problems and working together as a team are important. Students quickly realize that teamwork is the only way they will succeed in meeting the deadline.

Each student has a role. One is the project manager, one is the assistant, one might be a cameraman, and one might be responsible for capturing the footage onto the computer. In all, there is a role for each of the twenty-five to thirty-five students in the media classes, and everyone learns his role. They work together as a team, and they celebrate the completion of the project as a team. Of course, some students do more, but they know going in what is expected of them, and the boys choose their role. The system works well for everyone because students know that eventually they will be project managers. It may be for a smaller project that involves fewer people, but there are plenty of projects to be done, and they all take on a leadership role at least once in the class.

The project is intense, requires a lot of time, and is exhausting, but it is something that bonds the students, brings out their creativity, inspires teamwork, and, in the end, showcases their work to a large, appreciative audience. As an educator, I love it.

PRODUCTS THAT ENGAGE

One recurring theme in the accounts of lessons resulting in created products was the energizing effect of sheer engagement in the production process. The quality of engagement appears to be transitive to interest in and mastery of subject matter to which students might not otherwise respond. In the following example, an American biology teacher engages his students' understanding of the immune system through the creation of original comic strips:

In seventh-grade life science, students create a comic strip about the immune system. They create it individually. I have created a note packet that has all of the information that is required in the project. I lecture over the packet for about sixty minutes split between two class periods. During these periods, I show several animation clips that detail different parts of the immune system. Students then do a blood typing lab that uses simulated blood and antibodies. Students determine the blood type of a crime scene sample in order to solve a crime and develop a better understanding of antigens, antibodies, and agglutination by doing this laboratory experience.

The comic strip details an infection by a chicken pox virus. It starts with primary exposure as a child, details the first primary immune response, and includes a section where the person, as an adult, becomes exposed again to the chicken pox virus. The comic details the role of memory cells in lifelong acquired immunity to the chicken pox virus.

Students have two forty-minute class periods to work on their comic strip and have about two weeks to complete the project. Students can do it all by hand or use a variety of computer software programs to draw. Their comic strips must include a required set of scientific detail that is given to them in a comprehensive assignment sheet and rubric. This assignment is the assessment for the unit. Some students love it, and others say they would rather take a test.

Students are allowed to make corrections to the comic after it has been graded. I have several examples from previous years that I let the students view briefly. I don't let them read it because I don't want to hinder their imagination by having them get too many ideas from the examples. They just get a quick feel for the format of the comic. I allow students who have special learning needs to read through the examples closely after they

> have been working on it by themselves for about an hour so as to make sure that what they are doing is matching the objectives of the project.
>
> The rubric has a checklist that mimics the required components in the assignment sheet. Five percent of the grade is given for creativity, and I grade fairly easily on this component. I look for some side dialogue among characters and not just a pure fact-driven narrative. I also assure them that artistic ability is not graded, and my examples are ones where the artistic ability is not superb.

A Canadian mathematics teacher reported a gratifying increase in his students' engagement when he assigned them to produce an appealing compact disc cover that would require their effective employment of mathematical functions and conic sections:

> In grade 11 mathematics, where the topics of functions and conic sections are heavily taught and discussed, I had the students complete a project that I had done in previous schools for the past five years. The project requires students to create an original and eye-catching CD cover for a fictional or existing musical group or singer by using only functions and conics.
>
> I have found this project to be the most successful and engaging project for my students, both girls and boys. Students are to call on their creativity to create the best possible CD cover that matches their tastes and personality while incorporating the use of technology, primarily the use of graphing software. Many students even went on to use graphic design software. But in the end, it was important for students to show the equations, domain, and range for every function or conic used in their design. They then submit a final cover design inside an actual CD case, which must also contain the rough work done at each step of their project.

Sexuality as a topic for scholastic consideration is a lightning rod for all manners of intense feeling on the part of schoolboys, including discomfort and a disinclination to engage. This Australian science teacher reported overcoming such obstacles, and achieving gratifying results, by inviting his year 9 boys to create an instructional storybook for younger children:

This is a lesson spanning around a week in a science course focused on human reproduction with a class of twenty-two ninth graders, approximately fifteen years old. This topic typically generates much hilarity among pubescent boys, who generally have little to no real understanding of human reproduction. Moreover, there is a common reluctance among this class group to ask questions and engage in any type of open classroom discussion on the subject.

To break down the typical taboos among pubescent boys, I elected to have the students prepare a storybook targeted toward four to six year olds explaining "how babies are born." To add gravitas to the assessment of their work, I was able to use the services of my five-year-old daughter to act as audience and marker. An added benefit of the target of four- to six-year-old children ensured that the boys prepared work of an appropriate standard.

The structure of the task was based around group work. The class was divided into six groups of three or four boys, and they were provided with written instructions and guidance on the preparation of a PowerPoint "storybook" to be presented in class of an approximately four-minute duration.

The boys spent the first lesson researching human reproductive systems for men and women from the subject textbook and investigating relevant Web sites. A further two lessons and associated homework were then given over to collating their research, allocating roles and responsibilities for work, brainstorming a suitable theme or story line, and structuring their presentation.

From the outset, I was impressed by the enthusiasm and engagement shown by the boys in their race to prepare a storybook. They were focused on preparing research and forcing each member to synthesize his understanding of human reproduction to a simplified format for a story line suitable for four to six year olds. With only one exception, the quality of the boys' presentation was of the highest order and highly enjoyable and humorous. My daughter was able to follow each of the story lines and recount the boys' presentation. My favorite was a group that used the man's "car" parking in the woman's "garage" and then "mixing petrol." For the one group that failed to simplify their story and had insisted on presenting material almost directly taken verbatim from the textbook, their inferior attempt was obvious to themselves and their peers. By their own volition, they resubmitted a vastly improved piece of work.

Many of the teachers participating in this study noted the increased engagement their students exhibited whenever scholastic material seemed to bear meaningfully on their existing or future situations. The challenge posed by this Canadian teacher of economics to his eleventh-grade students was to augment microeconomic studies by composing an actual business plan:

Each year in my grade 11 economics class, I have the boys develop business plans in small groups. This is one of my favorite assignments because it is open-ended and allows the boys to put into practice many of the economic concepts we have been learning through the first half of the year.

At first the boys try to identify problems or needs that people may have. Once done, they then try to find a solution to that problem that they think people would be willing to pay for. As their plans evolve and we move deeper into the business plan, the task becomes more complex, requiring them to start dividing the task (and the business into departments).

Each department evolves separately but still requires close communication with the others so that the overall plan is cohesive. This is a very challenging task as many of the boys are used to working independently. Often they get too far ahead in their planning and need to backtrack to get consistency across the whole company.

I offer a lot of feedback, but the project is really driven by the boys and so they are very motivated. I just facilitate them around roadblocks and group conflicts, but ultimately the projects are all theirs. I seldom judge anything unless asked, but offer guiding questions to make sure they do not get completely lost or bogged down.

The project unfolds over about a quarter of the year. We usually start getting the boys thinking about it before Christmas and start in earnest in January. They have to submit a good draft by our spring break in the middle of March and receive feedback on it immediately after break. They use this feedback to make any improvements before they submit their final copies, which are sent to a group of experts (usually parents and old boys of the school who are involved in business in one way or another) in the middle of April. At the end of the project, the boys present their plans in our annual New Ventures Fair. They submit business plans, make a pitch, and answer the judges' questions. They then get feedback from the judges on how to improve their plans. I use this feedback as well as my own observations during the development of the plan to evaluate them.

This is a summary activity to see what they have learned about business organization, costs and revenues, government policy and regulation, labor and capital markets, as well as many of the fundamental concepts of the course like supply, demand, opportunity cost, and scarcity.

The creation of a product like a video or instructional manual or a storybook for children proved to be transitive to student involvement in a variety of scholastic pursuits. This American teacher of advanced Spanish found that an original video project deepened her boys' engagement in the course's central text, *Don Quixote:*

The following activity is one I have used as a final class project for students in advanced-level Spanish classes. The students have read numerous selections of Spanish literature and are intimately familiar with characters, themes, plots, and writing styles of the given author. The teacher may choose to allow the students to select from a few literary pieces, or all students may be given one literary selection to use.

The students work in groups of three or four to write, act out, film, direct, edit, and produce a video depicting an original ending to a piece of literature. Most successful among my students have been the groups that choose to create an original final chapter for *El ingenioso hidalgo don Quijote de la Mancha*. Because there is such humor and often absurd happenings in this novel, the students thrill at the chance to represent the zany deeds of the characters they have come to enjoy like Sancho Panza, Dulcinea, and of course, the hero himself, don Quijote.

Each student is asked to take part in all phases of the production of this ten- to fifteen-minute video. There must be ten to fifteen minutes of dialogue, with the rolling of credits, silent slow-motion scenes, or panning the scenery excluded. Although there may be one main director or producer, each student must act in the video to earn credit. The grade for the project is based on the originality of script, the richness and precision of the grammar and vocabulary used, the proper pronunciation of the lines, and the appropriate connection to the original literary piece. The students are encouraged to film in a variety of locations and are given two or three weeks of class time to work on the project. Many students choose to include guest actors and incorporate music into the background.

Each group is asked to present the final video of their original video on the final day of classes or during exam day. This presentation day is treated like a screening of a new film, and audience critiques are encouraged. Each group is asked to make a copy for the teacher to keep while they keep one for themselves.

THE BOYS RESPOND

The boys' reports of their favored lessons strongly corroborated the special engagement and empowerment their teachers observed in the process of being required to make things. The boys' language reveals their pleasure in being utterly absorbed in the creative task but also, as this Australian seventh grader writes, in successfully manning the "marvelous machines":

The boys' reports of their favored lessons strongly corroborated the special engagement and empowerment their teachers observed in the process of being required to make things.

My most interesting and engaging subject during my time in year 7 has got to be my technology lesson, learning and making a clock. My clock took about a term to make but I'm just going to tell you one lesson which made my day in technology. It was one morning in technology and we were making our clocks. I got my clock and started to use those magnificent machines in the technology room. For that period in technology I was using the sander machine which sands off wood on your project. I was also drilling holes in my clock where the clock magnesium goes in the clock. Just using those machines was a great experience because I had never used anything like it before. In the end, making my clock was a great success and I was proud of it. I will never forget the day using those marvelous machines and making my clock.

Boys expressed their appreciation of mentors and coaches who gave them ample instruction to proceed but who also left room to discover and innovate. A Canadian seventh grader whose favorite lesson required him to build a ramp using his knowledge of the Pythagorean theorem noted that his and his classmates' creative experience was not only intrinsically valuable—it was fun—but that it also resulted in gratifying tested results:

What I really enjoyed about the project was that we were free to express ourselves. My group and I finished early so we could decorate the ramp and attach company logos to it. The construction phase took about three classes and then we made and presented a PowerPoint to the class. The PowerPoint was made during two intervals of seventy-five minutes. It consisted of daily logs which we took throughout the project and it also thoroughly explained the Pythagorean Theorem and the reasons for all of our decisions that had to do with the ramp. The PowerPoint was presented on the sixth and final day of the project. All groups contributed to our amassed knowledge on the Pythagorean Theorem. When we had the test, the class average was in the high eighties. I enjoyed this project because we got to learn math and also got to construct. Since kindergarten, I have loved to build things, which is a hobby I think most thirteen-year-olds share. Projects like this that involve thorough interaction help us learn and I yearn for more projects like these in our classes.

Another Canadian middle schooler expressed a similarly gratifying sense of accomplishment in his successful construction—with judicious faculty guidance—of a robot:

[It] was something that was really fun, and I learned a lot from it. I learnt how to build a robot, I learnt the gears and what type of gears made the robot the fastest, I learnt about what wheels made the robot go faster and slower, which had the most control, which had the least, etc. The programming taught me how to read pictures and use common sense in telling what each did, and in the end our group ended up winning. This was something that was very fun, and something that was a great learning experience. I think that the main reason that I won't forget this project was because it taught us a lot but at the same time it taught us to work well with other people. Also this project really was straight-forward, there were no hidden secrets or traps. It was really something that we learned. For example, the teacher didn't teach us anything that we had to learn alone. Instead our teacher taught us everything that we had to learn, and we then had to use what we learned to make the project work.

Much has been written over the past two decades about the need to understand and to honor the multiple intelligences of children—and not to overvalue the intelligences most frequently assessed in schools: verbal and quantitative cognition. And while *multiple intelligences* has become a buzzword among educators, there has been little visible progress in altering either pedagogy or curricula in ways that recognize and exercise noncognitive abilities. By contrast, both boys and teachers in this study attested to the skill and self-confidence gained in the process of conceiving and creating products. Such, certainly, was the strong conviction of this far from eloquent but very feeling Australian ninth grader:

In Industrial Design and Technology my most memorable lesson was when I was in the workshop in a class and we were just starting our Dove Tail box job. I had been told how to cut a dove tail joint and my teacher was extremely motivating. Because of this I was now able to create great wood work jobs. Once I had finished my job I showed my teacher and I was congratulated because of my good effort and job completion. This class motivates me every time I am in Industrial Design and Technology because I have a great feeling of being able to create something with a good accomplishment. With a great teacher who is very nice and smart and the subject, it made me way more confident because my teacher trusted me to do a good job and allowed me to create an even better job than what I could ever create. This subject is my favorite subject in school and I find it incredibly engaging when doing a job. This subject makes me enjoy school a whole lot more because doing wood work is a lot of fun and it makes you feel very happy when you complete a job. I feel that Industrial Design and Technology is a great subject and this lesson is very memorable because I created something that actually was good to me and my teacher.

CHAPTER

3

LESSONS AS GAMES

Many teachers' reported devising a game or adapting an existing game to advance a variety of scholastic aims. There are obvious reasons that the introduction of a game in a scholastic setting might appeal to boys—as a break in routine, as an outlet for competitive spirit, as sheer fun. Those aspects of games were clearly apparent in many of the lessons reported, but teachers did not typically employ them for their own sake. We were struck by the range and variety of learning outcomes claimed for the game-playing activities and also by the positive results teachers reported in employing games to advance necessary but often tedious course work, especially memorization of foundational skills and material: basic grammar, spelling, vocabulary, and review for examinations. Enjoyable as many of the lessons using games appear to have been, it is the transitive capacity of the game to stimulate and enhance essential learning that impressed the teachers.

GAMES FOR FOUNDATIONAL SKILLS

Learning foundational skills necessary to do advanced work in any school subject is often met with resistance by students who do not see the point of mastering them. Many teachers reported success—even their best success—in devising games that overcame such resistance.

This New Zealand classics teacher reported success in gaming the process of reviewing Latin grammar:

In Latin, I decided to make a competitive game of grammar review before examinations (students versus me). I place verb/noun forms for conjugating/declining on the board, and I get them up to the board to answer them. Each form they get wrong is point(s) to me, each correct form a point to them. I ensure that the game is always close by taking off points for untucked shirts, socks down, and so on.

In this way, the game is always close, and thus competitive. It rewards them for getting answers right, which should encourage learning. I build it up, stating that I've never lost and that they could be the first class to beat me, but "only if you know your Latin!"

They love the competitive nature of it, and when used sparingly, it is an effective tool for encouraging necessary learning in a fun way.

A New Zealand English teacher reported strengthening the spelling skills of weaker students through the creation of crossword puzzles—which proved to be unsolvable unless the entries were spelled correctly:

I have been teaching a group of year 10 boys who struggle with English. One area where I have focused is their spelling. Each week I give out a spelling list that they are to learn for a test the following week.

Each list is made up of twenty words: fifteen words are teacher chosen, and the other five are words that they have spelled wrong throughout the course of the week. For the teacher-chosen words, I have worked alongside their science teacher picking chemicals and other terms that they need to know how to spell. This gives continuity between subjects.

After giving out the list, I also make sure they have an understanding of the meaning and context in which the word should be used. I have used a range of activities to do this, including filling in the gaps in sentences, searching the dictionary online or the book, and looking through articles to see words in use.

One activity that I found particularly useful was to get the boys to create their own crosswords. They needed to make sure the spelling was correct, and they used this correct meaning of the word as a clue. The boys created the crosswords on puzzlemaker.discoveryeducation.com.

The boys finished their crosswords and printed them out. We then had a competition on who could complete the crossword in the fastest amount of time.

This activity showed me a number of things: those who could not spell the words properly could not put the crossword together properly, and those who didn't understand the context also couldn't make it work—this was the same for both the maker of the crossword and the answerer.

This activity was really simplistic, but I found that the competition and the interaction with the computer really engaged the boys and gave them a fun alternative to learning spelling.

An American teacher of Spanish reports the effective employment of a game designed to speed and deepen her eighth graders' mastery of verb conjugations. The game she devises incorporates a number of transitive elements, including teamwork, competition, and active physical movement:

As the eighth-grade Spanish teacher, I understand that not all of my students share the joy I get from conjugating verbs. So when they've got to memorize the conjugations of several verbs at once, I like to use an activity we call *Terminamos*. As part of a team, the boys try to conjugate a given verb more quickly than their classmates on the opposing team.

As a first step, usually the students and I go over the verbs and practice the conjugations. This usually starts with the boys writing the verbs in their notes, then practicing them aloud, and finally using a rapid-guess quiz approach (sometimes with a ball) in which I "throw" a verb and a verb form at a student and encourage a quick, accurate response.

The night after I've presented the verbs, the students usually do several short assignments that help them practice using the verb forms in context. These usually include an activity in which they choose between two verb forms to complete a sentence, then an activity in which they fill a blank with the best possible form of an appropriate verb, and finally they use the verbs to complete a short writing task.

A day or two after the students see the verbs for the first time, we play *Terminamos*, an activity that the students have come to anticipate eagerly. I divide the boys into two teams. We move the desks to the sides of the room, and the teams line up at the back wall, about fifteen feet from the whiteboard. I give the first boy in each line a marker, and I remind them of the rules. First, it's a silent game. If a member of team A talks, a point goes to the other team. Second, students may walk fast, but they may not run.

I start the activity off by giving the boys a verb in English. The boy first in line on each team speed-walks to the board and writes the first-person-singular conjugation of the verb or, if he doesn't know it, taps the board. Once he's finished writing, he speed-walks back to his team and hands off the marker (like a baton) to the next boy in line. The second boy then speed-walks to the board and checks the first boy's work, corrects any errors, and then adds the next part of the conjugation below.

When the team finishes the conjugation, the last boy to write speed-walks back to his team, which yells, *"Terminamos!"* (we finished!). I then come to the board and check that team's work. If it's correct, that team gets a point. If not, I advise both teams to keep playing.

At the end of the class, the team with the most points wins the game. Sometimes I give the winning team a piece of candy, and other times the losing team puts the desks back in order. The boys always have positive feedback about this game, and it certainly adds a little excitement to grammar study.

A South African teacher whose duties are to support weaker students' study skills found that an improvised "horse race" was an especially effective way to promote his boys' comprehension of their daily reading assignments. Once again, there is an element of active, on-your-feet movement in this game:

The boys had been required to read a particular text for homework. I needed to check their comprehension before moving on with the text. Instead of giving them the usual "written comprehension exercise," we played a horse-racing game. Boys were divided into pairs and assigned a distinctive postcard: a printed quiz with space left for the answer and a copy of the text being studied. Postcards were lined up on the left-hand side of the board, with the number of columns across the board matching the number of questions asked in the race. The rules are that both boys look up the answer together; only one question can be completed at a time; one boy is the appointed scribe for the answers, and the other is the "runner." When they have an answer, the runner takes the written answer to the teacher; the teacher decides whether it's correct. If it's correct, the runner gets to move his postcard/horse forward.

GAMING DIFFICULT OPERATIONS

A number of teachers reported the efficacy of gaming not just foundational skills but especially difficult or challenging operations, as did this New Zealand classics teacher:

A difficult aspect for third formers in Latin is learning declension patterns (five declensions, with singular and plural forms). I found boys respond well to turning this into a competition, where they are challenged to beat the "world record" for reciting these declensions aloud (in front of the class). I then turned this into an interclass competition with another class at the same level. Each class put forward its three fastest decliners (plus the teacher), and a special competition was held. Classes were encouraged to make up their own supporters' chants in Latin, so the event took on the character of a sporting fixture. The teachers were included in the teams so that a class identity or cohesion was encouraged (not just the students, but the teacher also!). Since the teachers were not as fast as the students, this also enhanced the humor for the students. All instructions and judging were done in Latin, although the team leaders' pep talks to their teams were allowed to be in English. Impartial students from another class were employed as timekeepers, and a "celebrity" judge (the head of department) ruled on questions of accuracy of pronunciation.

Concerned that his otherwise willing students were resistant to engaging the issues raised in Nathaniel Hawthorne's *The Scarlet Letter*, an American English teacher was inspired by a popular sports talk television show to devise a game:

Earlier this semester, I was in the middle of teaching *The Scarlet Letter*, and I began to become frustrated by the general lack of enthusiasm put forward in discussions. The boys were not whiny about the novel. Overall, the boys here value good education, and as such, they realized that studying this nineteenth-century romantic novel was a necessary, if not important, part of their educations. That said, the novel did not readily bring out their curiosity. I was beginning to have to lecture more than I like, and some of the weaker students were undoubtedly beginning to gravitate toward study aids like SparkNotes, CliffsNotes, and the like. Such aids do not give enough content to earn A's, but they allow students to get by.

In the case of *The Scarlet Letter*, the payoff for the dense reading was not there, and I knew that I needed to change my approach. There is always a temptation to make contemporary connections to the novel's subject to entice more discussion, but I did not want to have just an analog discussion; I wanted the student to find a way to get excited about what Hawthorne actually wrote.

The Scarlet Letter is a powerful, seminal novel. I wanted to find a way to discuss it, not just modern stories like Hawthorne's novel, and I also wanted the boys to talk and think, not merely listen to me.

I was watching a sports talk show, *Around the Horn*, when I thought of a way to get the boys to talk. So many of the boys are "ESPN junkies" that they almost all knew of the show. I created a list of critical questions pertaining to *The Scarlet Letter* and handed those out to the students. I then split the class into four teams. I gave the teams a day in class to prepare ideas and evidence for their responses, and then we had three days of competition. There were eight rounds where one team member spoke up for his group in a fast-paced debate. Students gained points for good insight and effective textual references and lost points for vague, inaccurate, or poorly communicated responses. The competition turned out to be a great success. The pace of the discussion, the competitiveness, and teamwork excited the boys, and that excitement carried over to their study of the text.

What I like about this particular exercise is that it energized our study of this difficult and somewhat distant novel without compromising our study of Hawthorne's intricate art. *The Scarlet Letter* offers great insight into the problems of theocracy, overcoming both national and personal history, and humanity's inclination to scapegoat certain individuals. However, the novel is not merely a vehicle for discussion of these larger issues. There is richness in both the writing and the depth of thought that Hawthorne put into his writing. To use the novel merely as a discussion prompt is to undermine its value. I like the "Around the Horn" exercise because it contemporized our engagement of the novel without sacrificing the rigor and the content of our discussion.

A Canadian chemistry teacher reported the effectiveness of a competitive game he devised in strengthening his eleventh-grade students' review of challenging chemical reactions:

When reviewing energy in chemical reactions I created a thirty-five-question PowerPoint review contest. The class of sixteen boys was broken into teams of two. Each team created a sheet with TRUE written on one side, FALSE on the other side. Each question was difficult, requiring analysis of information or application of knowledge. A time of one to three minutes was given for each question. Partners would discuss (and often disagree on) what answer they would go with. At a designated time, each team would flash up their TRUE or FALSE answer. A running tally of each team's score was kept on the board. Each question on the PowerPoint had a follow-up explanation of the correct response. Teacher input was intentionally kept to a minimum. The exercise took about an hour to complete. Nutritional prizes were provided at the end of the class. The PowerPoint was then provided online for students to use as a test review.

GAMING FOR RETENTION

Many teachers noted the effectiveness of an improvised game in reviewing material at end of term or for exams. Games, such as this highly interactive example devised by a British science teacher, were found to strengthen retention of a wide range of material:

Games were found to strengthen retention of a wide range of material.

I have been using quite an effective [exam review] activity for my exam classes in recent years. The activity itself would last approximately thirty to forty minutes, but there could be more time spent on it for preparation.

The idea is to revise a topic or a body of work such as "oil" or "waves" or "digestion" to give three examples from science. It could, however, be used for any subject that requires students to remember a mass of connected information. All of this material has previously been taught, but this lesson requires the use of a prepared resource: all the useful information on the topic written out on a piece of paper in the form of a spider diagram. This could be produced by the teacher or by the students beforehand.

The activity requires the students to split into groups of four and for them to spread themselves around the room. They should be clustered around a piece of plain paper that they can all clearly see. At the front of the room—in my case, on the front bench—I put four or five copies of the resource, face down on the bench. I then explain the activity to the students as follows:

> One person from each group is to come up to the front. On my signal, they may turn over the resource and look at it for thirty seconds. When thirty seconds are up, they must go back to their group and write down what they remember, setting out the points as they were on the original resource.

After a predetermined time, ask another student to come up and repeat the exercise. The aim is to "reconstruct" the original resource, with all members of the group responsible for piecing it together. It is up to the teacher how many "visits" to the resource should be sufficient.

When you have decided to stop the game, you can ask the groups to swap their versions of the resource and assess their rival groups' versions by issuing each group with an original. You could ask them to highlight in one color the areas that were done well and another color for areas done less well. The groups can then feed back to each other or the whole class.

I normally then ask the students to return to their individual seats and issue them a fresh piece of plain paper. I ask them in silence to write out again, from memory, all the points on the resource.

Another British teacher found that her modern language students' review of end-of-unit material was enriched by the aid of an improvised Monopoly game:

The lesson is intended for the end of a unit to help consolidate language covered and highlight any misunderstandings that have arisen on the way. The lesson would ideally be placed before a unit test, where the same language is being tested. It replaces drier methods of reviewing material.

In order to prepare for the lesson, it is necessary to devise a Monopoly-like board with squares allocated to four hotels. Each hotel has a particular meaning—a grammar hotel or a vocabulary hotel—depending on what is being reviewed. Lottery squares can also be added, so that if the boys land on them, they lose a certain amount of euros or, indeed, win some. All language on the board should be target, and it is helpful to write in the middle some key game-playing phrases such as, "It's your go [your turn]." Once the board is ready, a revision sheet should be prepared, and the exercises should be divided into four categories and a hotel assigned to each.

At the beginning of the lesson, the class should be divided into groups of four. They should all be given a revision sheet and be asked to spend the first few minutes working out the answers to the hotel questions they have been allocated. They do this on their own, with reference to their books, and must not let the others see their answers. As an alternative, depending on the ability of the group, the boys could work out answers together by joining forces with other "Hotel A's," or the teacher could issue them with the answers.

The boys should then move so that they can all sit around a desk in their groups and they start to play, as they would Monopoly, except that when someone lands on their square, they ask them a question from their hotel; if the answer is right, they take the reward that is marked on the board. Someone in the group keeps track of the money won.

The game should run for about fifteen minutes, and then the boys return to their seats and see if they can fill in the rest of the revision sheet on their own and ask any questions.

An American colleague in modern languages found a variation on the game "Hangman" to be especially effective in vocabulary building:

Practice: To create a way to use vocabulary within the context of a game or competition between teams/partners.

Example: Hangman. Best used to practice or review current/previous vocabulary, perhaps before a quiz or test or to break up the monotony of reviewing for semester exams.

Preparation before class: Create several phrases or sentences that use as many vocabulary words as possible.

In class: Draw spaces for your hidden phrase on the chalkboard or electronic Smart Board. Also draw gallows (or other method of recording incorrect guesses) for each team. Divide the class into teams of three to five students. Inform the class what the prize will be for the winning team. Explain the basic rules of Hangman and the additional rules of playing the game in Spanish. For example, any student heard speaking English during the game will cost his team a point. Next, ask the students what kind of things they might need to know how to say in Spanish in order to play the game of Hangman without speaking English—for example, "Give me a 'b' " or "Give me an 'e' with an accent." Next, assign a team captain who will be the one who makes the team's official guess known to the teacher.

Remind the students that captains change every round. Then begin the first round with teams taking turns guessing. Award points to teams that correctly guess the phrase. Finally, award the prize to the winning team.

Observation: Other than an occasional inadvertent slip-up when a student is excited and says something in English, all teams generally play the entire game (ten to twenty minutes) speaking only Spanish. They are so concerned about not hurting their team's chances of winning that they work really hard to remind each other to speak in Spanish and to help one another say something in Spanish when a team member is confused or can't remember how to say something.

This American classics teacher, while wary of relying on games to amuse his students, found that his students' engagement and enthusiasm were heightened when he improvised a competition to see which "team" could best identify grammatical rules at work in translating English into Latin:

I find that competitive activities are often useful in getting the boys to use Latin grammar in an active way. For instance, in a Latin prose composition exercise, I had the boys in a class work in teams of two. Their objective was to take a paragraph of English prose and find all the Latin grammatical rules that they would apply to it in order to translate accurately into idiomatic Latin. The team that could find the highest number of applicable rules was the winner. I observed that the boys were excited by the idea of competition and approached their task with a little more enthusiasm than if I had just asked them to translate the English into Latin. They had to think carefully about how an English passage would be stated differently in Latin. They were also forced to review the Latin grammar that they had already learned throughout the year. After each group had finished going through the passage, we discussed the different Latin grammatical constructions that would have to be used in their translations. I am not an advocate of using games regularly in class, but in this instance I believe that the competitive nature of the exercise increased my students' enthusiasm for the work.

An American math teacher reported that his very "best lesson" is derived from a popular TV game show, *The Price Is Right.* The adapted game, he said, engages boys in the most difficult operations in the course:

I believe that the best lesson I teach is the game of Plinko from the show *The Price Is Right* for my precalculus and statistics class.

In the game of Plinko, a contestant is given a chip and has the opportunity to earn up to four more chips. To determine how many additional chips will be given to the contestant, the contestant is shown four products. For each product, an incorrect price is given. The contestant must decide whether the first digit or the second digit in the given price is correct. For each correct decision, the contestant earns one additional chip. Thus, after this portion of the game, the contestant will have one to five chips to drop onto the Plinko board.

After the number of chips is determined, the contestant releases the first chip from any of the nine slots at the top of the Plinko board. As the chip makes it way down the board, it will encounter twelve pegs where it can bounce to either the left or the right. If it encounters a peg that is directly adjacent to a wall, it simply falls in the only available direction (www.amstat.org/publications/jse/v9n3/biesterfeld.html).

By reflecting the Plinko board, the probability of success (bouncing to the right) remains constant for each trial; therefore, the students may use a binomial distribution.

A binomial distribution is a difficult concept for high school students to grasp. By my use of this real-world example (and a show that all high school kids watch when they are home sick), they are better able to master the concept.

I begin the lesson by showing a video clip from youtube.com that shows the game of Plinko from start to finish. I also show clips from the game that rarely occur (the plink chip gets stuck on the board two times in a row). The boys are then tasked with determining which slot has the highest expected value (will win the contestant the most money) and which slot has the highest standard deviation (is the riskiest). The game of Plinko can also be simulated using the TI-84 graphing calculator.

The boys seem to love this lesson because of its real-world application and of its ability to teach difficult concepts: binomial distribution, expected value, and standard deviation.

This first-year math teacher builds retention of course material by simulating another popular American game show, *Jeopardy:*

Another activity that the boys enjoy is a *Jeopardy*-esque game I use to review before an exam. In this exercise, I split the class into two teams and then ask each team to come up with a name. I begin the game by asking a student from one of the teams to come up and answer a question on the board. If he answers it correctly, he earns a point for his team. If he does not answer the question correctly, a member from the other team has an opportunity to solve the problem and "steal" the point. Next, regardless of the outcome, a member from the second team (the one that could steal the point) is invited to the blackboard to solve the next problem. All the while, students are required to work on the problems at their desks.

The students really enjoy this activity for two reasons. First, the boys enjoy the interactive nature of the game. They can speak up and get excited without (much) risk of being scolded for interruption—they can have fun! From a teacher's perspective, the interactive nature of the game keeps the students' energy level high, which in most cases keeps them involved in and focused on the class activity. Second, the boys love competition. Even when there is no material prize to be won, the boys are very interested in coming out on top. And with the object of competition being math problems, they naturally have to focus on the problem at hand and thus review for their upcoming assessment.

> *Even when there is no material prize to be won, the boys are very interested in coming out on top.*

This American mathematics teacher's most effective lesson derives from a popular diversion among sports fans, the game of fantasy football, adapted for his middle school boys as Fantasy Football Math:

My most successful lesson with students has been a project—Fantasy Football Math. I read about using fantasy sports in math classes in the

September 2006 issue of NCTM's publication *Teaching Mathematics in the Middle School.* I've adapted some of the lessons into an eight-week project.

Each student drafts a fantasy team (while staying within our salary cap), keeps track of his players' statistics, and computes each player's fantasy points over a period of six weeks of head-to-head competition with his classmates. The salary cap helps level the playing field, so that even those who are not too familiar with football have a chance to do well. Also, players can be selected for more than one team so that even a football novice has access to all the best players.

Players gain points for passing, rushing, and receiving yards and touchdowns; they lose points for throwing interceptions and losing fumbles. At the start of the season, the class is given a formula that will be used to compute player points. Each week they gather their players' statistics from box scores on the Web and use the formula to calculate the points their team has earned. I provide a schedule for the season so students will know whom they face each week. The team with the highest score wins for that week.

Once the season is over, students also analyze the data they collect to determine which players were good values and which were fantasy busts. They use circle graphs to compare each player's salary as a percentage of the team's salary and another circle graph to compare each player's total points for the season as a percentage of the team's total points.

One aspect I like about this project is that it can be adapted easily. I've used this project with seventh- and eighth-grade boys. Each time I've used the project, I've adjusted it to fit what the class was working on at that time. One year we were discussing integers and absolute value during the fall, so the formula included those topics. Another year we discussed decimals during football season, so the formula included decimals. This project also incorporates multiple skills, including using formulas, reading and understanding box scores, using the order of operations, using a scientific calculator, and creating and analyzing graphs on Excel.

The appeal of games based on popular national sports is by no means limited to football. College basketball serves equally well for the sixth-grade students of this American geography teacher:

The purpose of the lesson is to work on our map skills of a designated continent. A major part of the sixth-grade geography class is learning the countries of the world. We typically introduce this game during the NCAA [National Collegiate Athletic Association] basketball tournament in order to play off an event the boys are already excited about. The "tournament games" consist of rounds of questions the boys ask one another about the map.

When the boys enter the room, the desks are arranged in pairs of two facing each other. On the board is a tournament bracket drawn with all of the boys' names listed in a particular spot. Usually I try to arrange the names so that the stronger students, based on quiz average, do not play each other until the later rounds (similar to a real tournament).

Each round of the tournament consists of ten questions. The first boy quizzes the second boy on five questions, and then they rotate. Next, the boys check the five answers to see what the "halftime score" is. Then they repeat that process to complete the full round. Questions can range from asking the capital of a country and the boy must answer with the correct country, to spelling a certain country name. Sometimes I give a blank map that is numbered, and the boys can ask a question like, "What country is number 7?" In later rounds, the boys can ask directional location questions—for example, "What country is directly north of China?" Once a boy is mathematically eliminated from the match, the match is over.

If we are studying a large continent, we might break the rounds down into the different regions of the continent. For example, round 1 is North Africa.

One downside of the lesson is that there are eight losers after round one. To combat this problem, I draw up a loser's bracket tournament on the board that allows kids who lost to keep competing. Since some rounds take longer than others, the next available competitor will play a game in order to limit the amount of time waiting.

Depending on the amount of time to compete rounds, I adjust how many questions are asked in each round in order to finish the whole tournament in one class period.

This lesson allows the boys to focus on the material we are covering, have fun competing, and get out of their seats, which is great for a sixth-grade class. The boy who wins the match gets to go up to the board and write his name in the winner's slot after each round, which the boys really enjoy. In the end, we have a tournament winner who is crowned Champion of the Map.

This American French teacher reports that her sixth-grade students better retain and enjoy their new vocabulary as a result of playing an improvised ball game. Like a number of the other lessons converted to games, this one involves a good deal of movement—and a ball:

I find that my students particularly enjoy activities in which they are each actively participating. They love to do activities that get them out of their seats and moving around the classroom, and I find that they retain material better if they are physically interacting with it. To this end, whenever I present new vocabulary, though we first go over it in a teacher-centered activity in which the students repeat the new words while looking at them in a vocabulary packet and then complete written exercises using the new vocabulary, we always "play" with the vocabulary words through various interactive games. One such game is called "*Qui a le bal a la parole*" (Whoever has the ball can talk).

Typically this game is played at the end of a period after we have already completed group work that requires them to identify the vocabulary words and use them correctly with their notes for reference. I tell them first to put away their notes and to form a circle on the floor. I then give one student a small ball and turn on some French music. Once the music starts, the boy with the ball gently rolls it to another boy in the circle, who rolls it to someone else, and so on. They keep rolling the ball until the music stops. I stop a given song roughly ten times, and when the music is not playing, that is their cue to stop rolling the ball. Whoever has the ball at that time must then correctly give me the French equivalent of a vocabulary word that I give him in English. If the student correctly responds, he is allowed to stay in the game and is given one point. If he is unable to produce the correct word, he must sit out a round and look over his vocabulary list while he waits to get back in the game. He does not receive any points. In order to get back in the game, he must also correctly respond to a "reentry" question. I keep track of the points that each boy earns throughout, and at the end, the boy who has the most points gets a coupon equivalent to one quiz point.

After we play the game, I generally ask the students to continue to review the vocabulary that evening, either by making flash cards or writing clues to go along with the vocabulary. The next day, they are to come to class prepared to show off their knowledge of the vocabulary through a warm-up activity, a game of bingo, or a pop quiz, for example.

GAMING INQUIRY

A number of participating teachers reflected thoughtfully on the importance of guiding their students into the inquiry, or problem-solving, mode. Some of them, moreover, saw activity with games as an invitation to inquiry itself.

This American science teacher devised a game that challenges her students quite literally to unlock intriguing mysteries:

As the standard chemistry class of fourth formers [tenth graders] enters the classroom, they see a sturdy metal box on the front desk, closed and sealed with a combination lock. Immediately they are drawn to the box, and questions about its contents come from all directions. Several boys test the lock, and others feel compelled to test the weight of the box by picking it up. Eventually I ask the boys to gather in predetermined teams of three or four. As the boys take their seats, I distribute a list of practice or review problems similar to problems they have worked on in teams in the past. During those previous team problem-solving sessions, I have emphasized the importance of each member of the team leaving with the knowledge of how to solve those particular problems to encourage cooperative approaches and shared learning. There are too many problems for any one boy, but if the work is distributed, there is plenty of time to complete the task. I explain that their objective is to discover the combination to the lock and then open the box. The team that does so will share the treasure within (snacks, school supplies, late homework excuses, and so on).

Increased speculation begins, and the boys' competitive natures kick in. I continue to explain that the combination can be derived only by correctly solving the problems they have been given (all have numerical answers) and then, according to written instructions, manipulating and combining those answers to arrive at a three-number combination.

The quest for the combination begins immediately. Team leaders delegate problems to team members in various ways, and the boys begin to work. The environment is dynamic: boys are encouraging each other, helping teammates who are struggling, reporting their progress, projecting themselves as the winner, playfully taunting other teams. Finally one team approaches with a possible combination. The sound level in the room drops noticeably as many eyes focus on the box, although some boys continue working with confidence that the secret combination has not been found on the first attempt. The first team tries its combination, pulls down on the lock, and nothing happens. Cheers erupt from the others as they all reengage, while disappointment is evident from the previously hopeful team. The team leader brings me the combination, and I offer feedback such as, "The first and third numbers are correct." He returns to his team, and they work to find the error. Eventually the combination is discovered and the box opened. The victors claim their treasure (often sharing it with the class) and return to their seats. We talk about which problems were most difficult and why, what strategies were most effective, and the importance of all teammates being as prepared as possible. As class ends, claims of "We'll win next time," and discussion of how to be better prepared when the next box appears follow the boys into the hallways and can continue for quite some time.

This Canadian mathematics teacher invites her eighth-grade students to higher-order inquiry by challenging them to devise an algebraic "Scrabble" game, in which the very nature of algebra must necessarily be considered:

At the end of the algebra unit, I had the students create an algebra Scrabble game. This took four to five seventy-five-minute periods.

The preparation for this activity was twofold. First, we began by discussing traditional Scrabble: rules, procedure of play, scoring, game board, and so on. Second, we summarized all the algebra covered in the two years these students had been learning it—for example, simplifying, solving, and exponent rules. Within this discussion, we characterized which aspects of algebra were the trickiest.

The students selected their own groups of four. Then they were given guidelines on how to create their own game. The guidelines were written on a handout but were just that: "guidelines." Nothing was set in stone. The handout contained a handful of suggestions, but each group was encouraged to be creative. In addition, they were given a marking rubric for the final product that clearly depicted what I was looking for in presentation, teamwork, methodology, and final product.

Supplied with materials, the students selected the size of their game board and how many playing squares they wanted. Some groups took the initiative to add special squares to the board for "double-point" or "triple-point" scores.

The next step consisted of making the playing tiles. These had to match the size of the squares on the board and were sorted by color. Each color tile represented something unique: integers, operators, equal signs, or variables. Considering that the procedure the students were presented with were merely guidelines, some students added exponents as possible tiles, as well as fractions.

The third stage took the longest. The students had to derive their own rules for their respective games. How would play proceed? How would scores be tallied? Most groups chose that a player's turn would consist of putting down a complete one-variable algebraic equation. This player would replace the types of tiles used in his play from a supply pile on the side of the game board. The next player had to solve the equation just put down before he could play an equation. If he solved it incorrectly, he lost his turn, and play moved to the next player. The player who correctly solved the equation then got his chance to put down an equation, stringing it to an equation already on the board.

Scoring also varied from group to group. Most groups decided that a player would be awarded a certain number of points for solving an equation correctly. This was a flat amount. If an answer was incorrect, the player would lose points—for example, a player earned five points for correctly solving but lost three for incorrectly solving. Other groups issued the value of the variable solved for as the points for that player. Either way, every student was very aware of the equations he was putting down on the board; he did not want to give points away to the next player. The equations had to be difficult enough not to be a giveaway, but players were restricted to what was in their hand during the moment of play.

The groups were asked to type up their respective rules in a formal manner. Some chose to make booklet with diagrams, as seen in a real board game. Once completed, the boards were set up in the classroom and were used as a study tool before the algebra unit test. The groups got to play each other's games.

An American physics teacher devised an intriguing game of dice that cannot be resolved—or "won"—without engaging in the deductive thinking and pattern recognition that characterize true scientific inquiry:

One of the big ideas that I try to convey to my introduction to physics students in the first semester of their sophomore year is that scientists often look for patterns in nature in order to understand how a particular phenomenon works. Finding patterns is a skill that requires critical thinking and problem-solving skills, so I introduce a couple of activities in which the student is given the opportunity to try and develop the skill set of finding patterns.

The first activity involves a game called "Petals Around the Rose" that uses rolls of five dice. The only rule of the game is that you can't tell someone else how to play it once you figure out how to play it yourself. The

I know the activity is engaging because the students who didn't get it by the end of class continue to work on it until they do.

only clue to how to play the game is the title of the game itself, and the students receive six sample rolls of the dice with a corresponding numerical answer. By looking at the sample rolls and the numerical answer, they have to deduce the answer to subsequent rolls by seeing the pattern in the previous examples. It is a challenging puzzle that is surprisingly simple, but it requires the student to test and eliminate a large number of possible solutions. Some students find the pattern within minutes, and others struggle with it until the bell rings. I know the activity is engaging because the students who didn't get it by the end of class continue to work on it until they do. I've had some boys work on the puzzle for days.

GAMING A PROCESS

Sweeping expanses of history, the confluence of current events, and the complex interactions of multiple variables of any kind can overwhelm students. Some teachers felt they had successfully engaged students, even younger ones, in the magnitude and intricacy of such processes by asking them to play a component part, as a competitor in a game. Such was this American geography teacher's approach to teaching his sixth-grade boys about African nation building:

In our sixth-grade geography curriculum, we spend the final weeks of our year exploring Africa's past. We focus on the idea of exploitation as we note the slave trade and era of European imperialism in Africa.

In groups of four, each group was assigned a European nation (Germany, England, Denmark, France, and so on). The boys battle for control of different nations in Africa. After memorizing the location of each nation, they fight to acquire control of nations. I place a blank map of Africa on the Smart Board, and tap a ruler to a nation. The group that provides the name of the country first gains control of it. I then mark that country with the group's assigned color. After all the nations are taken off the board, the group's next task is to figure out the resources that they have acquired by gaining control of such nations. They refer to the back of their textbook to find information about each nation's resources as they record their commodities.

From there, they estimate the number of people they will now govern, the various ethnic groups, and different languages spoken. In this part of the activity, they begin to realize that there will be obvious difficulties to try and keep these diverse nations controlled under their imperialist rule: the people who inhabit the land.

The final part of the activity involves a point system I designed that weighs the pros and cons of imperialism for the imperialist country. Points are awarded for natural resources and deducted for multiple languages and ethnic groups to show that while acquiring resources from Africa is beneficial to these European nations, there are difficulties as well.

The boys are given the chance to drop countries they consider "not worth the trouble" and focus on areas where the pros outweigh the cons. They often find that the most valuable countries in their game match up with the nations coveted historically by Europeans.

In conclusion, the boys are asked whether revolts and uprisings will potentially ensue in their regions of control. They are also asked how African tribes and peoples would respond to imperialist rule. Through these questions, the boys see that while the game being played in class is a numbers game, in large part about benefiting the European country, the people who are native to such African regions are being entirely ignored. I reference that this game is not too different from the game played by such European powers years ago.

I wrap up the activity by asking what made these Europeans think that imperialism and the exploitation of African resources for economic gain were justifiable. Many conclude that they spread their rule because they believed they were superior and thus had the "right" to expand their empire globally to enlighten those they consider inferior. Some conclude more directly that they needed to keep their nation competitive during European global expansion in a rat race.

This activity is effective because it gets the boys thinking about competition and acquisition of resources as it begins as a fight for "the most." However, it ends as a reflective discussion of "why this happened" and addresses the victims—those who were first ignored.

In the end, the boys have learned about Africa's nations, many of its resources, and European exploitation and imperialism in Africa through an interactive group activity.

A Canadian teacher of mathematics and computer science found that she was able to exploit the attraction computer games held for her programming students in a way that enabled them to see and ultimately master the processes that produced them:

> Computer programming is a complex activity involving understanding of commands, syntax, algorithm development, and debugging skills for both syntax and logic errors. It can be taught slowly with drill and practice and repetition of commands, but I have found that I can teach a great deal of material quickly by using games as the basis for student assignments. Not only do we cover the material quickly, but students have a thorough understanding of the programming constructs. This is because they are completely enthralled by programming their own computer games. Boys, in particular, are easily "hooked" on video games, and although the games they create are crude in comparison to the games they purchase and play, they are still quite motivated to learn how to add functionality and features to their games.
>
> In the past, I have used commerce-type applications for teaching programming (for example, a bank interface) but nothing else seems to get the students' interest more than games. They become very involved in the assignments, help each other out, and ask far more questions—they are insistent about learning. A cross-curricular effect is the need to bring in math skills to develop more sophisticated animations.
>
> The games involve simple animation with user interaction and scores. Students can be creative by adding their own features. Two of the most successful assignments use a race game involving shapes and a very simple "space invaders" type of game. I start by introducing the idea of an algorithm; then the students watch me create partial programs on the projector. For example, I show them how to make a shape move, and then they do it. Initially they copy my code. Then I ask them to make variations on the program (move in a different direction, speed up or slow down, loop the animation, and so on). By this time, they understand how the animation works.
>
> A second step involves decisions using if statements and introducing variables to control actions. With these three concepts, along with simple input and output functions, they can program games.

This unit is successful because it is very student centered and involves the students in "doing" something. Initially the classes are mostly lecture. After two classes of copying my demonstrations, they start to put the pieces together and begin working more independently. As the unit progresses, they spend more time in class working on their assignments and learn by doing. I become a coach working with students individually.

Debugging takes up quite a bit of time as students test their programs. This encourages independent thinking, and I help by asking leading questions to find the problem. This shows them that they know the answers and models a problem-solving structure for them.

I don't believe many of our students go on to become computer programmers, but I do believe that the process of thinking logically, developing algorithms, and debugging programs may transfer to other courses by improving their problem-solving skills.

As a teacher, it is particularly satisfying when some students take on the role of coach/teacher to help other others debug their programs. It is also very fulfilling when I hear students say, "Wow" or, "This is the best class today!" or, "I wish this class was longer," because they are enjoying the course and they are completely engaged in the task.

THE BOYS RESPOND

In no other area of this study was there a stronger concordance between boys and teachers than in their agreement about the power of games to bring new energy and interest to the classroom.

In no other area of this study was there a stronger concordance between boys and teachers than in their agreement about the power of games to bring new energy and interest to the classroom. Even learning activities as seemingly game resistant as memorizing factual details bearing on the Tudor and Stuart monarchies can become, in this New Zealand senior's experience, pleasurably enhanced by formatting the exercise as a board game:

This year in my history class, there was one memorable moment that stood out for me. In this lesson we were learning about English monarchs such as Queen Elizabeth, King James, and King Charles. Normally I find it quite hard to concentrate in this class, but in this particular period, the teacher made it a lot more enjoyable by turning revision exercises into a board game. This board game consisted of a die and a number of multiple-choice questions based upon Queen Elizabeth's reign. The game went like so. You start at the starting point on the board and roll the die and move the number the die shows. When you land on the number you have rolled you have to answer the question; if you got it right you have to stay on that question till your next turn of rolling the die. We did this in groups of three with one person in charge of reading the answers. The point of the game was to get to the end of the game without answering any questions wrong. This activity built a good sense of competition among the class, making it obvious that they all were getting something out of it. I found it good instead of constantly copying notes off the board day in and day out, and getting bored out of my mind when I am trying to learn but can't because of the same old routine. This activity taught me a lot about the topic in such a short space of time (forty minutes) and got me highly motivated.

This British tenth grader appreciated an improvised game's capacity to draw out the creativity necessary to dramatic performance. Such games also led this boy to dramatic activity outside school:

One of my favorite lessons was a Drama lesson, in which we had speech lessons. During this time we played a variety of games to improve our public speaking skills. Seeing as it was early on in the term it helped everyone to get to know their fellow classmates and generally have a laugh. One of the games required us to stand in a circle and try and describe our first day of life. Personally I found this very interesting because it really allowed people to show off their imaginative side, and for some of us their funny side as well. There were only about eight of us in this Drama class so you really felt like you were learning something because there were not twenty boys shouting for attention from the teacher, but a smaller group all gaining a solid and fun learning experience.

Another game involved passing a tennis ball around the room and when you caught it you had to say one word to add to the story, and after a few minutes we had built up quite an interesting story with different parts reflecting on the variety of characters in the group.

Unfortunately we do not take Drama in year ten any more, which is a shame. But those lessons really got me into some out-of-school drama activities. I believe those lessons build up confidence for later life, and have definitely helped me in social activities as well as some things in school. I would definitely recommend those drama lessons to anyone at the school, because of the skills you can learn there.

Students as well as teachers noted how well games enhance routine yet essential classroom work such as reviewing for examinations, as this American biology student writes:

The experience that stands out for me the most during my time at this school occurred during my ninth grade year in Biology Class. We had a test the following Friday, and we were thinking of a way to study most effectively. My Biology teacher decided that we should play a review game that is fun and effective at the same time. The teacher described to us a game called "Trashball," where the separate teams (three or four students) were asked questions, and if they got the question right, they could shoot a ball of tape into a trash can for extra points (farther away from the trash can means more points). The teacher would read off the questions and one player could answer a question for five points, or get help from his team for two points. If they were wrong, the question is passed to the next team. The winner of the game receives two free points on the next test. My class played this game many times, and my team won the game once. The two points I received helped me boost my grade a third of a letter grade, and I learned some material that I otherwise would have missed.

Students also noted the more durable kinds of learning advanced by well-conceived games, as in this British senior's account of learning the essentials of global economics:

My favorite and most interesting lesson was an Economics lesson at A level. It was a game that the teacher set up before a lesson (double-period). The game was set up to demonstrate to the students how globalization works and how international markets bargain and trade. It was called the "International Trading Game." Four tables were arranged around the class and each table had some resources. The class was split up into four equal teams and the aim of the game was to make the most money. The way money was made was by cutting shapes of a certain length, width or radius, out of paper. Three shapes were used. A circle which was worth the most money, a triangle which had the second highest value and a rectangle which was worth the least. To claim any money, a team had to produce five of a particular shape. Once five of one particular shape had been produced, you could trade these for money (Monopoly money was used). To create these shapes, though, a team had to have resources. Paper, scissors and a ruler were needed for all shapes, and a pair of compasses was needed to make a circle. Each team was supplied with certain resources. One team had a lot of paper, two teams had all resources except for one with a lot of money, and one team had a lot of scissors. The teams with a lot of resources were representing MEDCs [more economically developed countries], as they have a lot of power in the world economy, and the two teams with less resources represented LEDCs [less economically developed countries] as they don't have as much power or money. The game started and straight away teams were bargaining and trading and using what resources they had to their advantage and everyone could clearly see what the game was set up to show. This lesson will remain in my memory as it was such a clear representation of how world trading works. It made what can be quite a complicated theory, very simple. Not only did everyone learn and gain from the lesson, but everyone left the class talking about how fun the lesson was and the fun factor proved essential to the success of the game.

The transitivity of the gaming process seems to apply to the broadest possible range of subject matter, whether contemporary or in the remote past—as in this

Canadian tenth grader's experience converting the progress of Odysseus through the Aegean into a game:

> At my school there are dozens of activities to choose from, but my favorite one was a project in English. Our class had read a book about the adventures of Odysseus and our teacher had thought it would be fun to design a board game. With the map of the ancient Greek story, as a group we designed a board game. There was plenty of planning that had to be done with all of the 3D objects that had to be put on the different parts of the board. The most challenging part to the project was making the question cards because it used up most of our time. It was an enjoyable experience because I had not done anything like this. At the end of the project we finally played the board game. There were some small mistakes in the game but we played it anyway. At the end this was the funnest experience I've had at school.

Quick to note the expansive pleasure they take in classroom games, many students also acknowledge the substance of what they seem, sometimes inadvertently, to learn. This Canadian eighth grader, for example, was regularly delighted to engage in the Dictionary game, as opposed to a less transitive form of vocabulary building. Willing to acknowledge his own less-than-stellar scholastic standing, he holds out—with some thanks to games—the possibility of improvement:

> One of my most memorable things that I experienced during my middle school years (grades 7–8) took place in grade 8 with the famous Dictionary game. Before I explain what the Dictionary game is, let me just tell you it is the funniest, most amusing and politically incorrect game ever, which is what makes it so fun. The whole point of this game was to go in a group of friends that may be large (over 5 people) or small (3 or 4) and we are each assigned papers and a dictionary. Each person gets a turn to look through the dictionary and find a strange word that is hard to find the

definition for, and then everyone else in the group must use their smarts or imagination to try to guess what the word means. Of course, as a group of teenage boys, we tend to get a bit creative in a sense that everyone finds humorous. The point of the game, in my opinion, was never to actually get the word right, but to basically have a good time, and I think that this was the most effective form of learning. I don't believe that learning should be all about throwing a book in front of you or simply writing down a few math problems, but to explore the nature of learning through fun and games and other things that reach out to students of my age a lot better than dusty old books and boring lectures. Unfortunately, the reason I am not doing as well as most of my peers are due to this belief, but I don't think it's too late to change.

CHAPTER

MOTOR ACTIVITY

The role of movement in boys' learning has been closely observed and in one form or another prescribed since the ancient Greek pedagogues incorporated rhythmic exercise into their program for teaching boys. In schools today, physical education tends to be a discrete subject aimed at healthful conditioning, basic instruction in athletics, and simply providing an outlet for physical exertion and play. Little attention has been given to the role of active movement in ordinary classroom instruction.

Contemporary observers of child behavior have documented differences in female and male motor development, noting, among other things, the earlier development of fine motor capacities in preschool and primary grade girls and the tendency of boys the same age to prefer large-muscle activity—running, jumping, riding vehicles: a tendency generally to what the developmental theorist Erik Erikson called "intrusive play."

The teachers participating in this study reported in large numbers and positively on the transitive power of physical movement in mastering tasks and incorporating concepts. Of special interest here are accounts of boys' "embodying" a process under study—a chemical reaction, the human digestive process—in order to embed it more deeply in long-term memory. Claims for the positive effects of motor activity in ordinary instruction can also be seen in the entries under several other categories, especially games, role play and performance, competition, and teamwork.

EMBODYING A PROCESS

Motor activity plays a part in most kinds of instruction, but a number of participating teachers recounted lessons in which movement, including vigorous movement, was expressly and intentionally linked to specific learning outcomes.

This Canadian science teacher gets her students up on their feet and moving to teach her seventh-grade students the various properties of mixtures in solution:

In a grade 7 science course, I had to explain why certain pure substances have affinity or attraction to each other, while other pure substances can more easily be involved in mixtures. The scientific theory has to do with particle theory and explains why grass stains come out when mixed with certain detergents but will not come out with just plain water.

The boys stand up as a group and divide into half (half being grass particles, the other half being water particles). I then explained to the grass particles that they were to behave like young boys of grade 3 age playing basketball on the playground. The water particles were to be young girls who were walking by the playground. I asked the grass particles if they would be interested in leaving the game to join up and talk to any of the water particles. The answer was clearly NO. I instructed the groups to return to their respective starting locations and did the experiment again; this time the water particles were a detergent and the grass stain particles were not grade 3's playing basketball but some grade 7's and 8's. When the detergent particles passed through, I asked if the grass-stained particles would be interested in branching off for conversation. This time a fair majority said yes and left the group playing basketball. After a bit of time, there were not enough playing basketball to sustain the game, and they eventually broke up and joined the detergent particles in conversation. Through this activity, I was able to demonstrate a key component of the particle theory.

Nearly any observable operation can, with imagination, be embodied. This American biology teacher devised a lesson in which eighth-grade boys "act out" the process of cell division:

1. Read about cell division (interphase, mitosis, cytokinesis).

2. With a partner, use the model to act out each phase and stage of cell division.

3. Walk around and ask if they have any questions to clarify.

Next long period

Cell division play: The class is split into two groups, and each person is assigned an organelle (a part of the cell).

4. They must work cooperatively and talk about how they are going to act out each phase, stage.

5. Rehearse.

6. Each group will act out its play with the other group watching. There is a minor competition bonus, which usually boosts cooperation and creativity.

EMBODYING CONCEPTS

The reported effectiveness of physically embodying the subject under study was not limited to scientific processes. Concept could also be embodied by students, as this New Zealand economics teacher demonstrated with his senior students who were studying the concept of diminishing returns:

The lesson objective was to demonstrate to students diminishing marginal returns and develop an understanding of why it occurs. To do this, I cleared all of the desks from the center of the room and marked out a track on the carpet approximately 1 meter wide and 8 to 10 meters long. At each end of the track, I placed a bucket and at one end a bag of thirty [field] hockey balls. I selected one student and told him his task was to transfer as many hockey balls, one at a time, into the bucket at the other end of the track. If he successfully emptied the bucket at one end, he was to transfer them all back again. He was to be allocated one minute to complete the task.

At the end of his time, I recorded the results and then selected a second boy, so there were now two boys transferring hockey balls, and I repeated the exercise. Then I added a third, fourth, and so on. The boys got right into the task, and it became something of a competition among the boys to see who could make the greatest contribution to total output. I had not tried this experiment before, so it was to my relief that diminishing returns started to set in after about six workers, and we carried it through to about ten workers. It took only a little prodding from me to get the boys thinking about why marginal output declined as workers were added, and throughout the year, we could refer to that experiment every time a question about diminishing marginal returns came up in a test or exam.

As a footnote: The next lesson, a few students came back to say they had been thinking about the experiment and had come up with a way of improving their technique, and so we tried it and were able to demonstrate how productivity gains from new technology lower costs as well.

In the following exercise, an American science teacher engages his students in a consideration of atomic structure using three different methods—drawing on paper, manipulating marbles on a Chinese checkers board, or "acting out" (embodying the structure by physically arranging themselves)—and then asking each boy to choose which method worked best for him:

In my class, I spent a considerable amount of time describing the electron cloud model of the atom. This is very abstract for the boys and requires a number of different strategies. We first worked with drawing an atom on paper. Students found out what the atomic number was and filled in each orbital with the correct number of electrons. I have a marble board that resembles Chinese checkers and allows the boys to create an atom by placing each electron, neutron, and proton in different wells of the game board. For the last activity, I had the boys acting out the atom in the center of the room using color-coded index cards with N, E, or P written on them. On the last page of the atom quiz, I asked the boys for feedback about which model worked the best for them in the class. Here are some quotes:

Favorite Model: Drawing on Paper

''When you draw it you can see what an atom is and you can count the electrons easier and it is not as loud.''

''I like drawing the electrons. They were easier to see.''

Favorite Model: Marble Board

''The marble board has a few good things. First, it is to scale, unlike the drawing and acting. Second, unlike the drawing on paper, the marble diagram shows protons and neutrons. Finally, unlike drawing it with paper, the marble board is more hands-on. Overall, the marble board is the best model used in the science class.''

''I like it because it is easier to correct mistakes and I think it is more fun.''

Acting It Out: Favorite Model

''I like acting it out better because you get to have fun and stand up plus playing with the marbles distracts me. Also acting out helps you remember it better.''

''I really like acting it out, because it is active, fun, and shows the electrons moving which makes it a better model.''

Expressing opinions regarding each model, each boy in the class really helped me realize the different approaches each student has when learning the material.

Each boy in the class really helped me realize the different approaches each student has when learning the material.

Scholastically productive motor activity took many forms other than reenactment and embodiment. This Canadian mathematics teacher recounted how his eleventh-grade boys' foray into the practice of origami increased their understanding of certain concepts in topology:

As an alternative lesson/break from teaching curriculum, we did some origami. I found this activity in the book by Thomas Hull called *Project Origami*. I gave them all some plain paper, cut into squares as per the activity outline. I gave them each instructions on folding a crane with their piece of paper, after showing them a completed version to inspire them. They immediately set to work—their hands were busy, and the room was quite quiet. Some worked very well, and others were frustrated by the instructions, which are prescriptive enough to do the activity, but leave enough out to make it somewhat of a challenge. Some students had experience with origami and were done in minutes, while others took almost an hour. I had two other much more difficult origami pieces (constructing a box and a "butterfly bomb"—from the same book) to keep those students busy when they finished the crane.

This activity, in fact, relates to graph theory. When they finish the crane, they then need to unfold it and mark the creases with a pen. We then discussed map coloring and how we would color the maps we had just created. They (at different times) came upon the idea that it took two colors. This could open into a discussion of the four-color map theorem as well, which I was able to get into only as a brief mention, unfortunately. The neat catch at the end is that they are then asked to predict what will happen to their two-colored maps when they are refolded into cranes. The answer is that because the cranes are two-dimensional, one color ends up on one side of the crane, while the other is on the other side of the crane! It surprised almost all the students, and although some of the mathematics is beyond most of them (at least within the curriculum and time restraints), they are left with a bit of a feeling of wonder of the magic of mathematics.

An American mathematics teacher reported success in employing a highly specific motor exercise, shot putting, as a stimulus to engage students' understanding of how parametric equations can model physical motions:

There are a number of things that boys love to do simply because they are boys. They like to compete, they like to throw things, and they like to use technology. This lesson allows them to do all of these things, while we learn to create a mathematical model for motion in two dimensions using parametric equations.

Parametric equations are used to compute an *x* and *y* coordinate based on another variable, usually time. This allows us to model the motion of something both horizontally and vertically as a function of the time the particle has traveled. Parametric equations are frequently used to create a graph for the motion of a thrown or fired object such as a ball or a rocket. In this lesson the projectile we use is a high school shot put weighing twelve pounds, and each student creates a mathematical model for the path of his throw.

After we've introduced the concept of parametric equations and worked through a few examples, we then determine mathematically what should be the "deal" angle of release of the shot to achieve the greatest distance. With this information in hand, we head out to the shot-put circle. After a short demonstration on proper shot-put technique, each student is coached through some practice with the shot, and then we film two attempts by each boy. A meter stick is placed vertically next to the shot-put circle for scale. The distance of each throw is also measured for an additional data point. The film is then downloaded to a computer, and, by using a software program named "VideoPoint," each student can create a series of data points for his throw. The "VideoPoint" program displays the path of each throw, and the position of the shot in each frame of the film is given an *x* and *y* coordinate. These points are then downloaded into the student's calculator so he can do an analysis of the data to create a mathematical model of the throw.

At a more concrete level, this American teacher of introductory Spanish exercises his students' mastery of basic numbers by having each boy embody a number and then engage in combinations on command:

This is an exercise we do at the beginning of the form I [seventh-grade] Spanish class. The boys have just learned the numbers from 1 to 20. They are able to count, and they learned the simple task of basic mathematic operations: addition, subtraction, multiplication, and division.

First, the students count in consecutive order from 1 to however many there are in the class. Each student has to remember his number and represents that number for the game. Then I ask them simple math questions—for example, "What is five plus seven?"—the boys who represent numbers 5 and 7 have to stand up. The solution to that problem, number 12, has to stand up as well, restate the problem, and solve it: "Five plus seven is twelve."

This is much more difficult than it sounds. It requires the memorization of all the numbers and the vocabulary for basic mathematical manipulation. It also requires the ability to hear fine nuances in language; for example, "dos mas doce" (two plus twelve) is very hard to distinguish, since the words for two and twelve almost sound identical. This makes the boys pay close attention and trains their ears in a way a regular exercise would never accomplish.

There are several reasons that this exercise works in the classroom. Every boy has to pay attention. Since it requires the "numbers" to stand up, each boy is on alert. They have to hear and recognize the numbers in the problem and know the mathematical manipulation, since any one of them could be the solution. This creates funny situations in the classroom: you might have four or five boys standing up because some might have misunderstood the math part and others the numbers. The boys then correct one another until they come up with the right trio, restating the problem and solving it.

This American English teacher uses abrupt transitions to motor activity—in this case, forming "lineups"—to bring energy and focus to especially compelling points in the texts being studied. In forming these "line-ups," boys physically, and not just cerebrally, commit themselves to various points of view:

An effective practice that I have employed in teaching boys is "lineups." Lineups may be used at any time. At the start of class, it sets an active tone and provides a strong visual impression. During class, it changes the pace, gets the boys out of their seats, and recharges their batteries. At the end of class, it can provide a gauge for any number of things that happened during the class, whether direct feedback for me as the teacher or a chance for the boys to give their opinion about something we discussed during the class.

A lineup is essentially a line of people, arranged by height, arranged by date of birth, arranged by shoe size—whatever. In the English classroom, a lineup is more sophisticated than that. I ask the boys to come to the front of the classroom and arrange themselves, for example, according to their opinion of Blanche DuBois in *A Streetcar Named Desire.* If you think Blanche is insane, go to the right. If you do not think she is insane, go to the left. If you are not sure, go to the middle. Talk about Blanche with the other students in your group. Decide how you rank among all those who think Blanche is insane, among all those who think she is not insane, and among all those who are not sure. Voilà! A lineup representing the class's opinions about Blanche DuBois!

At that point, I might go down the line and have each boy comment on how he arrived at the position he finds himself. This will involve talking about Blanche's behavior, what we have learned about her past, what she says, what other characters say about her, and so forth. After each boy has checked in, we would probably go back to our seats to continue a discussion of Blanche. Or—we might go into another lineup, this time registering reactions to Stanley Kowalski, Blanche's male counterpart in *A Streetcar Named Desire.* The prompt might be something like, "If you think Stanley's character is a positive portrayal of masculinity, go to the right; if you think Stanley's character is a negative portrayal of masculinity, go to the left; if you have mixed feelings about Stanley's character as a portrayal of masculinity, go to the middle. At this point, as before, talk with the other students in your area to determine how you rank in your section of the lineup."

Lineups can be done at any grade level, at any time, and with any area of the curriculum that the teacher is imaginative enough to find a way to adapt the lineup to the content. As implied by the examples, though, I believe that lineups are particularly well suited to literature.

THE GENERAL TRANSITIVITY OF MOTOR ACTIVITY

Engaging students actively in pursuit of mastery and understanding appeared to deepen and strengthen learning of all kinds. In some cases, the selected physical activity did not have a clear or "logical" connection to the task at hand. As in some of the examples in this chapter, the movement appears to be transitive to the mastery and retention of the subject matter under study.

In the following account, an Australian teacher of Shakespeare's *Romeo and Juliet* to year 8 boys indicated the transitive effect of stage combat on the overall engagement in and understanding of the work:

> I have used the discipline of stage combat as a way to introduce Shakespeare to year 8 boys. The boys are taught the basics of stage combat in regard to swordplay and, using practice weapons, are drilled in the basic techniques. This is then tied to act 3, scene 1 of *Romeo and Juliet,* where the characters of Mercutio, Tybalt, and Romeo all duel, resulting in the deaths of Mercutio and Tybalt. The students are required to act out this scene, including choreographing the swordplay of the duels as part of the dramatic action.
>
> This works very well with the vast majority of boys because they are physically engaged in the action of the scene, not just purely the language. The "hook" of learning about weapons and combat not only motivates them to be involved in the scene but also helps them to be responsive to the larger issues in the play and to sustain interest in what seems at first to be a difficult text.

In the following example, the motor activity selected—passing a beach ball—bears no thematic relation to the task at hand: the mastery of Spanish subject pronouns on the part of seventh-grade American boys:

> An effective practice that I employ with my seventh-grade Spanish class is the passing of a beach ball. It is special because the beach ball has the subject pronouns divided on each side of the ball. Every color has a subject pronoun written on it. The ball is initially passed by the teacher;

thereafter, the student passes it on to another classmate. The student has two responsibilities: know the verb he is to conjugate and what subject pronoun his hand will be on when he catches the ball. This allows the student to demonstrate his ability to conjugate any verb given and use tactile methods to do so. There is more engagement and a high level of energy when this practice is executed versus directly asking a student to conjugate a particular verb from his desk.

Even when the point of instruction is mastery of movement—as in physical education, athletics, and stage performance—motor activity may prove transitive to other objectives, as in this American drama teacher's account of his efforts to build an "ensemble" spirit in his student performers:

Whether warming up physically and vocally, participating in theater games and improvisations, or performing monologues or scenes, much of theater class is about getting students out of their seats and encouraging them to learn about dramatic arts through self-expression. Through exploration and risk taking, students discover much about the world, the people and stories that inhabit it, and, most important, themselves.

One of my favorite theater lessons that highlight's self-expression is a crash course in becoming an ensemble member in a musical theater number. In an hour and a half, students are directed to sing, move, and act in a high-energy song that teaches them to be an integral member of an ensemble. It uses mind, body, and voice and challenges students to work together to create a group piece where every individual is important to the whole.

This lesson comes at the end of the musical theater unit, which encompasses a look at its powerful beginnings (*Show Boat*) and covers the substantial changes leading up to present-day productions (*Wicked*). The goal of the unit is to educate students on the unique identity of this very American art form, the talented people who have and continue to create it, and that musical theater is alive and well and continues to enthrall, enlighten, and entertain thousands. The song I use for this class is "Jacob & Son's" from *Joseph and the Amazing Technicolor Dreamcoat*. It's an ideal number for an all-boys' school since it contains all male characters. The characters are "the Narrator," who introduces the cast in the song; "Jacob," the father; and his twelve sons—fourteen in all.

During the process of staging the number, I make sure to compliment the performers often, taking special care to encourage those who need to be more energized. They are telling the audience a story and must use voice, body, movement, and gesture in order to be successful. Also, encourage each performer to make a choice about his character. Is Jacob authoritative or benevolent? In what way can we individualize each brother? Am I the confident son? Am I the nerd? Am I the loving son? As I give the students these instructions, the number becomes richer, and they begin to take ownership of the number. The pride the students take in being able to perform an entire number in a very short amount of time comes through in even more energy and many calls for "let's do it again!" If you aren't already there and have a stage you can use, announce that you're moving to the theater to do the number. This increases the excitement and energy. Add lights and maybe even an audience, especially other teachers from the school.

At the end of this lesson, students leave with great enthusiasm, some still singing and moving. The preceding days of musical theater discussions and recordings have come alive in a very real and visceral way. One other and very positive outcome is to see some of the students from this class attend the auditions for the next musical.

The range and variety of invigorating motor activity are limited only by the imagination of the teacher.

The range and variety of invigorating motor activity are limited only by the imagination of the teacher. This American Spanish teacher builds her students' facility in spoken communication by challenging them, in groups, to negotiate an obstacle course:

In Spanish II, the students review and master commands. They also learn the vocabulary necessary to give directions. This lesson incorporates these two things into a fun activity to give the students a break from normal classroom learning. The idea is to have a maze/mini-obstacle course that the students have to navigate in groups of three. The first student is blindfolded and has to rely solely on the directions given by his group members. The second student is in charge of giving the commands that lead the first student through the maze. The third student is there to make sure that the first student is never in danger of hurting himself. The three students rotate roles until everyone plays each part once. If the numbers do not work out so that the students can be paired in groups of three, a group of two works. One student has to both give commands and watch to make sure that the blindfolded student is safe at all times. Students are encouraged to take their time and move slowly throughout the course.

First, the class needs to review the command forms and the types of directions they will need to use during the activity. The class should go over direction words, command forms, and parts-of-the-body vocabulary. The students can help in setting up the course. The teacher should make a decision whether this activity should be assessed. Some classes may require some sort of evaluation in order to make the students work to their potential. If it is already a highly motivated class, it may not be necessary to assess. If the teacher chooses to give students a grade, he or she may want to end with a paragraph reflection in Spanish. The teacher could also add some sort of worksheet before the activity to make sure that the students are well prepared.

In order to prepare for this lesson, the teacher needs to have blindfolds or scarves, desks, mats, or chairs ready and access to a space large enough to accommodate the activity. If the regular classroom is big enough to set up the course, this is the most convenient option. If not, the teacher should ask if there is a small gym available to use and if there is equipment that could be used to set up the course.

In an exercise he calls the "movie lesson," this South African teacher assigns his boys of mixed high school age to assume active roles in movie production and to simulate making a movie of a poem. The activity is transitive, the teacher reports, to total retention of the poems selected:

> This is called a movie lesson. Choose a suitable poem. Ask the boys to bring props for the movie. The teacher is the director, the pupils the actors, cameramen, clipboard operators, and so on. They then read the poem and act out the poem. The director stops them when he is not happy with the reading or acting. It is all fun, but the boys learn the poem by heart without realizing it.

THE BOYS RESPOND

It is far from startling to report that boys find it refreshing and occasionally even thrilling to be released from the close confinement of much classroom business and to be allowed to engage in vigorous physical activity. Many of the boys seemed to recognize, as their teachers did, that such release can serve the intended learning objectives.

This New Zealand senior relates an incident in which a brief physical "work-out" advanced his and his classmates' understanding of some essential physics principles:

> The most motivating class which I have taken during my time here is year 11 physics. There was not one lesson or unit in particular which made it a good class. It was more down to the more relaxed class atmosphere because the teacher was not extremely strict but was entirely capable of controlling the class if we got off track and would steer us back to concentrating on the subject matter at hand. The constant use of practical examples to which we could relate made it so much easier to learn and therefore minimized the difficulty of understanding physics. One such example was in the middle of the year when he got all of us to run up a flight of stairs while he timed us to demonstrate the principles of work: work = force × distance, and

showed that the smaller members of the class could be faster than those of larger mass but that the larger people would still have a much larger energy output than the smaller ones. The use of practical sessions made it so much easier to understand material which seemed rather complex at the time. Learning for me becomes so much easier when you have a teacher who rather than yelling and seeming to expect you to remember every little thing actually attempts to teach to the best of his ability and tries to make sure that you understand what is being taught.

This British eleventh grader relates how an unexpected infusion of physical exertion in effect "reset" his and his classmates' receptivity to material under review in his biology class:

We were having a double period on Friday afternoon and so everyone was not in the mood for learning. We watched a video about water regulation in the body but many of us were not concentrating and were either sleeping or talking with each other. So, as a result of this lack of concentration, our teacher decided to take us outside and let us run around the building to wake us up. Then, we came back in and he gave each a card and drew a diagram of the kidneys and the brain. He then gave us five minutes to arrange ourselves in the right order, from the diagram on the board, and for half of the class to give a presentation about what would happen if there was too much water in your body and vice versa. I enjoyed this lesson as our teacher made us concentrate by making us run, and then gave us an interactive lesson rather than just listening to a boring video.

The transitive power of movement and play need not always precede—or stimulate—specific learning outcomes. In this British twelfth grader's account, the play served as a reward, or reinforcement, for successful learning:

This year, one lesson that I found to be both fun and educational (yes it is possible) was a mechanics lesson spanning two periods. The lesson took place in the staff snooker room and was split into two parts: applying principles we had learned; having fun. During the first period, we were charged with finding figures for the following: the coefficient of restitution between the billiard balls; the coefficient of restitution between the billiard balls and the cushions; the friction coefficient of the table surface. To do this we were given crude measuring materials, having to find ways to overcome not only the basic provisions, but also the obstacles of external forces not covered in the syllabus (such as air resistance) that would distort our findings. After a dodgy start, especially regarding our initial misuse of formulae, our team regrouped to see where steps had been miscalculated and where we could improve upon our practical experiments. The collaborative effort paid off as our group managed to draw figures which even surprised our teacher with their accuracy. We then waited for other groups within our class to come out with their figures (producing successful efforts also) before a discussion over the practical methods and calculations used to derive our answers. Having completed this mentally taxing ordeal, we were granted permission to use the table in the way it was originally intended to be used, although with woeful results when compared to our previous exploits.

All the students found the lesson stimulating as it allowed us all to participate, putting theory we had recently learned into practice, giving us a chance to evaluate it, rather than just being taught to accept the writing on the board. Overall, the lesson was particularly enjoyable as I felt that I was taking an active participation in it, and I look forward to more lessons of this nature.

The specific type or amount of physical movement necessary to boost engagement in and retention of material can vary considerably. For this American seventh grader, the mere fact that his class moved to a cupola at "the highest point" on his school's campus drove a particular English lesson home with unusual force:

One English class, we were going to discuss Ray Bradbury's *Dandelion Wine*. The story starts with the main character waking up in his grandparents' cupola and his sudden realization of summer's inception. He thinks of the rituals which he knows will take place in the weeks to come. He realizes what it truly feels like to live life to the fullest in these first few chapters. My English teacher took our class up to the gazebo from 1913, which is the highest point on campus. This setting for our class was symbolic of where the book started off. We had a Socratic discussion (reminiscent of that which we have around a Harkness Table [a large oval-shaped table seating a dozen or so students and a teacher]) about the main character's outlook on life, and how we choose to live our life to its fullest and furthermore what the purpose of life is. This is not only my most significant class experience but possibly that of my whole life. I realized that in coming to an independent all-boys' school that I would learn much more than academics, and my purpose as a human being.

Some of the schools participating in the study, particularly those in Australia, maintain a separate facility situated in relative wilderness, in which boys by age group are run through a progression of outdoor orienteering and leadership training exercises in the course of their time at the school. The boys tend to remember these "school camp" experiences warmly. Many report what they feel have been "life-changing" experiences of self-awareness and increased self-confidence in consequence of the exertions asked of them, as did this Australian eighth grader:

One extremely memorable experience was during the exciting year 8 camp. It was a five day camp and on the fourth day, we did worthwhile activities such as knot tying and rock climbing. Rock climbing was a major challenge because it required a lot of physical work and mental motivation to succeed in climbing to the top. Not many people achieved this, so climbing to the top was an honorable experience. The first time I attempted this difficult task, I only made it halfway as I didn't have enough confidence to climb to the top. After I was safely released down, I felt very miserable and regretful. Just before the camp coordinators were about to pack up the equipment and call it a day, I asked if I could do it again, because I would never be able to sleep at night, thinking I didn't make it to the cursed top. Luckily they agreed, so I thanked them thoroughly. I psyched myself up and prepared myself for the daring climb. I went off to a good start and made it halfway quickly. After that, I found myself in a very uncomfortable position. A few people below me were cheering me on, and I didn't want to let them down, so I continued climbing. In a blink of an eye, I had made it to the top that had eluded me. I have never felt more cheerful and triumphant in my life. After that moment, I realized that almost everything is possible if you put enough motivation in it.

Another Australian, a ninth grader, reported that the wilderness solo required by his school's bush camp program had expanded not just his self-reliance but his perspective on his relative place in the world. As in the preceding account, the rapt appreciation this boy expresses reveals something of the transitive potential that physical exertion holds for boys in every aspect of their schooling:

When I was in year 9 at school camp I had to complete one of the biggest tasks of my life, the solo. This was a major learning experience for me because it made me realize how lucky I have been in my life. On this solo we were put out in the bush for 15 hours and made to survive by ourselves. We were supplied with dinner but it was still something that I have never done before. The 15 hours did consist of a night, though. I spent the night thinking about how I have been brought up in a very protected society and that many in the world don't get to have the luxuries I have been given. When I woke up the next morning I was a completely different person. I was no longer only concerned about myself. I now knew that in fact I was very lucky and that it is others that I should be concerned about. This solo experience is a very important thing to have in all schools, especially the ones with richer students, so hopefully they too can realize how lucky they actually are. Although I only talk about this one solo experience, the whole camp in general is a big learning curve and very enjoyable. The camp is made to try and develop our knowledge about the bush and to make us into stronger people (not strength wise but inner strength). I would advise all schools to develop a school camp or outdoor education camp as it will be an advantage to all students in the short term and in later life. The skills that you learn are essential to becoming a stronger and more well-rounded person.

CHAPTER

ROLE PLAY
AND PERFORMANCE

Many teachers found that requiring boys to take a role—whether an imper-
sonation or as part of a purely physical process—was transitive to a deeper,
surer understanding of the material under study. In many cases too, the requirement to perform before others contributed to the student's sense of responsibility
for and ultimate mastery of an assigned task. Performance and role playing
require a significant degree of motor activity, which, as seen in the prior chapter,
plays a central part in effective lessons.

In a related way, the responsibility of presenting important material to class
mates—material they must master and retain in order to complete an assignment
successfully—appears to deepen the boys' engagement and result in superior
work.

Teachers are often struck by the realization that they had never been true
learners until they found themselves responsible for teaching others. The sense
of urgency and the drive to mastery one feels when one is responsible for what
others must do and know are clearly transitive, deepening one's own knowledge.
In many of the lessons in this chapter, teachers identified the effectiveness of
putting boys in charge of consequential outcomes.

ROLE-PLAYING A PROCESS

A number of teachers reported the effectiveness of embodying an observable process. This New Zealand biology teacher devised a lesson in which a highly specific biological process, human digestion, was broken down to the extent that students performed the key roles in each successive step:

I was teaching the human digestive system to a year 11 lower-stream class. This was the summative lesson in a series in which we had learned about each stage of digestion. The students were able to describe the need for digestion and recall the organs involved in the digestive process, but I needed an activity to help them conceptualize the entire system. I saw this as an opportunity to use a role-play scenario to illustrate the journey of food through the digestive system.

So we set the classroom up as the human gut, moving the tables and chairs aside to make room—the head at the front of the room, the anus at the back. The side tables also doubled as some of the major organs that "feed into" the digestive tract. These included the pancreas and the liver from which pancreatic juice and bile were secreted. The "food" we used were balls labeled with nutrients: glucose, amino acids, fats, and oxygen molecules wrapped in layers of newspaper. Some students carried these food parcels into the "mouth" of the room, where they were met by a few students mimicking the chopping, tearing, and cutting action of the teeth, at the same time being coated with "amylase" from spray bottles. Then they moved into the esophagus and were squeezed along by peristalsis to the stomach, where the "hydrochloric acid" and "pepsin" coating were applied. Then students with other juices from the side tables moved into play. At the small intestine, the remaining wrappers were broken down, while the oxygen and nutrients were absorbed through "holes" in the small intestine back into the bloodstream. Finally, water entered the large intestine and was absorbed by giant sponges that mopped up the excess liquid. The undigested newspaper was stored in the rectum and then passed out through the anus into the rubbish bin. The activity was captured on video to ensure that a "walk-through" narrative could be played back to the class at the next lesson.

An American economics teacher reported the effectiveness of having her twelfth-grade boys enter into a fairly theatrical "Wild West" role play in order to introduce them to essential concepts in money and banking:

Teaching money and banking is one of my favorite activities in economics. I use the same lesson for both Advanced Placement students and those in the Introduction to Economics classes. The two presentations, questions, and a test take about four class periods—a week on our schedule.

To introduce the concepts of money and banking, I use an interactive presentation developed by Professor Don Wells at the University of Arizona, which Stephen Reff at an AP institute in Tucson shared with me. It's called *The Story of Pine Gulch.* Stephen has a video of himself presenting the story to his classes on his Web site at http://www.reffonomics.com/textbook/macroeconomics.html.

When I present this story, I dress as a cowgirl. I bring bandannas, hats, and cap guns for the boys. I encourage them to dress as cowboys, and I assign parts. I am usually the narrator. Boys are uniquely gifted in making noises, I have observed, so I get them to make the sounds of the horses, the robbers, and the wounded "Slim" as he goes down after the duel at the end of the story. I encourage the boys to make "rabble, rabble" noises as the townspeople gather, to shoot their cap guns to call a town meeting, and to shout out the lines of the crowd in the story.

In the story, Slim is hired to be the "keeper of the gold" for the townspeople. He eventually develops currency and fractional bank lending as a way to make things more convenient for himself and the townspeople. Students get the idea that money is whatever is generally accepted in exchange for goods and services. They also see that the money supply and the economy grow when Slim makes loans. It's a fun lesson that they remember.

ASSUMING REAL-WORLD ROLES

The energizing potential of role playing served a number of teachers in their efforts to illuminate contemporary and historical world events.

A New Zealand English teacher assigned his class to assume the roles of reporters, editors, producers, and on-camera presenters and to produce a news bulletin. In carrying out their assignments, students had an opportunity to see how news is shaped and colored by the various personal choices made by those who gather, edit, and deliver it:

Students were asked to watch a television newscast for homework and to look at the role of the presenters as well as the style of editing or continuity. I gave a few examples so the students had a reasonable idea of what to look for.

The next morning I asked for comments about the presenters' roles, attitudes, and delivery. Some useful discussion followed about body language, voice modulation, neutrality, and their change in register and tone for different types of news articles. We then discussed how news items were grouped and the techniques used to link various items. Some student comments were quite perceptive and included comments on inappropriate groupings and clever links.

After the ten- to fifteen- minute discussion, I played the class a video clip of a news bulletin, presented by two readers, and then asked the boys to fill in answers to a worksheet set. The worksheet drew attention to presenters and reporters and their different roles, as well as the editing or linking devices used in the newscast. Once we had discussed the answers, I told them that they were about to present a news bulletin, in pairs, as part of their oral assessment for the term and then briefly asked them to tell me why we had discussed the video clip and the homework bulletin. They were quick to bring up the idea of an exemplar and the need for some degree of emulation, and they also mentioned how they had not really thought critically about presentation or continuity before.

Students were encouraged to use "minimalist" props (hats and scarves, for example) as they assumed roles of reporters and presenters; each boy had to present two items and act as a reporter in the other two. They were also encouraged to use different mannerisms for these reporter roles—for example, accents, pace, and body language. They were given two lessons to work in the pairs.

I appointed groups of boys to discuss, divide, and plan their own news bulletin, which were required to be three to five minutes in duration. Weekend homework was assigned to learning and rehearsing their parts, and then they were asked to present the bulletins to the class. They were told they could use notes but that in the absence of Teleprompters, they would need to establish eye contact and therefore know the bulletin fairly well.

After the presentations, students were asked to nominate the best presentations. Eventually the one selected as best was, luckily, the same as the one I had awarded highest marks to, and students were asked to give four reasons that it was best. The discussion that followed this "voting" was valuable in what it said about oral techniques and creative presentation.

A New Zealand history teacher's "best lesson" was the result of collaboration with a colleague in which their classes together reenacted a consequential moment in national history:

The practice detailed here was undertaken with a form 4 [grade 10] social studies class of thirty-five students. The topic was the Treaty of Waitangi, and the subtopic under investigation was the New Zealand Wars. Prior teaching experience had indicated this was a not a well-liked aspect of the course; nevertheless, the students were required to have an in-depth knowledge of a single battle in the New Zealand Wars to satisfy curriculum requirements.

The preparatory phase of the activity ensued over three periods, beginning with two evenings of independent student research into the predetermined battle of Rangiriri, a significant turning point in the colonial movement south from Auckland in the 1860s. This independent student research was followed by one teacher-directed lesson on the finer content of the conflict, one period for student discussion on costuming, and a final session preparing the logistics and movements for the day in question. Put simply, the aim was to reenact the battle of Rangiriri on the neighboring Mount Eden in Epsom, Auckland.

The time afforded for the actual activity on the day was a single forty-minute period, plus lunchtime. My class was instructed to undertake the activity from a British colonial army perspective, while a colleague informed his class, running parallel with mine, of their instructions to undertake the activity from a native Maori perspective. Both sets of students were informed that the purpose of reenacting the offensive and defensive ambitions of each side was to bring history to life in such a way that a sense of being there could be achieved.

On the day of the actual lesson, students arrived and changed into elaborate costumes, with bamboo as rifles and spears, and proceeded to the surroundings of Mount Eden where the preorganized Maori occupied the summit of a steep ridge and the British formed at the base. From that point onward, the students representing the colonial army acted out a planned invasion reminiscent of the tactics and realities of official accounts from Rangiriri. The other class responded as the local Maori of the land defending their "fortified pa" [turf] from high ground. All of this action was caught on video for postevent review and laughter. Students completed this module of work by reuniting as a combined cohort to watch the footage and the acting talents of their fellow class members.

ROLE-PLAYING CRITICAL DECISIONS

Role playing was also effective in helping students identify and assess their own values in critical personal matters.

Role playing was also effective in helping students identify and assess their own values in critical personal matters.

An Australian social studies teacher reported building such awareness in the course of a presentation about military conscription, in which boys, in the role of potential draftees, were challenged to commit their service, or not:

My most recent aha! moment was teaching a year 10 class about military conscription in World War I. After reviewing a text input on why young men in Australia volunteered to fight in World War I, we constructed a list of reasons from that material, plus any other reasons the boys could think of, that would lead them to fight for another country in another land. Not surprisingly for twenty-first-century boys from comfortable backgrounds, this was quite a short list. Several boys immediately took the view that almost nothing would make them join the army if they didn't want to because "no one had the right to tell them what to do . . ."

I then began a scenario where a close ally of Australia was under a threat from a near neighbor. I asked the boys to stand along a continuum across the room as to whether they would volunteer to fight. A few stood to show they would; we discussed why, and really it was because they wanted the adventure (an entry off our earlier list). I then increased the scenario to add that the enemy were now massing on the northern border of Australia and using some colorful prose explained what was happening (numbers of troops, ships, aircraft, and so on). A further shift of boys occurred, and again they had to justify why they had moved. Debate was now starting between the boys as some shouted over to others to move or not to move and even hinting that they were being cowards (but within classroom behavior parameters), which we again discussed. Over the next twenty minutes, I sketched in more and more intense scenarios in a progression from data I had prepared earlier.

My use of known geography, towns, and places in western Australia contributed to the feeling of threat and being under attack. By the last part of the lesson, almost all boys were now standing as volunteers. By this process, we had clearly established that there is a point where boys and men would volunteer to fight even today given the right circumstances.

We then spent the next few lessons looking at the circumstances of a twenty-year-old Australian boy in 1915 and why large numbers of young men in fact chose to serve in large numbers. As a corollary, we could also look at how the classroom mentality reflected the community mentality during that period and the pressure that could be placed on young men at that time.

EMPATHIC ROLE PLAY

Many teachers' peak moments and "best lessons" occurred when boys were asked to identify personally with someone under study, to act and feel as that character would, and to produce an account of the experience.

This American English teacher asked his eighth-grade boys to assume the identity of a child soldier in Africa:

> After some decades of coed high school teaching, this was my first year teaching eighth grade and my first year teaching boys, so the data are a little sparse. However, the most distinct and memorable experience of the year was the boys' response to a relatively common assignment about Ishmael Beah's memoir, *A Long Way Gone*. Beah's book chronicles his life as a child soldier during the civil war in Sierra Leone. An apparently true story about boys and war, it was an instant hit with the students, though a certain "fascination of the abomination" paralyzed their usually active critical habits. They liked it in spite of bad writing and strained credulity.
>
> The writing assignment that closed the unit asked them, in part, to write a "personal response" to the novel:
>
>> Clearly, a good portion of *A Long Way Gone* will strike you as significantly different from your personal experiences. That said, I am hopeful that, as you read the book, certain moments, certain thoughts, and feelings that Ishmael has about his life will seem familiar to you.
>>
>> Here's what I'd like you to do. Choose a passage from anywhere in Ishmael's book that resonates with you in some personal way, and do two things with that passage. First, explicate it on Ishmael's terms; second, explain why you feel personally connected to the passage. The first section of this project, "the passage explication," should be one paragraph (seven to ten sentences); the second section, "the personal response," should be longer, since in it, I'd like you to use details and/ or an anecdote or two from your own life to support and develop your personal connection to the passage.
>
> What was good and surprising in the boys' essays was the degree of empathy that they were able to extend to the writer and the analogies that they were able to draw between his and their experience, despite the

dramatic differences between his experience as a child abducted into an army and theirs as children of privilege raised by mostly intact families.

The first part of the assignment, the "explication," required them to pay close attention to Beah's language and understand the emotional subtext—often the loss of self and the putting on of masks or roles—that allowed Beah to cope. The second half of the assignment, the personal response, asked them to see how this same psychological process can operate in their own lives, albeit under far less stress. Although they didn't use the word *integrity* in their pieces, many boys wrote about a loss of personal compass or judgment that they have experienced as a member of group. One boy in particular wrote about the erosion of "the concept of I" that Beah experienced in his cold-blooded soldiering that he, the student, experiences in his daily life in choosing to do what his friends ask rather than what he would do on his own. He even saw this loss of integrity operating in the everyday lies he tells himself and others: that his homework is done when it's not, that he was playing in the park when he was actually spending money in an arcade, that he got an A on a quiz but neglected to mention the D on a test.

Although Beah engaged in varsity-level coping by lying to himself about the inhumanity of the civilians he killed, the assignment opened many of the boys' eyes to the connections between Beah's and their own shifting, furtive responses to powerlessness in the face of authority. Their writing was engaged, fresh, truthful, and purposeful.

An American English teacher found her eleventh-grade students deepened their understanding of a series of quite different novels by assuming characters from the texts and interacting with others in the course of being interviewed on a simulated *David Letterman Show,* a late-night American television standard:

V Form English [junior year] is a study of American literature. We read *One Flew over the Cuckoo's Nest*; *The Scarlet Letter*; selections from Emerson,

Thoreau, Whitman, and Douglass out of *The Norton Anthology*; *A Streetcar Named Desire*; *The Great Gatsby*; and *The Adventures of Huckleberry Finn*.

For the midterm exam review, I assigned each boy in the class a character from one of our first-semester texts: McMurphy and Nurse Ratched from *One Flew over the Cuckoo's Nest*; Prynne, Dimmesdale, and Chillingworth from *The Scarlet Letter*; and Emerson, Thoreau, Whitman, and Douglass from *The Norton Anthology*. In addition, I assigned one student to be David Letterman. The assignment was to prepare for *The Letterman Show*, where David Letterman would interview his literary guests. The "guests" had to come to class prepared to answer questions "in character"; they had to know themselves well enough to respond in a convincing manner, consistent with all that these characters had said or done in their piece of literature. They had to bring in a typed outline of their character traits, with supporting textual evidence outlined in detail. They also had to bring in one specific question for every other guest on the show.

David Letterman had to come to class with two questions prepared for each guest. His questions could address the guest's feelings toward another character in his or her own novel or in another text; he could also solicit his guest's views on contemporary American life (religion, politics, war, health care, government, education, freedom of speech, gay rights, or something else).

The boys had a week to prepare for this exercise, and each student was graded on how truthfully and thoroughly he represented his assigned character; Letterman was graded on the thoughtfulness and appropriateness of his questions. Each student had a name placard and cup of water at his desk, to simulate a formal talk show environment. Many chose to come in costume; Hester Prynne wore her scarlet embroidered "A" on her blazer lapel, and Arthur Dimmesdale had his "A" hidden on his undershirt. I sat as an "audience member," taking notes on how well they represented their assigned character in their questions and answers.

What ensued was a lively and entertaining discussion, with every member of the class involved. Because they had to interact with the other characters from the other texts, I felt that they were well prepared for the exam. They had to review their assigned text well enough to impersonate their character, and they had to know the other texts well enough to ask and answer questions from those other characters.

Another American English teacher reported deepening eighth-grade boys' understanding of human diversity by assigning them to assume a secret identity, an alter ego, for four weeks and report impressions of the world from this seemingly alien perspective:

While teaching *To Kill a Mockingbird*, I have the students (a typical class has fifteen boys) consider the words of Atticus Finch, which he tells Scout early in the novel, that you never really know a person until you walk around in his skin. With these lines in mind, we begin a project I call either the "Filter Project" or the "Alter Ego" project.

First, we brainstorm individuals or groups of people who either have in the past or currently suffer from discrimination or who tend to be stereotyped. The list can end up rather long, but I end up narrowing the groups to six, based on prior knowledge of which groups work best for the activity. Typically these groups are women, poor people, African Americans, gays, non-Christians, and Hispanics. I then write the names of these groups on cards and invite the boys out in the hall one at a time to choose a card from the deck. They choose their card without being able to see what they are choosing. They are instructed to keep their choice a secret, lest their friends and family may act toward them in an artificially good or unpleasant way.

For the next four weeks, the boys will filter all their daily experiences through not only their own eyes, ears, and sensibilities, but also through the eyes and ears of an alter ego that they likely know very little about. Each week the boys report on their experience with their alter ego by writing a journal entry. They may choose to keep their character at an arm's length by writing the entries in third person, or they may go out on a limb and assume a first-person point of view, taking on the character himself or herself.

Depending on what card a boy has chosen, the first entries are often a bit tentative and unsure. But as the weeks pass, many boys find that they are indeed getting to know this alter ego by "walking around in his or her skin" for a while. Even a gay character, who normally would be a considerable threat for an eighth-grade boy, tends to receive a more charitable reaction once a boy has discovered how it might feel to actually be gay in a society that often is harsh toward that group. The "woman" card tends to be equally rich in possibilities, especially for boys in an all-boys' school. After four weeks and several journal entries, we finish the novel and have a coming-out party where guys admit to who their alter ego was.

BEING RESPONSIBLE FOR THE LEARNING OF OTHERS

Teachers also reported warmly about the improved preparation and overall quality of performance on the part of students who were required to present material to classmates—material that mattered in the latter's progress through the lesson and through the course.

An American English teacher recounts how student-conducted class business can not only meet teacher-determined standards but substantially exceed them:

As part of a four-week study of poetry, my freshmen both read and write poetry. This year I experimented with having the ninth-grade boys lead the discussion. For each day of class, I designated one of my fifteen students to lead the first twenty minutes of discussion of an assigned poem. I moved to a chair in a back corner of the class, moved one of the students to the front of the class, and listened as he led the students' discussion.

My principal job, which I usually fulfilled, was to listen and let the students do the talking. From Gwendolyn Brooks's "mothers" through Philip Larkin's "This Be the Verse," a student led the first twenty minutes (or more) of each class. Particularly memorable were discussions on Milton's "When I Consider How My Light Is Spent," Keats's "Ode on a Grecian Urn," and Stevens's "Emperor of Ice Cream." Near the beginning of the discussion on "Emperor of Ice Cream," I was sorely tempted to intervene, as the student leading the discussion was (in my opinion) reductively taking the line, "Let the wenches dawdle in such dress," as a reflection of the poet's denunciation of prostitutes. Keeping my silence, I was thrilled to see that the students disagreed with their leader's interpretation. The free-flowing discussion that followed was among the finest conversations about a Stevens poem I have ever witnessed. As I told the discussion leader the first chance I got, "You taught such an impressive class. Although you clearly came to the class having prepared for hours to share a particular interpretation of the poem, by listening to your classmates' skepticism, you showed the flexibility of letting the discussion develop into a richer reading of the poem."

This British chemistry teacher reported that "putting his boys in charge" of lessons resulted not only in thorough understanding of course material but also improved retention of that material:

I employ this practice with year 12 and year 13 [ages seventeen and eighteen] chemistry students as a way of making preexamination revision sessions more involving and effective.

After leading a few revision sessions myself on those topics that I think warrant the most attention for a particular class, we review the list of remaining topics in the syllabus, and each boy selects one topic on which he will lead a revision session for the whole class. In a lesson, we typically cover two or three such topics, so it normally takes about three lessons for each boy (out of a class of about ten) to have his opportunity. Each boy then prepares the revision session on his selected topic and runs it for the class.

I give the boys freedom as to how they run their session, and so the approaches taken by each boy vary, but they know the standard expected. They model their session on the ones I have run and on effective approaches they have observed in other teachers. They typically prepare a short description of the topic, which they present using PowerPoint or other aids; prepare a handout containing the key points; and prepare a worksheet with sample questions to be worked through and discussed as a group.

> I have not been disappointed by any session, and some have been outstanding. The approach creates a cooperative learning culture in the classroom. The boy leading each session takes pride in the quality of his session since it is judged by his classmates and not by a teacher, and the boys receiving each session pay close attention because they are keen to see how their classmate performs and they quietly assess how they themselves have performed, or will perform, in comparison. In addition, the boys receiving each session hear the topic explained in their own "teenage" language, which is different in many cases from a teacher's explanation. Many of the sessions would have scored high marks in any formal lesson observation of a teacher covering the same topic.

Students' sense of responsibility for the work they produce is heightened, in this American history teacher's account, by its appearance before a potentially worldwide audience:

> In my twelfth-grade elective course, Modern European History, the final examination is a group entry to the online encyclopedia Wikipedia for the Russian novel *Life and Fate*, by Vasily Grossman. As a group, we created categories that each member of the class is responsible for writing, editing, and submitting. The collaborative entry requires knowledge of the book and the period in which the novel takes place: Stalingrad in 1942–1943. Since the book has well over eight hundred pages and a character list of over one hundred, the boys are required to share many of the responsibilities and then collaborate on the final entry.

This American teacher of ancient world history reports measurably superior student performance as a result of assigning them to become resident "experts" in component parts of a larger unit of study:

History obviously involves a lot of reading—of the text and supplemental materials. That reading then needs to be discussed and extended to higher-level thinking. I've learned that the best way to do this is not to give notes and lecture. Instead, in my ninth-grade ancient world history course, one of the methods I use is a cooperative jigsaw, where boys are assigned a "chunk" of the reading to become experts on. They meet in an expert group and agree on what the main ideas are and then teach that material to their peers in small group (known as home groups) discussion. Usually I take the notes that the expert groups were giving to their home groups and use them to create a quiz on the material. This way, the boys have complete ownership of their learning, they are actively engaged with the material, and the quiz at the end raises their level of concern about their efforts. In addition, the jigsaw allows the class to move through a good amount of the text without having to read all of the pages on their own, which is another motivational factor for the students.

I recently used this strategy in my class to move through a good deal of material in the text about ancient China. Not only did the boys attain good information from their expert and home groups, but the class averages on the subsequent quiz was an A–, which is far above their normal performance on reading quizzes.

In this next lesson, a history class studying the U.S. Supreme Court is divided into groups responsible for conveying the substance of significant judicial decisions. Within each group, a "teacher" is delegated the responsibility of explaining and clarifying his group's work to the other groups:

This is an activity for the U.S. history survey course that has a variety of different content applications. This description deals with the John Marshall Supreme Court, but I have also used a similar exercise to assess the communitarian movement in mid-nineteenth-century America. It is important to have a large room available to do this assignment. Other material requirements are poster board or newsprint and colored markers.

Prior to the assignment, the students in two sections are divided into groups of four or five. At that time, they are given a series of readings covering one of the Marshall Court's major decisions. Each group reviews a different case. These readings are readily available on the Internet or in other sources in any library. I usually try to get one reading from journals such as *American Heritage*, *History Today*, or *American History Illustrated*, plus at least one legal rendering of the case. They are also encouraged to use the text.

As a boarding school, we can have evening meetings in lieu of the regularly scheduled classes. Since this assignment involves two classes, it is easier to take an hour to an hour and a half in the evening to get the work done.

Each group is provided with a poster board or newsprint and colored markers. Their charge is to (1) briefly summarize the background of the case, (2) describe the constitutional issue under review, and (3) give the decision. They should also think about the application of the Court's decision and how it affects us today. They also have to draw a picture that represents the case. The object of creating this poster is to teach their fellow students about their case and the results of the decision.

Once the project is finished, the group selects a "teacher" and posts their creation at a designated station around the room. The "teacher" stays with his poster to explain the case to his fellow students, while the rest of the group goes to a separate poster and "teacher." The class begins with the "teacher" explaining the case as the students from a single group take notes. Key to this, and the part of the assignment that often provides the most humor, is interpreting the picture for the students who have no background on the topic other than what they have been told by the "teacher." After about five or six minutes, depending on the time available, and also taking time for questions, the groups rotate to a new location and repeat the process until they have reviewed all the cases under consideration and completed the circuit around the room.

Once the groups are back at their original poster and with their "teacher," they brief him about all the cases they have heard so he can take some notes and have the same information that they do about the Marshall Court.

THE BOYS RESPOND

Teachers in boys' schools are quick to assert that boys together are quick and often eager to suspend belief and imaginatively assume roles. This observation contrasts sharply with the cool, unto-himself adolescent male stereotype. The boys in this study strongly affirmed the pleasure—and the resulting learning—of being asked to get out of their familiar skin.

The boys in this study strongly affirmed the pleasure—and the resulting learning—of being asked to get out of their familiar skin.

This British tenth grader reports enthusiastically about a potentially lost history lesson being reclaimed by the sudden infusion of action and drama:

The history teacher had been given the cursed Friday afternoon lesson which normally consisted of pupils talking among each other and discussing what they were going to do at the weekend while the teacher valiantly tried to get through the material of the lesson in vain. However, the teacher said that we were to have a different lesson that day. He took us all to the drama theater and passed out a plastic sword and shield and we lined up on the stage. The teacher explained that we were going to reenact the Battle of Hastings. Throughout the lesson we reenacted the battle, half the class as Normans and the other half as Saxons, with the teacher giving step by step analysis of the battle while we acted out what he said. By the end of the lesson we had finished the battle and had even seen a death scene from a student!! The lesson is particularly inspiring for me as the teacher had made a real effort to make the lesson fun and the pupils resolved to make an effort from then on during the Friday afternoon lesson. Also I hadn't realized that history could be so interesting. I know that the lesson was etched onto my brain because when I took an exam I remembered the lesson vividly.

An Australian eighth grader explains the way simply changing the mode of presentation from critical analysis to active role playing enlivened the reading of a required text:

In English, our class had finished the novel we had to study. Our teacher had given us a play that we were reading aloud in class. The play was *An Inspector Calls* and was a play about how a high-class family in England tied in to a suicide case. The family originally thought that they were all innocent, but all found out that they all had large parts to play in the girl's death. The play also pointed out how different people reacted to the accusations and the truth that came out under interrogation. We enacted this play in class. It was enjoyable because the audience had a laugh at their classmates expressions, voices and acting, while absorbing the underlying message. In the third or fourth session of the play, I went up to act as the inspector. It was really fun. I found it easy to get into the role of the inspector. The class laughed when we forgot lines, but were subdued in the more serious parts of the play. Although to an outsider, it may have seemed like we were not listening, everyone absorbed the play's meaning, the characters' personalities and why it was chosen for the play and other specific details. The story was different from what I usually read and enjoy, but because everyone was having fun watching and acting, I enjoyed following the story as much as I liked playing my part.

I would have enjoyed reading something more to my taste. The advantages to reading and acting the play aloud were that we did not get bored even when the plot was not at its most exciting. The lesson was most enjoyable, and I would have liked to do something else like it again.

The engagement may be heightened when students are asked to impose themselves imaginatively on a text under study. This Canadian seventh grader was assigned to act out and perform an "unseen moment," which he identifies as "a moment that was missing from the book," in John Steinbeck's *Of Mice and Men:*

During English class in grade 7, the whole class read out loud the book *Of Mice and Men*. This was memorable because the book was probably the best book I've ever read in my lifetime. We had so many discussions on whether a part in the novella proved the American dream or friendship and more. Reading the book was fun and motivating because we had to act out the characters with their accents. The story setting was in the country with the people having rather western accents. Including the accent was fun and made the experience funnier in perspective. While reading the book each student individually had to write down notes that they would use for their final examination essay and fill out a few pages of activities on the book each night or so. Before the essay, and using our knowledge of the book, we had to make a play with a partner that was part of our final English exam mark. The plays went on during two full hour-and-a-half periods with 30 different plays to listen to. Each play was rather a success. It was surprisingly fun to put on the costumes and imitate accents. We had to do an "unseen moment," a moment that was missing from the book. My unseen moment was before the book started. I had a great time making my play and reading *Of Mice and Men*.

A fascinating feature of the boys' positive responses to being asked to assume roles was their realization, in some cases years after a particular lesson or exercise, just how deeply the imaginative engagement in subject matter had been embedded in their learning.

This Canadian eleventh grader mused thoughtfully back to eighth grade and the emotional impact of having been assigned to represent a particular country's national interests in the course of important "negotiations":

Although I am highly motivated in all class activities and assessments, one Grade 8 Geography project sticks out as truly engaging. To simulate real-life political affairs as effectively as one could to middle school students, the teacher separated the class into six/seven groups, identifying each group as a country. For about a month's worth of time, each group did various assignments at will. These assignments included the creation of passports, mini-constitutions, bills/acts, and summaries on various sectors of the country. To make it more interesting, each group was allowed to choose any form of government, thus creating greater variety. Each group was awarded points of varying magnitude for every assignment it completed. After the month, to simulate war, the teacher had all the "countries" engage in a simulated military conflict, with the accumulated points serving as military strength. Basically, each group had the opportunity to create alliances and contemplate strategy. At the end, after a definitive winner was established, "peace talks" were held. I remember how this project had the entire class completely immersed in its work. Most students, myself included, treated "country development" and "war" as if it were reality. I have rarely come across a project which could be so engaging yet so educational in my academic career.

This Canadian eleventh grader reached back to fourth grade to locate his most formative lesson:

There are many experiences that have been especially memorable for me during my tenure at my school, but one that seems to be especially significant was in the formative year of fourth grade. . . . The school work was not very challenging, and looking back on it, I probably worked too hard. . . . The most fun and influential experience was Business Day. Our class spent about a month in the spring preparing for Business Day in which we would sell our masterful product to the rest of the lower school. I was lucky enough to be elected president of the company. I was a pretty timid young student, and this was one of the first times I was put in a position to lead anybody. Because of my newly appointed position I had to stand up in front of the class every other day and lead a stock-holders' meeting. I can't remember the specifics of what we talked about, but I do remember being nervous. It was the first time I felt personally responsible for the success of a group I was working for. I learned how to make sacrifices for the good of our company. One time, for example, I had to kick one overzealous shareholder out of our meeting for talking out of turn. This was probably the first time I had hurt somebody's feelings, and I felt bad about it. However, experiences like that helped to prepare me for my role on the Honor Council, when cases sometimes result in expulsion from our school. Also, it helped me gain confidence. First, I learned my classmates trusted me. That was the first time I thought of myself as any kind of leader. Also I learned that I could stand up in front of a group and speak with some success. In conclusion, Business Day was a very beneficial diversion from our normal school work. Especially in lower school, experiences like this help students to like coming to school, but also increase their ability to work together. The skills learned in these early years really become more useful as the obstacles that school and life present become more challenging.

CHAPTER

6

OPEN INQUIRY

A prominent and recurring feature of many of the lessons reported as especially effective were those in which problems with indeterminate outcomes were posed. The goal was not for the boys to discover or compute a "right answer," but to formulate a solution according to their own research and best lights. Science teachers referred to this approach approvingly as "doing science" as opposed to "studying science." They noted the energizing autonomy and the self-confidence revealed in the course of open investigations carried out in a wide range of scholastic disciplines.

EXPERIENCE AND THEORY

Well-established theories and laws, principally in the sciences and social sciences, tend to be accepted by students as authoritatively and remotely "given." A number of teachers remarked on the empowering sense of understanding boys exhibited as they explored the relationship between actual experiences and the theory to describe them.

This New Zealand mathematics teacher had his students test some probability assumptions by designing a series of in-this-world trials to be tabulated and assessed:

I have chosen to report on my fifth-form [eleventh year] NCEA Mathematics class, which has a wide range of mathematical ability, despite being a midstreamed class.

This year, I began the section of work on probability by using some simple practical activities. I had printed out a results sheet and used the data projector to explain how the students should fill it in, using tallies.

There were four different experiments that I expected the students to get through:

1. Toss two unbiased coins, and record the number of heads obtained. Repeat this at least 10 times in the time allotted.

2. Roll a die 20 times, and record the outcome of each throw.

3. Select 3 cards randomly from a standard pack of 52, and record the number of red cards obtained. Return the 3 cards to the pack, shuffle it, and choose another 3 cards. Repeat 10 times.

4. Drop a paper clip from a height of approximately 20 centimeters onto a sheet of paper with large squares already drawn on it. Note if the paper clip lands completely inside one of the squares or if it touches the side of a square.

Enter the data gathered onto the common spreadsheet projected onto the screen at the front of the class.

This was such a different lesson from the ones they have come to expect from a math lesson, where much of the work comes directly out of a textbook. Students commented on this fact immediately. There was plenty of movement and a fair bit of noise as they went from one task to another, but the students remained focused. They were clearly having fun "playing with the tools" and were eager to get the tasks completed so they could enter their results for the whole class to see.

I thought that the main benefits from this introductory lesson were truly felt later on in the module. For example, students were able to discuss and see the difference between theoretical and experimental probability using their own experience as "proof." The teaching of the vocabulary associated with probability was made easier. Words like *trial, outcome, event, frequency,* and *simulation* were not simply definitions out of a book, but had specific meaning based on the activities. When we came to the section on probability simulations, students had a much better understanding of which experiments and tools they could use. They also had a better grasp of the concept of independence and conditional probability: you can always tell the moment when a student suddenly "gets it." Perhaps the biggest compliment paid was by students who had been struggling with other areas of math who asked if they could do more experiments in class because this one had helped them to learn.

In a similar manner, this American mathematics teacher challenged boys to investigate the mathematical law of sines by puzzling over the area of a given cardboard triangle:

One exercise that I found was particularly effective in teaching the law of sines to advanced algebra II students and precalculus students involved the use of simply made manipulatives. When I started using this technique, I simply cut out a cardboard triangle on which I marked the degree of all the sides and angles. I passed it around the room and asked the boys if they thought they could calculate the area. It was not a right triangle, and they were not allowed to use any measuring device. They had only the lengths of the sides, which were marked, and the measures of the angles, which were marked. Eventually one of them would invariably suggest dropping a perpendicular to one side and using the fact that the area is one-half the base times the height, so they could calculate the area.

Usually I had them work in groups, and different groups came up with the same area using different bases and heights. Since all of the sides were labeled with letters as well as lengths, I asked each group to write the "formula" that they used to find the area using the variables for the sides and the angles. Usually different groups came up with formulas using different sides and lengths. I then asked them whether these should all be equal, and they quickly agreed. Then we were able to set the various expressions equal and manipulate the equations to eventually derive the sine law.

One modification that I found worked when I had the time was to make paper copies of a single triangle and hand it out to specific groups to work separately. This had the advantage of separating the groups more so that they worked more independently.

An American economics teacher assigned senior boys to test one of the foundational laws of economics, the law of demand, with consumer responses to a product they had conceived themselves:

In the second unit of a typical Advanced Placement microeconomics syllabus, one introduces the theoretical foundation of market demand—the amount of a certain product that consumers are willing to buy under various price assumptions. A common approach, taught in both secondary and higher education, is a presentation of the theoretical determinants of the relationship between price and quantity demanded, as well as the graphical representation of this relationship on a two-dimensional graph. A typical economics course does not delve into the world of real data.

My approach to this lesson is a week-long project in which each student conceptualizes a fictional product or service that would be of interest to members of the school community and then estimates, through actual data gathering and analysis, the real market demand curve for that product. In the past, boys have imagined products and services ranging from "dorm room cleaning," to "personalized bumper stickers," to "summer lacrosse camp," and every conceivable product in between.

The project starts with the creation of a valid sampling technique and survey questions, which are tested out on the class first. A typical survey question would be, "Would you rent a dormitory refrigerator for twenty dollars? How about thirty dollars?" The data gathered through the survey are input and analyzed in Microsoft Excel and eventually presented to the class as a market demand curve, along with a written summary of the student's process, conclusions, and vulnerabilities of the analysis. Students are allowed to work alone or in pairs.

Throughout the unit on market demand, students are encouraged, in class and in writing, to apply new theoretical concepts back to the actual market for their fictional product or service. When I introduce the concept of "substitute" goods and the resulting shift in market demand, I ask a student who modeled a market for a snack bar to discuss the impact on his market of a change in the menu at the school's dining hall. When I introduce "complements," I ask the student delivering groceries on campus to describe what would happen to the demand for his service if the school outlawed fridges in dorm rooms.

DESTINATIONS WITHOUT MAPS

Across disciplines, teachers noted the energizing effects of setting boys to tasks for which successful resolution was perhaps possible but by no means certain—or easy. Such was the experience of this American geometry teacher:

Over the past several years, I have been giving my tenth-grade honors students series of challenge problems throughout the year. These problems are designed to be more difficult and thought provoking than typical assigned problems. The students are allowed to work in small groups and have a variety of resources available to them, including compasses and a computer program (The Geometer's Sketchpad). I try to assign problems whose solution is not obvious. It is good for them to struggle and have to try different approaches for a single problem. I have found that by varying the groups, kids have to play different roles in the process. It is thrilling to see kids working on math and arguing about various approaches. It is good to see them thinking their way through various approaches and why (or why not) it ought to work. They also have to wrestle with what their results mean and when it means they have found a dead end.

I try to assign problems whose solution is not obvious. It is good for them to struggle and have to try different approaches for a single problem.

This South African science teacher reported gratifying results from challenging his students not merely to carry out an experiment illustrating a principle but to design such an experiment themselves:

Teaching science is exciting in that experimental work is part and parcel of most lessons. Boys are given an experiment to perform and then learn from what they observe. These lessons in themselves bring out the "hands-on" approach that boys identify with. This approach, though, can be taken a step further. Instead of providing experimental procedures and a listed method, I have found that actually getting them to design the experiment takes the learning process (and excitement level!) to a new level. One example is the examination of the relationship between extension and load (Hooke's law). They are also asked to compare two springs. They are then left to design the experiment (guidance is provided, but no answers given), and they are left to come up with a comparative graph of extension versus load for each spring. This particular experiment is for the grade 8 level and forms part of the component on force. No introduction or explanation of the law must be given; a brief demonstration of apparatus is all that is required.

This South African mathematics teacher reversed standard practice in teaching the factoring of mathematical expressions by presenting the answers, to which ninth-grade boys are challenged to discover a process that would result in such an expression:

In teaching grade 9 factorization of quadratic trinomials, I like to use a method of self-discovery so that the boys learn how to factorize these expressions without actually realizing that they are learning "factorizing" per se. At this stage, they are proficient in multiplying out, so I ask them to "reverse" the procedure—that is, if I give them the "answer," they identify the question. Once they are able to produce the factorized version of the expression in several cases, I tell them that they have "factorized" the expression and what this means.

An American mathematics teacher reported that his most effective lesson was to challenge boys to consider a variety of complex, real-world variables in order to predict a consequential outcome:

I have found that the most effective teaching method that I have used is a hands-on real-life approach. Every year, I have tried to find real-life examples that can be used to illustrate the material that we are covering in class. A particular group lesson using the cost of postage combines individual thinking with group organization.

The task I set before my students was to create a model of the price increases that our country faces when having to buy postage. I supplied the students with data on the prices of postage stamps over the years. Their job was to work together and find a way to predict the prices in the future. This was done using the graphing calculator to find a model that best fits the data.

The use of technology and a hands-on problem-solving approach really pushed my students to think outside the box and use the tools given to them. The excitement of problem solving was apparent with every student, and at the end of the lesson, they realized that it was possible to predict price increases with a high level of accuracy. I have found that boys enjoy solving problems and, more important, solving problems that affect their lives in some way. The combination of technology use with real-life data in my opinion makes this teaching method a very good one for teaching boys.

ENCOURAGING PERSONAL PERSPECTIVE

A promising means of helping boys bridge the gap between their personal concerns and seemingly remote scholastic subject matter is to devise lessons that draw on the former to illuminate the latter.

In this lesson, a Canadian English teacher encouraged her seventh-grade boys to impose their own experiences and viewpoints onto John Steinbeck's *Of Mice and Men:*

This is an assignment spanning five or six class days in a grade 7 English class consisting of twenty students, between twelve and thirteen years of age. This task was assigned after the students had read and analyzed the novella extensively. We focused on Steinbeck's character development and his brilliant use of dialogue. Most of the boys seemed to genuinely enjoy reading and discussing this poignant work of literature.

Their task was to write a script and perform a scene that could have, or maybe even should have, appeared in the novella. They worked in pairs, and I allowed them to choose their partners. The scene had to be two and a half to three and a half minutes in length. They could set their scene before, during, or after the story. Both group members had to be involved in the writing of the script. Because they were assessed on the quality of their performance, they had to memorize their lines. Simple, effective, and appropriate costumes and props were also required. Their scene had to be plausible, meaning they had to create an episode that would have made *Of Mice and Men* a stronger, more complete story. They were asked not to parody the characters or events in the story in any way. Some of the scenes that were performed included Slim and George at a bar after Lennie's death, Curley meeting his wife for the first time at a dance, and Lennie and George right after Aunt Clara's death.

An American English teacher deepened his students' appreciation of the way editorial choices shape seemingly "fixed" and inviolable texts by having his twelfth-grade boys recast a selected scene from *Hamlet* according to their "best guesses" of what, given varying earlier editions of the text, was the playwright's real intent:

In a two-day lesson offered in the middle of our six-week study of *Hamlet*, I introduce my students to the work of the editors and scholars who put together editions of old works. I have my sixth form students create their own version of a scene from *Hamlet*, using only the original sources available to editors and critics. Students weed through digital images of the *First Quarto of 1603* (notorious among Shakespeare critics as "the Bad Quarto"), *the Second Quarto of 1604–5*, and the *First Folio of 1623*. At first glance, students note that the *First Quarto* is the shortest of the three; it also uses markedly different language from the other two editions. The *Second Quarto* and the *First Folio* are generally quite similar, but subtle distinctions abound, such as wild differences in punctuation and capitalization. Students quickly realize that there is no "correct edition" of the play—we have no idea what "the director's cut" of *Hamlet* might be; we have only what critics have pieced together using sound scholarship or even sensible hunches about what the Bard intended. Using their own best guesses about what a modern reader would find helpful and mindful of the balance between "authentic" and "readable," my students then type up their own "edition" of the scene complete with footnotes and explanatory material.

After comparing their various editions and hearing their specific questions and comments about punctuation, spelling, and word choice, we walk across the street to the university library to view one of the 238 surviving copies of the *First Folio*. Our wise guide there answers student questions about the publication of old texts, comparing the *First Folio* the boys now know fairly well to a medieval Bible manuscript, a page from a Gutenberg Bible, and even some quarto editions of other Shakespeare plays.

My modest hope is for my students to understand the differences among various editions of Shakespeare plays. My grander aim is to encourage them to question and challenge the validity of any text and to seek, whenever possible, the original source.

THE BOYS RESPOND

Running through the boys' accounts of their favored lessons is a consistent, sometimes almost urgent, appreciation of being given the opportunity, time, and room to carry out an assignment or solve a problem on their own. As they report,

There is no substitute for the boost in confidence and pride in accomplishment the boys feel when entrusted to "figure it out themselves."

it is reassuring that teacher assistance and expertise are close at hand, but there is no substitute for the boost in confidence and pride in accomplishment they feel when entrusted to "figure it out themselves."

This New Zealand eleventh grader felt stirringly challenged to exceed his former level of writing competence by being challenged to compose virtually "anything," guided only by examples of best work of former students:

A class experience that stands out for me is my year 11 class in narrative writing. My teacher's approach to this topic was unlike many I have had before. He inspired me by showing us some of the best previous work and encouraged us to write by not only giving us freedom, but also showing us the true scope of what that freedom could entail for us. The student work from previous years was truly outstanding. To know that these pieces were written by students no different from me was important to me because it gave me the confidence of knowing that I too could achieve that level of accomplishment. The fact that these were the best was also important because they inspired me to match their level of writing. This was the motivational side of the project. In terms of the content I enjoyed this topic because we were given the freedom to write whatever we wished. In English this is often daunting, and best work is not always produced when given this freedom because students struggle to choose the right subjects. . . . This was not the case with my teacher. Without putting any limitations on what we wrote about he managed to get us all writing on subjects that were good for an English essay. He got us all to think about actual experiences that we ended up writing about. I found this good for my writing because my own experiences never got too far-fetched because they actually happened. This is how I managed to do very well in year 11 English and why I enjoyed this particular topic more than most others.

For more than a few boys, the sheer relief of being liberated from standard classroom rigor was not just an opportunity to "loosen up" but also to unloose untapped imaginative potential. This seventh-grade Canadian boy, for example, experienced in an especially relaxed drama class:

> Our Grade 7 Drama class is one of the most interactive classes of them all. We have it twice in our ten day cycle every Wednesday, but it only lasts one term, then we switch to another program. It is a treat or vacation compared to the rest of the day and it is a time where we can sit back and relax while expressing how we feel or what we're thinking by acting it out in front of the class. We're always "chilling" and we aren't afraid to present to everyone else what we came up with. We sometimes fool around but the teacher understands that it is a time where we let out all our energy from sitting at a desk all day; it is our moment of liberty. It is not a specific class of drama that affected me; it is all the classes together. We play acting games that bring out our creativity and imagination which let us bring out the craziest of ideas such as the wax museum where we pose in a certain position to illustrate a theme that the curator (a student in the class) has to figure out while trying to catch anyone moving. Our teacher often lets us vote on the activity, which enables us to participate in a democratic society. I highly favor the idea of letting the students vote on activities or topics in class due to the fact that it lets us decide the best course to follow, but guided by the limits set by the teacher. I think that the school should either integrate more drama classes into our curriculum or have the other classes use similar ways of proceeding.

Of course, academic elbow room comes with a measure of uncertainty and risk, which, this American eighth grader found, can also be a learning experience:

> This year, in 8th grade Science, there was a lab called the sludge lab which was somewhat of the final lab that summed up the whole unit of Science that we had been covering. We were paired into groups of two and given a jar of liquid and other unidentified materials and asked to

somehow separate and identify the seven substances using the methods we learned throughout the unit. It was exhilarating to have free rein over the lab materials but at the same time I felt in control because I had to be careful and take all precautions because this wasn't a watered down textbook lab. The most intense part of the lab was the time when our teacher burst through the door, came running right at our lab station, and took an evaporating dish we were using from us and put it out the window. He later explained that there were mothballs in the sludge and if we were to release these harmful chemicals into the air, people could pass out and have to be hospitalized. Luckily that obstacle was avoided. Overall, this lab experience was both beneficial for my learning, and gave me the opportunity to have more responsibility which made me feel mature and in control.

For most students reporting, the energizing, transitive factor in being able to solve problems and execute tasks independently was the implicit trust extended to them as they went about their business, as in this Australian eighth grader's account of being entrusted to operate sophisticated power tools in the course of completing his assignment:

My favorite lesson was in a Technology class in term 2, year 8. This was a practical class. We were building CO_2 dragsters. I guess the reason I enjoyed this class so much was the independence given to us when using tools such as a scroll saw. The structure of the class was a five minute instruction, then work for 40 minutes and finally an evaluation with the teacher about what we had achieved that day. While we were working, the teacher came around to supervise us and monitor our progress. I do not think it is just the subject that I enjoyed but the structure of the class to work independently. I believe all classes except Mathematics should be planned like this. The teacher should give us a research task every lesson and I think this would really motivate me.

Among the several features of open inquiry that the boys appreciated was the opportunity to link the scholastic and personal dimensions of their lives. For this American tenth grader, that link was forged in a satisfying way in the course of completing a "personal narrative" of his choosing:

> I would have to say that the moment that stood out to me most was a project in English class. This project can be described as a personal narrative. For this we were given the option of choosing a moment in our life that had the biggest impact. It had to be about three to four pages long and we had the freedom to pretty much write about whatever we wanted. But it had to have some sort of impact on us. For my personal narrative I wrote about how I had Bi-Lateral Hip Arthroscopy. We had guidelines that were to lead us through the narrative. For the first day it was due, we brought a draft to class and we used peer editing to make our narrative better. We were then given another day to have our second draft ready. Our second drafts were peer edited once again. The day our final draft was due we all had to read our work to the class. The teacher then had us talk about our stories very briefly. This whole process took about one week and each day in class we would either peer edit or just on our own write more to our story. I thought that this project had the biggest impact because I improved my skills as a writer and it also gave me the freedom to write about almost anything. The peer editing strengthened my editing skills and also helped me realize things in my own paper that I could edit myself. The class discussion was also beneficial because it helped me learn what the teacher is looking for. This was definitely the most memorable class project for me.

Setting students to open-ended or self-selected tasks does not imply that the teacher is somehow less essential to the process. Even in the most rapt accounts of independent student work, there appears an appreciative acknowledgment of the teacher's having determined just the right amount of room necessary to build autonomy without risking frustration and failure.

This ninth-grade Australian math student is aware that the independence granted him and his classmates to work on assigned math problems is strengthening him as a problem solver—and of his teacher's reassuring availability for help if needed:

An experience from school that stands out particularly for me is the work that we do in Math top set in year 9. I really enjoy Math classes and because of this I think that I learn better in these classes. Our teacher trusts us to work well and tries to cater for our needs, and is quite successful at this. Once he has set our work he mostly just sits at his desk, not disturbing us unless we become particularly noisy. However he is still there for us to ask him questions if we are stuck or have a problem. Because we have to solve the Math problems ourselves, instead of being guided through step-by-step, I think that we remember the method we used better and learn more, from both the methods that worked and those that did not. It also helps us feel independent and more motivated and able to extend upon the question if we please. In this lesson we were also allowed to work on our own or in groups of however many people we wanted. This lack of restriction allows us to solve the problem in a way that works best for us. I think that I learn more by not being guided step by step through the problems because if we were then we would only learn one way of attacking the problem and would not have had the satisfaction of knowing that we had solved the problem and not simply written down the answer. It also makes us feel more responsible for our own learning. I also think that devoting a whole lesson to solving a single problem that is particularly vexing is a much better way of learning than if we were to do a large number of simple, repetitive problems of the sort that we could solve with calculators without really thinking very much. These simple repetitive problems only lead to becoming bored and having a lack of interest in the subject. And therefore not enjoying it or being motivated in class which in turn decreases how much we learn or remember. I think that our focus on problem solving in Math is very important as that's what Math in the real world is really about: solving problems. Problem solving is also a great deal more interesting and "gripping" than straight forward sums and arithmetic. Surprisingly, because of the way in which my teacher runs our Math classes, I actually look forward to them and am quite pleased when I see them on the timetable.

CHAPTER

TEAMWORK AND COMPETITION

As the participating teachers reported their most effective lessons for boys, two of the most frequently stated claims were, "Boys like competition" and "Boys like to work together." It is clear from the previous chapters, especially under the categories of games and motor activity, that competition and teamwork are coextensive. In fact, the "competitive" element in most of the exercises cited is very mild: the victory or prize is usually no more than the collective pleasure of the pair or team in having finished first or having been voted best. It would be a delicate, and perhaps unfruitful, task to attempt to separate or compare the relative degrees of teamwork and competition in a particular lesson. That some exercises felt to be effective involved paired or team activity with no competitive prod indicates that teamwork and competition are indeed separable and that a mutually understood purpose can stand in for competitive advantage.

In schools' interscholastic athletic programs and more recently in scholastic instruction generally, serious criticism has been leveled at practices of any kind that pit students or groups against one another for differentiated rewards. In this view, competitive pursuits by their very nature produce a dispiriting and desensitizing effect on most children involved and should be replaced by cooperative activities (Kohn, 1986, 1993). Another view, again originating in athletics but with clear application to schoolwork, maintains that competitive structures rightly conceived can be a boost to the most effective kinds of mutuality and regard for others (Marx, 2004). From our study, a fair generalization might be that a wide range of teachers found that forming teams to complete a task that would in some way be judged competitively was transitive to learning and mastery.

ENERGIZING COLLABORATION

In some of the "best lessons" reported by teachers, the very process of collaboration seemed to drive the intended learning outcomes forward. In this American teacher's account, an eighth-grade English class derived characters from a common text and then combined those characters into a new story:

> *The very process of collaboration seemed to drive the intended learning outcomes forward.*

In my eighth-grade English language arts class, I have had success over the past several years with a cooperative writing project that arises from the reading of Pirandello's story "War," which thrusts a group of strangers together in a railway carriage during World War I. The characters are nameless. They have in common that most are parents of boys who have gone off to fight for king and country. The theme of the futility of war gradually emerges as the strangers converse and become briefly involved in each other's lives.

As a follow-up activity, I have the boys individually create a character, using a list of types of information they need to know about the nameless person they have drawn. Then once each has shown me his character sheet, groups of four or five boys are selected by a random process to work together. They then draw a sheet describing a setting and a basic situation in which their randomly assembled group of characters find themselves. Taking turns on a laptop computer, the boys then create a short story in which their characters' dialogue and action bring the problem to a climax and resolution. The boys get very much involved in their stories, effectively sharing the tasks of creation and revision. The results are usually some of the best writing produced all year. On several occasions, stories created in this manner have been published in the middle school newspaper. Similar cooperative writing activities have been developed and used successfully with other literature units, including Greek drama and a Shakespearean play.

An American teacher of history found that allowing his senior boys to collaborate on strategic matters—how best to solve difficult multiple-choice questions—produced unexpected and welcome benefits:

In a strong senior AP European history class that routinely featured pretty frequent tests consisting of four or five fiendish multiple-choice questions in addition to standard essay questions, my students bemoaned their repeated lack of success on the multiple-choice section. So I offered them an opportunity to have a test consisting of nothing but hard multiple-choice questions, but they could work together in two teams that each would turn in a single test that reflected their collective best wisdom and the team with the better test would get a five-point bonus.

Students prepared for this test with eyes more wide open. They analyzed previous test questions and uncovered patterns that revealed the kinds of subject matter on which I most frequently focused, and they came to recognize that some questions revealed my sort of hard left agenda, while others tended to treat conventional wisdom with a fair amount of irony. In other words, their metacognitive switches were fully engaged. Ancillary benefits also accrued during the actual test when on several questions, "smarter" and louder students' faulty choices prevailed over "weaker" students' more considered correct ones, and student discussions about the answers probed pretty deeply into the matters at hand with a sense of purpose and clarity often lacking in our class discussions.

Although the following exercise divided this American teacher's senior year philosophy students into groups advocating opposing sides of an ethical issue, the "competition" provided an occasion for exceptional collaboration:

The most effective practice I have used in class involved dividing a class in half and assigning each side the opposite position of a controversial topic. The topics have included whether God is omniscient and omnipotent, why bad things happen to good people, and the extent to which God actively participates in our lives and others'. In my ethics class, the topics have included stem cell research, abortion, the death penalty, and other controversial issues.

Each side was asked to collaborate on writing a seven- to ten-page paper in favor of the position assigned. Each group was responsible for arguing its own position, and everyone in the group was required to share in the presentation. The presentations were given without questioning by the other side. After the presentations, I asked each side to give me a list of issues they wanted to argue with each other. I put the list of issues under each team's name on the board and then began an open argument/debate between the sides. I assigned points for the effectiveness of the argument. At the end of the period, there was generally a winning side, but the scores were very close. I found that the boys were so invested in being prepared to outdo the other side that the topics were extraordinarily well prepared and the formal written work on which they collaborated was better than any work done individually during the year. The argument portion of the assignment was structured and regulated by me to maintain order and fairness in presentation time. When I have used this method, my classes have been better prepared, more interested, and personally invested in the outcome.

A Canadian mathematics teacher reported similar gains in allowing middle school boys to collaborate in pairs when tackling especially difficult problems:

I have found that by giving students assignments that consist of more challenging problems than those that they would normally find on a test or quiz, and allowing them to work in pairs, they have become effective problem solvers.

I give approximately eight assignments per year: four are counted for marks, and four are not. These assignments must be completed in class so that students cannot cheat by asking someone else (a parent, tutor, older sibling, or someone else) to help them with it. The assignment usually consists of four questions that must be completed by the pair during one seventy-five-minute class period. The strategy I suggest is that each student completes the assignment individually and then compares his solutions to those of his partner. At the end of the period, each pair is to hand in only one copy of the completed solutions to each problem.

The assignments differ from tests in that they consist of problems that are more challenging than those that the students would have previously completed in class. Furthermore, the students are allowed to use their class notes, textbook, Internet, and of course, discuss their solutions with their partner. They may NOT, however, discuss their solutions with any other group.

Sometimes I create the groups, and sometimes I allow the students to choose their partners. I have found that some classes prefer that I create the groups, and others prefer to do it themselves. The biggest problem that I have found when they choose their partners themselves is that they will fight over who will be paired up with the "smartest" student, or there is one student with whom no one wishes to be partnered. I have found that heterogeneous ability groupings work best for material that is new to all students, and homogeneous ability groupings work best for extension material (based on something previously taught but goes further). When the assignment counts for marks, I will not allow students whose marks differ by more than 5 percent to be partners.

I have used this method of teaching problem solving in coed schools, single-sex schools, and with accelerated math groups and remedial math groups. In all cases, the students like this method of learning and evaluation.

TEAMWORK WITH A COMPETITIVE EDGE

Across disciplines and across the lesson categories examined in this study, teachers reported the positive effects of forming teams of students who "compete" with other teams to produce the first or fastest solutions to the problems posed. This American English teacher reported success putting such collaboration and competition in the service of building her middle school boys' vocabulary and spelling skills:

For learning of vocabulary, I use a kinesthetic method of review that engages the boys. Boys are divided into teams of three or four. Each team is given a bag of small blocks with letters of the alphabet. Each team is given a few minutes to arrange their letters. One boy sits in the hot seat, which contains all the arranged letters. I read a definition of a word we have been studying, and the boy in the hot seat must try to spell out the word I have defined. The first boy to correctly spell the word earns a point for his team. The player in the hot seat rotates every turn. No one on the team may help the boy who is in play each turn. We play this game with anywhere from ten to fifty words at a time.

Another American English teacher engages competing student teams in "recomposing" literary texts from their scrambled component parts. The puzzle-solving energy becomes transitive to an understanding of the structure of literary master works:

Both on the playing fields and in the classroom, most boys enjoy and learn valuable lessons from competition. One of my more effective teaching practices in upper-school English classes fosters healthy competition and sharpens reading skills.

After grouping the boys in pairs, I give each team of two an envelope containing the same text: a poem or chapter from a novel they are studying that I have photocopied and cut into lines or paragraphs. The first team that correctly assembles the textual puzzle earns the satisfaction of a job well done and, perhaps of more incentive, bragging rights and bonus points on the next quiz.

This activity is valuable for boys, not least of all because it requires them to read closely: they must employ their critical reading skills in order to find the text's beginning, middle, and end and determine from context where lines or paragraphs make logical transitions. This activity also requires boys to negotiate with their classmates and to teach themselves, a welcome break from the routine that often results in their remembering better what they have learned.

My third formers [ninth grade] reassemble Shakespeare's "Sonnet XIX," which, in addition to being a surreptitious way for me to remind students of the sonnet's structure and rhyme scheme, generates rich discussions and leads the boys to make thematic connections to other works in the course. In reassembling a chapter from Douglass's *Narrative of the Life* or Fitzgerald's *The Great Gatsby*, my fifth formers [eleventh grade] not only sharpen their critical reading skills and test their recall of the previous night's reading assignment, but also gain more appreciation for the thoughtful composition and graceful prose of an important work of American literature.

TEAMWORK AND COMPETITION: PARTS COHERING INTO WHOLES

Several participating teachers reported productive student engagement in exercises in which each student was assigned a task that, when mastered and "taught" to classmates, resulted in the collective understanding of the topic or process under study. Such was the finding of this American teacher of middle school general science:

Most often this practice has been described as the "jigsaw puzzle" method. A question, situation, or problem is presented to the class as a whole. Each student is assigned a particular part of the whole. It is their responsibility to become the "expert" for their part, meaning they are to focus only on their particular task in regard to the larger problem. After a predetermined amount of time, that individual student meets with other students working on a different part of the bigger problem. It is each student's responsibility to report, or "teach," what they have found to the other members of the group, knowing the other might have no prior knowledge of these findings. After each student has taught his individual piece, the group as a whole addresses the larger problem or questions to come to a group decision.

An American chemistry teacher engaged boys over the course of a whole school year by dividing the class into teams organized on a "business model," the success of which depended on team members' combined productivity:

For the past two years, the science department has attempted to use cooperative learning exercises during sophomore-year chemistry classes. In order to achieve this goal, a year-long, student-run project has been established, wherein the students form teams and work together on a wide variety of assignments, including homework, quizzes, labs, and projects.

These teams reflect the format of the business world. Each team member occupies a different position (director, planner, public relations officer, and chemist), with different responsibilities specific to each assignment. For example, in a lab, each member of the team is responsible for a specific portion of the lab and lab report. He must prepare for his role by completing a pre-lab, perform a lab activity in class that ties in with his teammates' work, and write up a portion of the report. For oral presentations, the team brainstorms a topic with a prescribed assignment, and each member researches a different aspect of the topic and presents it.

The students are assigned both individual and team grades for their efforts, but they are also able to earn "stock points" in a personal portfolio for every grade. Better grades earn more stock points. For example, tests earn up to 1,000 points and homework assignments up to 100. The points are additive, and incentives are built into the program for maintaining strong, consistent results.

The value of those stock points is determined by the boys' average team performance. The sale of these stock points can be used to purchase many things that make their average school day more enjoyable, like food or hobby items, or they can use their stock points to improve their grades, along the lines of extra credit.

In addition, the stock program allows the students to relate chemistry content to real-world problems in a real-world format like business or politics. For example, while learning thermochemistry, each team poses as a company and researches a future source of energy. They then present their findings to a panel of teachers, who invest in their company accordingly.

The program is very popular among the students because of the excitement and competition it generates, as well as the focus on practical rewards. These are all sentiments that are useful when engaging boys. The team assignments can be homework, quizzes, labs, or projects, but in general, they all involve teamwork, visual stimulus, and procedures that are worked out by hand.

Another American chemistry teacher improvised a "business model" approach in which she challenged competing student teams of tenth and eleventh graders to form a company capable of producing a highly distinctive product—in this case, an Academy Award statue for runners-up:

The silver opportunity exercise is a group work activity where students pull together all the information that they have learned throughout the semester and apply it in a real-world setting. Students are divided into groups of two or three depending on the number of students in each class, and they are given two class periods and evenings to complete the assignment. The scenario is that they form a company to produce a silver Oscar for the Academy Awards to be presented to the second-place finisher.

As we begin our math unit in September, students study density and units of density, and then progress to percentage problems and factor label problem solving. We spend several weeks learning to write and balance chemical equations for the five simple types of reactions. In this exercise, they are required to determine a metal that will displace silver from a solution of silver nitrate. (They have studied the activity series of metals and know that a metal can replace any metal located below it in the series.) They are given pages from a chemical catalogue that includes prices for various types of metals and the different forms that may be purchased, like granular, wire, strips, or sheets of the metal. They have done a lab using aluminum strips to displace copper from a solution of copper II chloride and have seen me do a demonstration using copper wire to displace silver from silver nitrate. Students discuss which metals are possible choices for their single-displacement reaction and then narrow the field but looking at characteristics. They have read (I hope) the hazards given for each metal in the catalogue (for example, those that react violently with water) or know from class discussions which elements are poisonous. After selecting several metals that might work, they write balance equations for the metals to see which metal will produce the most moles of silver. Using the information from the catalogue, they do a cost analysis to further determine which metal to use and the cost of the raw materials. In the last steps, they determine the percentage markup for the Oscars with an explanation of why they chose that percentage, and they conclude with the cost their company will charge for the Oscar.

By the time they complete the activity, they have used almost every concept we have learned all semester. It is graded as one-half of a test grade, and bonus points are awarded for first-, second-, and third-place finish with the best answers. Help hints are available for a price of five points each in case they reach the point of total frustration.

There are endless variations on the "business model" approach to solving scholastic problems, as in this South African teacher's challenge to his students to devise a marketable procedure for separating salt from rock salt:

In teaching separations of mixtures to grade 8 boys, I have found a lesson that works well involves self-discovery and competition. The boys are given an introduction where they are told that their group is a company that has to develop a method of separating salt from rock salt. This is put into perspective in terms of industry and producing salt. Each member of the group has to take on a certain role (CEO, marketing, finance, and others). The boys are asked to plan how to separate the mixture. They then get to use any apparatus to put their method into practice. At this stage they often have the wrong method but discover for themselves why it doesn't work and make their own improvements. A few boys who really struggle need some guidance with thinking through their ideas. Once the group has completed the experiment, they write up what they have done. The write-up is submitted as a tender to the company (that is, the teacher) that is looking to implement a method on a large scale in industry. Each group then presents its report. The presentation includes the science, the costs, the marketing, and why their company should win the tender. After the presentations, the teacher, with input from the class, gets to choose the successful group. They are awarded with a bar of chocolate.

THE BOYS RESPOND

It would not require an international student survey to discover that school-aged boys enter enthusiastically into competitive activities. Of interest here, however, is the boys' pronounced appreciation of opportunities to both compete and cooperate in a scholastic setting. The heightened engagement resulting from such exercises is clear in the following accounts, as is the boys' awareness that such engagement results in substantial learning and improvement.

Of interest here is boys' pronounced appreciation of opportunities to both compete and cooperate in a scholastic setting.

As faculty and boys recounted in the Chapter Three on games, casting the most fundamental kinds of skill building as a competitive exercise can dissolve boys' resistance to what might be perceived as tedious drill. This U.S. eighth grader found a playful element of competition both enjoyable and productive in building his French vocabulary:

In French in 8th grade, we play a game where the whole group reads from a passage. Each person has one word to say, but if you pronounce the word wrong, you are out of the game. You go around the room pronouncing words and the last person standing wins. It is very competitive with my classmates and me, and sometimes there is a prize for the winner. I felt that my classmates and I were very engaged in the activity, and although we are having some fun, the game also helps us learn to pronounce all the French words.

In reading the boys' accounts of competitive elements in their favorite lessons, we were struck repeatedly by language approaching elation as they assessed what they had accomplished. This U.S. eighth-grade Latin student is anything but "cool" about his big day reciting the declension of Latin nouns:

Last year, my classmates and I were sitting in Latin Alpha when we heard some amazing news. Our teacher came in and told us about a contest, the Latin declension contest that would occur after every declension was learned. First it was easy, we had to recite the first declension endings singular and plural. Then we learned the second declension and it became harder. As the declensions progressed the contest grew harder and harder. At the end, we were supposed to recite five declensions as fast as we could and whoever was the quickest would be named champion. There were two heavy favorites in our class. "Mr. Latin" was the heaviest favorite. He had won all the earlier declension-offs and did not look as though he was slowing down. The second favorite was a quiet boy who was a killer Latin student. As all the boys filled into the room, I was quietly saying the declensions in my head as fast as I could. The contest began. Everyone dropped out fast, kids would either forget the declension or they would go too fast and the teacher would not be able to hear what they were saying. This contest had a two round format. The top three declensioners would go to the next round while everyone else would stop. I was sure that the two favorites would be in the finals so there was only one real spot open. It was my turn to go. I quickly rattled off all the declensions in 23.4 seconds, which had put me in second place with only one person remaining. This clinched my spot in the finals. I was pumped. So the finals were set. It was the two students and I in the final. I couldn't believe I was competing against the two smartest kids in the class to become the declension-off winner. One of the favorites went first, he said it in a record 11.3 seconds, but the teacher said he went too fast for anyone to hear, so he was out. It was the other favorite boy and I left. He was up next and he did it in an amazing 19.6 seconds. So I was last. There was no pressure because I was the underdog trying to beat the favorites. I started off and I don't know what got into me, I just rattled off the declensions in 15.3 seconds. I had won the competition! I beat the odds and won the declension-off. I was rewarded with a little candy and a medal. I was so excited, I couldn't believe I had won.

As in so many of the other examples of competitive classroom business cited warmly by the boys, there is also an acknowledgment of the special motivation provided by "delivering" for one's team, as in this American seventh grader's experience reviewing factual material in his English class:

> In English class in the seventh grade we were divided into two sections, and no student chose teammates. Each group sat in chairs on their side of the room and one player from each team went to the center for every round to compete against the other player. The players stood and waited until an English question was asked and the first person to pick up the object, which was an eraser, was allowed to answer the question. If you picked up the eraser first you had a limit of time to answer the question. I felt especially engaged because it was fun and almost every time I went up for my round I was cheered by my team and I answered most of the questions correctly. I usually beat my opponent to the object and I knew the answers to the questions. This was an experience where I felt engaged because the winning team received bonus points on the next test. It motivated me because I basically had a chance to test my English abilities and view my knowledge of the subject. This class activity is one of many activities that have especially engaged me during my career as a student.

Few schools in the United States subdivide their student bodies into "houses" (subdivisions of larger student bodies consisting of boys at each grade level), but many British, Canadian, and Southern Hemisphere schools do. Membership in a house provides students with a second, and more intimate, identification in the school. The house system also provides many opportunities for both traditional and improvised competitions. In assessing his "euphoric" victory in a particular interhouse competition, this South African twelfth grader reports that the ultimate reward was not merely "winning" but in contributing to the fellowship of his housemates:

> Normally my biggest highlight of the year occurs during a little festival we have called Cultural Week. We have six houses in our school and for this

one week, all the houses get involved through competition. My house has won the trophy for best house ever since I was in form 1.

As a result I have made it quite an ambition for myself to uphold the legacy of our house. Every single year I take part in a large number of events (often swamping myself with work!) to make a contribution. My strongest area thus far has been my directing of the form skits and my debating. All of my hard work and effort seem to pay off in the end when I hear my name called out for "Best Debater" and the ultimate pinnacle is the joy that the overall victory brings to the members of my house. I do realize that at the end of the day the only thing that really matters when I apply for university is the marks I attain in my academic career, and I do take it seriously throughout the year. Yet this one period of time is definitely the greatest feeling of euphoria I experience in a year. It feels good that I can make a big contribution to the house and bring my fellow peers something to be proud about!

Boys were also eager to report on the motivating effect of teamwork outside any competitive framework. The common feature to these reports were boys' readily expressed pleasure in "helping," that is, in making an important contribution to a collective effort. This Australian eleventh grader summarized the benefits of a sustained wilderness challenge that his school offered:

Last year, at the end of the year, all year 10 students participated in a ten day *Venture* through beautiful rugged terrain in the most picturesque part of Western Australia. Students bushwalk, and some parts of the journey require working as a team to sail and row. During the journey, everyone is required to work as a team, for instance: bush cooking, where everyone helps by sharing the jobs of cooking, cleaning, and eating! Or the bushwalking itself, where all members have to work hard to keep up the morale of the slower walkers. Another important team effort during the course is working together to build and maintain friendships. Each morning began with bag-packing for the days' trip, followed by a quick breakfast, and swapping of duties (disinfectant ownership, leadership, navigation, etc). The walks usually lasted eight-ten hours, with lunch typically eaten when we got to the new campsite. Upon reaching the campsite, hootchies [improvised tents] were set up, followed by hammocks, and exchange of dirty walking clothes for boardies [swim shorts] and a wash in the nearest river. After lounging around and relaxing, dinner preparation began. Afterwards, everyone got together for a group meeting about the things we learned about our environment's natural and local histories, each other, and our likes and dislikes about *Venture* that day. One night, after a long walk, our leader told us "it's all downhill from here, boys." The next day, however, we discovered that downhill meant first climbing Mt. Chance. A week into the camp one of the boys was complaining about the lack of technology and civilization; specifically the absence of television. So we all spent the evening creating our own forms of entertainment. The two most popular were the spear and the "insect pit," our substitute for TV, in which ants faced off beetles, and cockroaches battled with millipedes, and a giant insect that we found was paralyzed by a spider. The trip back was filled with awe (or sleep, for some) at civilization and technology (wow, look at those cars! And that streetlight!). *Venture* motivated me to work as part of a team, and was possibly the most engaging learning experience of my young life. I can see that I really enjoy helping people. It makes me very happy to help people, and I learned that I am strong. I was able to motivate the people in my group, even when they thought they were in pain. The *Venture* experience provided me with a practical application for the principles of altruism.

What his Australian contemporary learned in the bush, this British tenth grader experienced in his French classroom:

One of my most memorable lessons I gained the most from was a French lesson last year. We were learning vocabulary and were in groups of four. The teacher had told us we had to stand up before the rest of the class and recite vocab using a memorizing technique (e.g., a poem, a song, etc.) after learning the vocab for ten minutes with the rest of your group. My group and I had turned the sheet of vocab into a type of song and sang it to the rest of the class. I learned a very good way of memorizing vocab in that lesson and I can still remember that vocab today as it was such a good experience. I also learned a lot of other vocab learning techniques from my fellow classmates including using a theme tune from a popular program or film and fitting the vocab in. We shared our techniques and ideas as a class and benefited greatly for it as almost the entire class scored very highly in the vocab test the following week. I enjoyed the fact that we didn't do the usual "sit and listen to the teacher" sort of lesson and it was refreshing to have our French vocab learning techniques, our actual vocab and our skill of working as a team. It was definitely a good team building exercise and I am very fond of it still. I would recommend this type of learning exercise to everyone.

The boys' clear appreciation of sharing and the stimulating mutuality of working in teams need not always be initiated by a teacher or coach. This Australian twelfth grader's most memorable lesson was the result of his class-mates' deciding to take responsibility for a lesson's success:

Walking into a normal standard year twelve Accounting class I thought that I had another long and tedious class in front of me. But this time was different. My classmates and I had been set a series of long questions to be completed by the end of the week. It was Wednesday and we had some doubt about completing these tasks. Instead of complaining my mates and I jumped straight into it, helping each other and taking on the challenge. All of us must have got through half the work within a day and a bit, creating a success. Although the motivation was minimal at the start by the end of the productive lesson, most of us were rising above the challenge and highly motivated to finish the task.

CHAPTER

8

PERSONAL REALIZATION

While the effectiveness of most of the categories of instruction reported by teachers can be attributed to what we have been calling the transitive capacity of the instructional method to the subject under study, the impact of some of the reported lessons lay in their striking an especially responsive chord in the boys' personal lives. In many cases, such lessons brought to clear consciousness matters of deep personal importance, clarifying and energizing boys' awareness of realities and values beyond what might be expected or required in school.

CONSIDERATION OF OTHERS

A point frequently raised by those concerned about the limiting effects of single-sex education is that essential knowledge of the other gender will be diminished, if not forfeited altogether. Counterclaims can be made that consideration of the "other" gender in the absence of cross-gender distraction and stimulation is especially effective. This American teacher of history favored a lesson in which her boys were engaged in a sustained consideration of historical feminism:

In an elective for eleventh- and twelfth-grade boys, Global Women's History, students explored women's movements around the world. For about three weeks, they read essays about the origins of twentieth-century women's movements and feminist movements in various countries around the world. The case studies included Egypt, Vietnam, South Africa, Brazil, Kenya, Korea, Japan, and Iran. The essays were supported with the use of primary sources. The students examined the relationship between an interest in gender equality and the sociopolitical context in each country. In some countries, they noted that the issue of women's rights is often co-opted into a nationalist movement when women's support is needed to gain independence from a colonial power or establish a new nation. In other circumstances, the students noted that women are often drawn into social activism for causes other than what might be labeled "feminism" at first, but that once involved, those women often slowly find their way to more explicitly feminist causes.

In exploring how, when and in what circumstances people are drawn to feminism, the students struggled to define *feminism* and *feminist*. While I planned different class activities, the boys usually got involved in heated discussion quickly each day. They were stimulated by the issues raised in each case study. As they worked their way through their ideas about feminism, they gained confidence about the history they were studying. As their confidence in understanding the history grew, they were ready to take their knowledge to a more personal level by defining *feminism* and *feminist*.

They still struggled with definitions of *feminism* and *feminist*. I asked them to use the historical examples of women's movements, the participants in women's movements, and the way people in different countries had self-identified as feminists to inform their own conclusions about what kinds of people can be feminists.

I decided that they needed an opportunity to demonstrate their independent definition of *feminist*. *Ms.* magazine had a page titled, "This is what a feminist looks like." The page included a collage of photographs of dozens of faces. The class discussed the message *Ms.* magazine was sharing with the collage of faces. I asked the boys to make their own photo collage answering the question, "What does a feminist look like?" Each collage was to be accompanied by a written explanation for why each photograph had been chosen.

Each boy interpreted the challenge differently. They brought their collages and explanations to class and presented them to their classmates.

The collages sparked interesting conversation as the boys questioned each other's definitions and choices of illustrations. The boys enjoyed explaining their collages to each other.

This study provoked a lot of emotions for the students, and that emotional reaction stimulated their desire to pursue the study.

I think that the boys were intrigued by the variety of forms that women's movements have taken around the world. They were outraged when they learned that nationalist movements in some countries had enlisted women's support by promising gender equality but then not delivered on those promises once in power. They were surprised to learn that in many countries, most women were not necessarily interested in the notion of feminism. Rather, many women were drawn into social activism for other reasons. The boys were fascinated to discover that often women slowly found their way into feminism only after getting involved in other social causes. The boys had not previously thought about how involvement in one cause might lead a person to another cause. They also had not considered that many women do not prioritize gender issues in their lives. The boys were intrigued by their discovery that what concerns most women are not gender issues but issues that may disproportionately affect women. Women's own slow discoveries of this phenomenon caught the boys' attention. I think the boys were stunned by the idea that many women have no time or interest in being labeled feminist.

There was nothing flashy about this unit of study. We read scholarly essays. Boys discussed them in small groups or whole class discussions. The format was fairly traditional. It was the emotional reaction that made the lessons come alive for the boys.

In the final stages of the unit, the boys enjoyed stepping back from the details of the historical examples to make assertions about patterns. They enjoyed taking control of the material in that way.

The final assignment of the photo collage gave them a chance to own the notion of feminism. They were proud to feel mastery and insight about the subject. They also enjoyed the opportunity to create their own version of it.

It was the emotional reaction that made the lessons come alive for the boys.

SELF-DISCOVERY

Many teachers' "best lessons" engaged students in taking a considered measure of themselves, including looking at themselves in unfamiliar ways. An American art teacher recounted the often lasting impact of her ninth graders' production of a ceramic self-portrait:

> The goal is to create a life-size terra-cotta self-portrait bust as a monument to each boy's unique individual personality at this time and place in their lives. Before the project is introduced, the boys are asked to make an extreme facial expression and are photographed from multiple angles. This is fun and automatically reveals a great deal of personality.
>
> The teaching begins with the history of classical documentary portraiture up to its role in contemporary art. Then human structural anatomy is introduced, as is "body language" as a universal form of human visual communication. Sculpting begins with about sixty pounds of clay, which is physically challenging and helps the boys maintain their engagement throughout the sculpting process.
>
> This is a fairly straightforward and traditional project and is therefore accessible to the full range of adolescent maturity levels. It is more often an advanced exercise at the undergraduate art school level. The project can work with teen boys because they respond to the challenge of scale and the direct tangibility of realistic rendering. The quality of the resulting sculpture depends (like most other three-dimensional art projects) on the levels of concentration maintained throughout the process.
>
> The finished portraits adorn our campus, informing our community of the creative potential of each boy. Parents are incredibly proud of the sculptures, and years later the busts trigger memories of the boys' special years at the school.

An American teacher of philosophy and religion reported striking a resonant chord in her ninth-grade students by asking them to consider the role of honor in their lives:

> With my freshmen Gospel of Mark course, I employ a technique of striving to make the text applicable to boys today. One theme that boys resonate

with greatly is honor. When examining the text of Mark, there are multiple examples of Jesus lifting up honorable behavior as the best course of action. Whether it is in his dialogue disputes with the Pharisees or a parable of how to live one's life, I find that when the boys can see that living right has its own rewards, they come alive. They so want to do the right deed, to be thought of as honorable. The more stories I can share that exemplify that, the higher the bar is that they set for themselves.

At the conclusion of the course, I ask the boys to write a modern parable that illustrates a moral truth. Over half the class inevitably writes a parable that demonstrates doing the honorable course of action in the face of overwhelming temptations. This is a course that is historical in nature, and yet by the course's end, modeling our lives in the example of Jesus is something the boys take away from the class.

MASCULINITY

In a variety of ways, and not just in the lessons categorized here as personal realization, teachers indicated that "best lessons" often engaged boys in considering their lives as males and their masculine identities.

This American English teacher asked his students to ponder "manliness" through a consideration of the values and behavior of Atticus Finch, the hero of Harper Lee's novel, *To Kill a Mockingbird*:

A couple of my favorite classes this year occurred when I used a topic in a novel as a jumping-off point for a discussion of a vital life lesson. An example of that, and one that is particularly cogent to this study, was a discussion I led on "masculinity." In Chapter Ten of *To Kill a Mockingbird*, the Finch children learn a lot about what it means to be a real man. The chapter begins with Scout explaining, "Atticus was feeble; he was nearly fifty. . . . Our father didn't do anything. He worked in an office, not in a drugstore. Atticus did not drive a dump-truck for the county, he was not the sheriff, he did not farm, work in a garage, or do anything that could possibly arouse the admiration of anyone."

The kids believe that their father is the least manly father in the whole town, and it is a source of shame to them. He doesn't do any of the things a masculine father should do, like hunt, fish, farm, gamble, smoke, play in the church football game, and so on. Later in the chapter, however, Atticus is forced into a situation in which he must reveal a more "masculine" side of himself. When a rabid dog approaches the house, it is Atticus who shoots him. He doesn't volunteer for this position, but rather the other residents beg him to do it. Scout and Jem learn that their father is actually the best marksman in the entire state. Certainly that is a manly thing. And while for Scout it is the shooting ability that makes her proud of her father, the more interesting and more important lesson is Jem's revelation that Atticus had intentionally kept his marksmanship a secret. Atticus wanted his children to learn that shooting a gun and other things of that nature are not what make a man.

This is the jumping-off point for our class conversation. We now move beyond *To Kill a Mockingbird* to have a discussion about the idea of masculinity in modern society. For the rest of class, I have the boys list the things that we consider masculine in our society (money, power, capacity for violence, access to beautiful women, athleticism, strength, toughness, and others) and examine whether those characteristics are really virtues. Thankfully, the boys come to the conclusion that those "masculine" characteristics do not make a man. I label these characteristics as part of a cultural phenomenon known as false masculinity. We then shift the conversation to explore what characteristics a good man should have. A good man is a man with integrity, honor, courage, compassion, purpose, and loving relationships. We spend a lot of time talking about the relationship aspect of being a good man and how a man can be judged by his relationships. Is he a good son, brother, father, husband, teammate, friend, colleague, boss? At the end of the lesson, I felt that the boys had a much better understanding of what it really means to be a man, as opposed to the false masculinity espoused in our culture.

INTRINSIC SUBJECT MATTER

The effectiveness of a number of lessons related in this study resided, the teachers believed, in addressing life issues especially pitched to boys: their money and future work, their treasured possessions, their obsessions, their character, their social place, and, as in the following example, their understanding of masculinity itself. This American teacher found that addressing sensitive points of masculinity went deep with his American literature students.

My junior American literature class reads *Moby Dick*. Inevitably, there are the snickers when we read in Chapter Four that Ishmael and Queequeg sleep together at the inn before they depart on their voyage. But I restore order by pointing them to the line where, when the two of them wake up the next morning and Queequeg has his arm around Ishmael, he extracts himself from the embrace "by dint of much wriggling, and loud and incessant expostulations upon the unbecomingness of his hugging a fellow male in that matrimonial sort of style." That seems to take care of it for a while. We set sail.

As Ahab becomes more obsessed with his pursuit of the white whale, he inspires all of his men, including Ishmael, to take an oath and vow "death to Moby Dick." Yet Ishmael, being the romantic that he is, soon realizes the folly of his participation in his captain's vengeance. In the chapter called "A Squeeze of the Hand," he renounces his oath, and thus he attains ultimate salvation. It's a difficult but crucial chapter, and I want the boys to understand its importance.

In this scene, Ishmael and several of the men are sitting around a tub of the "sperm" that has "concreted into lumps," and they must squeeze it back into liquid. Here, only Melville's words will do:

I forgot all about our horrible oath; in that inexpressible sperm, I washed my hands and my heart of it. I felt divinely free from all ill-will, or petulance, or malice, of any sort whatsoever. I found myself unwittingly squeezing my co-laborers' hands in it, mistaking their hands for the gentle globules. Such an abounding, affectionate, friendly, loving feeling did this avocation beget; that at last I was continually squeezing their hands, and looking up into their eyes sentimentally; as much as to say,—Oh! my dear fellow beings, why should we longer cherish any social acerbities, or know the slightest ill-humor or envy! Come; let us squeeze hands all round; nay, let us all squeeze ourselves into each other; let us squeeze ourselves universally into the very milk and sperm of kindness.

In my class, we sit around a Harkness table [a large oval table]. It's perfect for this lesson. I ask the boys to join hands to form a circle with me. They are reluctant at first, but after the obligatory rolled eyes and shrugged shoulders, they finally go along with it. Leaving nothing to chance, I am the one who reads the passage aloud. They listen. Slowly, glancing like a dozen Ishmaels from one pair of eyes to the next, they begin to sense the purpose of the exercise. As my reading of the chapter progresses, they themselves become the crew, and they start to feel and then understand the deep brotherhood and mutual dependence that defines one of the central themes of the book. At last, as the chapter ends, I send a squeeze of the hand around the circle, and they release their grips. The physical moment is over, but the lingering stillness signals that the impression has been made.

Investigating a wilder, darker side of boyhood—in this case, being geographically dislocated and orphaned—stimulated the students of this American teacher of sixth-grade boys:

One of my favorite units of the year involves introducing my students to *The Lost Boys of Sudan*. We begin by having a discussion about sharia and the disadvantages of having a government based on religion. During this discussion, we compare life under sharia to the religious freedom we have here in the United States. For homework, the boys read one of the vignettes from Joan Hecht's book, *The Journey of the Lost Boys*. The next day in class, we have a brief discussion of the story, followed by a viewing of the film *The Lost Boys of Sudan*. This is a wonderful documentary that follows several Lost Boys as they make the transition from a Kenyan refugee camp to their new home in the United States. Usually class time does not allow for an entire viewing, so their homework for the night is to either read another vignette from Hecht's book or write a reflective paragraph on what they read the night before. The next class is dedicated to finishing up the film and discussing the immense difficulties the young men faced as they flee their homes and then once they arrive in the United States. I am very fortunate to know a local Lost Boy who generously gives an hour of his time to speak to the boys. The students are thrilled to meet a Lost Boy, and they are typically moved by his story. The next day, we follow up with a discussion of how fortunate the boys are to have a loving family, a roof over their heads, the opportunity for a wonderful education, clothes on their back, and food on their plate.

I enjoy this unit because I find that it is very eye-opening for the boys. Many of the Lost Boys were the same age as (or younger than) my sixth-grade students, so they can relate to the hardships these Sudanese refugees faced. The unit contains great lessons in courage, self-sufficiency, and overcoming adversity. Overall I stress the fact that these sixth graders are incredibly blessed, and therefore they should feel an obligation to help those who are less fortunate.

My goal is to eventually add a service component to this unit. In the past, the school has made a financial contribution from a larger fundraiser to a charity operated by Lost Boys living in America. In the future, I would like to lead the sixth grade in a fundraiser in which the proceeds go to that same organization, with the goal being that the boys experience making a positive impact on the lives of children they will more than likely never meet.

The beckoning appeal of the sinister was incorporated productively into this South African English teacher's challenge to boys to enter the world of Raymond Chandler's crime fiction:

The task that I want to share is a writing exercise for grade 10 boys. The unit is entitled "Writing in the Style of Raymond Chandler." The unit comprises a series of structured and scaffolded tasks that introduce pupils to the writing of Chandler before finally asking them to write the opening chapter to a private detective novel. The tasks work well as they all build on the previous one, and most of the preliminary tasks can be done in pairs or groups. Boys have always responded well to the task, and the reasons I think are:

1. Gangster and detective genre stories appeal to boys.

2. The scaffolding of the tasks helps the boys develop confidence in their ability to write.

3. Pair and group work is fun and generates good ideas.

4. Boys enjoy adopting the voice of a detective and imagining his shady world.

While boys' preoccupation with violent and dangerous pursuits is an abiding contemporary social concern, this South African history teacher guides her eighth-grade students' fascination with grisly combat to broader cultural considerations:

Studying the history of Vietnam with a group of Remove boys [grade 8], I found they were fascinated by the blood, gore, killing, hardship, and so on of the war. I taught five separate classes in the year group. I inveigled my coteacher, who had one class, to join me in a project near the end of term. Much of the content and facts had been covered in class, so they had all the basic knowledge and had done some reading. The year group was divided into groups of six. Each group was given one aspect of the war to research, for example, the capture of Hamburger Hill or the tunnel rats. They had to research their topic fully and write a script for a short five-minute dramatization. The script had to be factually based. Each boy had to take turns being the narrator. Each script had to have an introduction giving the context of the dramatization and a conclusion stating what happened after.

The dramatizations were presented to parents at a Vietnamese evening after which the parents enjoyed a Vietnamese meal and the boys watched a Vietnamese movie. The boys by the end of this knew their history inside out! They had learned it without realizing it as they had researched it, written about it, acted it, discussed it in their groups, and then watched each other. The best of inadvertent learning experiences ever!

This American mathematics teacher found boys especially responsive to an application of a mathematical principle that carried the promise of conferring a real financial benefit to them:

I am the mathematics department chairman, and I consider myself a teacher of teachers as well as a teacher of boys. The practice that I am going to narrate involves the practice of showing your students real-life examples of mathematics that can be used throughout the curriculum from anywhere, grades 6 to 12. I have many of these types of topics, but I will limit myself to the idea of compound interest during this discussion.

The formula for compound interest is relatively simple. The formula is: $A = P(1 + r/n)$ raised to the nt power. The formula has five unknowns:

A = amount of money at the end of the investment

P = amount of money at the beginning of the investment (principal)

r = rate of interest (must be converted to a decimal for the formula to work)

n = number of times the interest is compounded in a year

t = number of years in the investment

If I am teaching algebra I, I could give the following:

John wants to invest $1,000 in an investment that promises him 4.5% interest compounded monthly. How much money will he have at the end of 5 years?

If I am teaching algebra II, I might give the following:

John wants to double his money in 6 years. If the investment is to be compounded daily, what rate of interest does he need to achieve?

If I am teaching precalculus, I might use the following:

John had an investment that was worth $5,000 after 3 years. If he invested $3,000 8 years ago, what was his annual rate of interest? (This is usually referred to as APR in investments.)

An American economics teacher also found his eleventh- and twelfth-grade students responsive to investigating and mastering operations that promised financial gain:

For my eleventh- and twelfth-grade elective course in economics and personal finance, we have designed a stock-picking and investment selection contest that seeks to use in a "hands-on" practical way many of the concepts about financial analysis, finding good advice and making good investment judgments that I teach in the course. Each student is provided with a balance of $50,000 (not real money at this time, although that might change in the future) and is asked to use all manner of investment advice and analysis to select five common stocks traded in U.S. dollars in U.S. financial markets. In an accompanying form, the boy provides the name of the corporation, its trading symbol, industry area, price per share, and "reason for buying." The last information can be analysis, news, advice, or speculation. The boy is required to hold on to these stocks until the end of the next marking period (about three weeks or so), at which time they may trade for other stocks, take profits, or absorb losses.

I require that their portfolios be diversified (not heavily weighted in any particular areas). After the initial investments are made, they may have more than five stocks, including a foreign stock when we study foreign markets. As an incentive to participate and do their best, I award extra points on the term and marking period averages of boys whose gains are most impressive: five extra points for the winner, four points for second place, three for third place, and so on. I do not deduct points for portfolios that lose value, but a boy must have some amount of profit to gain any points at all. In a falling stock market like the past year's, not many boys have shown profits, yet a small number of assiduous and diligent "investors" are in the black.

Students are welcome and encouraged to use all legal forms of obtaining investment advice and information, including professional advisors to their family, family members, the financial press, investment advisory services, and the Internet. One of the many goals of this project is to teach young men to do proper research, use the Internet effectively, and invest responsibly. It fosters a healthy sense of competition such as they will encounter in their future lives. On the advice of one of our speakers, we use Yahoo Finance as our investing site. It offers bountiful investment information and advice for free and is very easy to navigate. I keep the password to the account so that any trades or portfolio changes must go through me as the "broker."

We allocate a certain amount of class time for stock trading, and boys are able to check their own portfolios on their own laptops, although they do not have access to their peers' information or accounts.

A Canadian mathematics teacher challenged her algebra students to use algebraic tools to explore buying the car of their dreams:

In mathematics, my teaching partner and I created a project to have the students do some research and apply their algebra skills acquired in the algebra unit. They had to research a model of car of their preference online, select options of their choice, select a payment plan, and see how much it would cost them per month for a lease for this car. We also supplied them with average costs for other expenses, such as gas and down payment. They used all of the information to figure out what their total expenses would be per month and created an algebraic expression for the amount of money spent over a time period of one year. In the end, they had to prepare a presentation to present their information to the class.

Subject matter close to boys' hearts of course extends beyond material acquisition. This American mathematics teacher tapped into her eighth-grade boys' immersion in major league baseball:

This topic is covered near the end of a prealgebra/algebra I course. I use chalkboard demonstrations, ask questions referring back to previously learned material that bear on the lesson, give the boys opportunities to practice the routine, and answer any questions they might have subsequent to trying to do the problems.

Class begins with a discussion about baseball. Who is their favorite team or ballplayer? We discuss the hardest positions to play. Through the discussion, most boys throw out numbers that they have heard on TV or the radio—for instance, "Jones is hitting .302!" or "Maddox has a 1.25 ERA." We talk about the meaning of a batting average and earned runs against a pitcher.

Today's class will begin with the following formulas on the board:

Batting average (AVG) = Hits/at bats
Earned run average (ERA) = (Earned runs × 9)/innings pitched

We continue to discuss what constitutes an "at bat" and when a complete inning is or is not pitched.

I produce the newspaper sports page and use specific baseball data from the night before. I ask the selected students to calculate a few AVGs and ERAs from the data.

I write on the board and have them calculate the following:

Consider the following two pitchers:
Jones: 1 IP, 4 ER = ?
Smith: 8 IP, 1 ER = ?
Total: 9 IP, 5 ER = ?
Jones: 6 AB, 3 H = ?
Smith: 5 AB, 1 H = ?
Total: 11 AB, 4 H = ?

From here the boys will notice that all the AVGs are decimals and not the whole numbers that are used when speaking about the AVG. They previously learned that a percentage is something out of 100. They will see in the batting averages that their AVG is based on how many hits they get out of ten at bats. ERAs are calculated in the same way but are whole numbers with some decimals. I then stretch the calculations to the whole team's batting average and ERA.

We then move on to more complicated calculations such as slugging percentage. The following information is written on the board:

Slugging average is calculated as: Total bases/(official at bats).

Official at bats are calculated as: Plate appearances − walks − hit by pitch−sacrifices.

Total bases are calculated as: Singles + 2 × doubles + 3 × triples + 4 × home runs.

We then pick more data from the sports page and calculate a batter's slugging percentage.

PEDAGOGY DESIGNED FOR BOYS

The great majority of the reporting teachers indicated that they believed their approach to instruction was in one or more ways pitched to boys' learning; others, especially beginning teachers and those beginning their teaching in boys' schools, were not sure, and a few stated emphatically their belief that their approach had worked or would work equally well with girls. Difficult to verify as such claims may be, the telling point here is that the teachers selected lessons they found to be "especially effective," and the recipients of those lessons were all boys. This section looks at a sampling of teachers who intentionally and explicitly designed lessons directed to what they believe are distinctive features in boys' learning.

A New Zealand English teacher, with three decades of teaching experience in both coed and boys' schools, reported that teaching boys to write essays works best when the process is highly structured, as boys do best addressing "short, sharp tasks":

Whether teaching language or literature, I always highly structure each lesson. The lesson always begins with, "Tell me five things . . ." This could be about the last lesson, the text, or something else, followed by, "What shall we do now?" The lesson then follows with ten-minute (maximum) activities that are structured within themselves. For example, planning an essay begins with these steps:

- Task 1 is to write the first paragraph—and brainstorm ideas.

- Task 2 is, "Write the opening sentence only." Then we stop and listen to some examples. I copy the best one and say why I chose it.

- Task 3 is to take five minutes to write two more sentences. We stop and discuss two examples and discuss.

All steps are tightly timed—sometimes with a clock on the whiteboard (from the data projector).

Every step they take in structuring (say, a paragraph) is written on the board by a student. I try to get as many students as possible up and writing on the board each lesson—to keep them active. I place strong emphasis on the words and phrases of the instructions using words like "*list*" and asking, "What are the four steps . . . ?" as these are less elusive than "*discuss*" or "*analyze*." The lesson always ends with a summary, for example, "What were the three most important things . . . ?" I use this structure for most of my lessons as I feel the boys like structure, simplicity, short tasks, and pressure. It ensures there is plenty of writing going on as opposed to very little with open-ended tasks. They like clear deadlines and limits.

I think it is connected to boys needing short, sharp tasks, as they can concentrate for only short time periods. I believe boys respond to things being timed and have clear limits.

I feel the boys like structure, simplicity, short tasks, and pressure.

They are wired for dominance (fastest, strongest, and so on), so activities that light-heartedly encourage this are popular. They need more recesses so a change of activity can seem like a "rest." They like established and monitored rules and routines and deadlines.

A New Zealand colleague underscored the value of crisp process and clear structure, especially with his senior English students:

The following lesson was conducted with a high academic sixth-form class. The subject of discussion was Wordsworth's concept of time in its relationship to the process of the creative imagination.

I invited the pupils to interpret the following statement and then cite evidence from the poem "Tintern Abbey" to establish its validity: *When the reaction of the senses, chiefly of eye and ear, to the external natural world at a given moment in time is suspended and exquisitely fitted to the mind by way of the creative imagination, that initial, transient, sensory experience dissipates and the soul, at a later time, feels an eternal kinship with transcended and spiritual meanings.*

Before they could cite evidence from the text to establish the statement's validity, students were required to interpret the statement itself. They were permitted approximately fifteen minutes to ponder the statement, then explicate the obscure implications inherent within the statement. To begin with, they were somewhat confounded; nevertheless, I persuaded them to look at operative, individual words and word clusters and engaged them in a discussion that would unravel precise meanings.

I employed the method of repetition, reinforcement, and reagitation while maintaining sustained eye contact. Although the class of twenty-four intelligent and academic-minded boys was awed at first, they gradually began to apprehend the difficult concepts and engaged in rapport with each other as well as me. We then proceeded to apply the key concepts to the text.

I distinctly felt that constant repetition, reinforcement, and reagitation of crucial issues were the strategies that unified thought logically and effected clear understanding in the minds' of the pupils.

The pupils themselves, of their own volition, admitted that their minds were formatively infused and heightened by the thrust and meaning of the topic discussed. I asked the pupils to submit a brief written comment explaining what particular method or at what moment they began to gain clarity of understanding. The merit and success of the lesson is strongly attested by the following responses educed from the pupils.

"Dr. A. is both unimposing and never patronizes our class. His treatment of us as equals leads to a free and liberal but guided class discussion. In one particular lesson, another student in the class was struggling with a particular concept; I had not fully grasped it either. Nevertheless, Dr. A. suggested that I explain it to him."

"Dr. A. promised to help me along. By the end of the lesson, he had understood the concept and so had I. This is a method whereby he not only included us and taught us, but also gave us enjoyment."

"Dr. A. repeats, reinforces and reiterates words, phrases and ideas. He involves the class in discussions, making sure we all understand. He causes everything to sink in by following the discussions with extensive notes, making it easier to apprehend the text. He also tells the occasional story or joke to keep us interested."

"I found that it really helps me to understand the difficult concepts if it is explained by another member of the class. Dr. A. would invite

> other students to explain the concepts in their own words so that it is reinforced through the words of a peer."
>
> "Although the ideas were somewhat complex, I always listened because his reasoning was logical and he assisted us in the understanding of the subject. An old story or two kept us entertained."

In an altogether different vein, this New Zealand teacher of year 10 mathematics felt that shared male experience—the "man-to-man" anecdote—was a useful aid in driving home the importance scholastic points, in this instance, the Pythagorean theorem:

> When I was a pupil at secondary school, my father got me a job working for a local plumber and drain layer, Cliffy Johnson.
>
> Mr. Johnson had captained the national rugby league team—the Kiwis—and was a powerfully built rugged man, a veteran of World War II.
>
> On my first day on the job, Mr. Johnson told me I had to dig a foot-deep trench parallel to the boundary line of a residential property and then a second trench at a right angle back toward the corner of the house.
>
> After collecting the required tools from the back of his old blue Bedford truck, he threw me three wooden pegs, a hammer, and a length of fawn-colored string that had four black marks strategically placed, in order, 3 yards, 4 yards, and 5 yards apart.
>
> "See you soon," he said, and off he went to get morning tea and a newspaper.
>
> An hour later, he came back to find me still digging the boundary trench and asked how I intended making sure I got a perfect right angle back to the house.
>
> I suggested using my eye and judgment, which he insisted was far too inaccurate.
>
> "Haven't you heard of Pythagoras?" he asked.

I replied that I was familiar with his theorem, and as he walked back to his truck to read the paper, he barked out, "Well, you shouldn't have any trouble then."

Suddenly realizing the significance of the string and the pegs, I proceeded to stretch out and mark the arms of a 3, 4, 5 triangle.

By starting with two pegs and the "3" along the boundary line and estimating a right angle in securing a peg at the "4," I then stretched out the third arm of the triangle to see if the "5" matched up with the starting peg.

It didn't. The arm was too long!

I instantly knew my triangle had three acute angles and the "4" peg would need adjusting outward.

Measuring again, the arm was now too short, meaning I had an obtuse angle at the "4" peg.

After one more adjustment, I had my right angle and started digging.

About an hour later, Mr. Johnston came over to check on progress.

"Not bad," he said. "Your old man said you had a few brains. But you need to know two more things about plumbing and drain laying if you want to stay working with me, son."

I politely asked Mr. Johnston what those two things were and waited with bated breath for his pearls of wisdom.

"Well, firstly," he said, "pay day's on Thursday and secondly, shit doesn't travel uphill."

I thanked Mr. Johnson as we shared a healthy chuckle.

"Come on then," he said. "Time for lunch."

This Canadian English teacher takes pains to locate "masculine" elements in what his students assumed would be a "girl's" novel:

I was teaching Austen's *Pride and Prejudice* to senior male English students. Students first saw it as a "girl's novel." To counter this perception, I taught it as a novel embedded in its time—the romantic revolution—and suggested that it was a subversive work in the romantic tradition. I had them research the period and track the appearance and movements of troops in the novel and explain their presence. I also encouraged them to examine the social turmoil evident in the novel. Why was the ancient aristocratic estate that the Bingleys lease vacant? What is the Bingleys' background? Students became excited about reading the book in a "new" way and were soon pointing out their own examples of social upheaval. These were great opportunities for writing assignments, especially in interpretations of the ending: "cop-out" or not?

An American English teacher reported success in engaging his students in a difficult and potentially opaque text, Shakespeare's *Macbeth*, by radically "activating" the process of analysis:

Teaching *Macbeth* to sophomore boys proves simple on the surface but challenging at heart. The prevalence of violence, witchcraft, and political machinations in the narrative never fails to engage the adolescent masculine imagination, but the challenge lies in guiding boys to a deeper understanding of the major themes of the play: the question of fate versus free will, the relationship between gender and power, the nature of mortality. This challenge cannot be approached like other literary texts—novels, short stories, poems—for the simple reason that *Macbeth* was not intended to be read but rather to be viewed.

In order to foster a full appreciation of the play, I have developed a visual literacy unit centered on film adaptations of *Macbeth* that seeks to frame the students' understanding of the dynamics of the play through analysis of visual images, angles, effects, and relationships. The unit begins with an interactive discussion of film terminology. The terms covered include *camera angles, camera movement, elements of cinematography,* and *elements of frame composition.* The method of teaching these terms is twofold: first, I show selected film clips (mostly from popular films) and point out the concepts in action, reinforcing the concepts with questions (for example, "Based on what we just learned, is this a pan or a tracking shot?"); second, I set up a camera and monitor at the front of the classroom and have the students actively demonstrate the concepts for their classmates. For example, one student will work the camera and the other two will play the roles of Macbeth and Banquo; then, as the two actors are reading lines, I prompt the cameraman in terms of shot selection: "Over-the-shoulder! Reverse angle!"

After an understanding of the terminology is adequately demonstrated (using a comprehension quiz), the terminology is then employed in analyses of specific scenes from the following *Macbeth* adaptations: Orson Welles's *Macbeth* (1948), Akira Kurosawa's *Throne of Blood* (1957), Roman Polanski's *Macbeth* (1971), Trevor Nunn's *Macbeth* (1979), and Billy Morrisey's *Scotland, PA* (2001). In one class period, for example, we might screen three or four versions of Lady Macbeth's sleepwalking scene. Then, in group discussion and individual writing assignments, the students analyze the decisions made by each director and the meaning communicated through these decisions. (Sample questions: "Why does Welles use a deep-focus, continuous shot? How does it influence the meaning of the scene?") Each screening is followed by a discussion of which of the versions best adapts the essence of the play, which requires the students to synthesize textual literacy with visual literacy. Finally, after four or five screenings in class, the unit culminates with an out-of-class analytical essay in which the students compare two or three film versions of a scene not viewed in class. In addition, the class may complete an extra-credit project in which two or more students collaborate on a film adaptation of a specific scene from *Macbeth*, putting their understanding of visual literacy into practice.

Simply put, boys love movies. This, in itself, should not be a cause of dismay among English teachers, but an opportunity for curricular innovation. The key, however, is not merely to play into the typical passive relationship between film and spectator, but to transform the students' relationship to visual media through active analysis of the cinematic language. At first, they tend to be resistant to the change because they are used to watching films without having to think deeply about what's going on; however, once they become comfortable with reading films in addition to merely watching them, the majority comment that the experience has enhanced and transformed their understanding of the art of filmmaking. In addition, the unit is specifically aimed to make use of boys' natural predilection for active participation, teamwork, and performance.

An American Spanish teacher combines a number of strategies intended for boys—high drama, clear structure, and sports references—in building foundational vocabulary:

Introductory-level Spanish units are usually divided by vocabulary themes, and one thematic unit that usually piques the interest of the high school boys whom I have taught deals with sports vocabulary. The textbook that we use focuses on soccer, baseball, and basketball and the related vocabulary. As John Rassias from Dartmouth has taught his students and colleagues, I employ rapid repetition, full and frequent class participation, and theatrical definitions to teach the vocabulary for the unit without using English. I use props like a soccer ball or a baseball bat, and I try to conduct the class in a gymnasium or outside.

Before I start with the lesson, I explain in English what we are going to do, and from that point forward, the whole lesson is in Spanish. I give the students a sheet with the vocabulary and sentences made from the vocabulary. If the word is *mano* (hand), I point to my hand, and I say in Spanish *mano* twice without using the English. The students repeat this as a class. I then rapidly point to at least six students to repeat what I have said while holding up their hand so that they may associate the word in Spanish with their hand without translating. We do this for each vocabulary word that the students can visualize, including verbs. When the time comes for the verbs, not only is a visual definition of the action emphasized but also the correct conjugation is highlighted according to different subjects. For instance, if the verb is *lanzar* (to throw), I act out a throwing of the ball while saying *yo lanzo* (I throw). And so on. With the new vocabulary, I construct basic sentences and act out the sentence, and then the students repeat the sentence while acting it out.

When the students are familiar with this format, I encourage them to create their own sentences. They are given time to play each sport and are encouraged to say aloud and in Spanish what they are doing while playing the sport. After more written and oral practice with the vocabulary and verb conjugations, the final assessment for this unit involves each student acting as the Spanish commentator for a sports game while it is being shown without sound on the screen. They don't know what will happen in their two-minute clip of sports coverage, so the boys must be ready to think quickly in the target language and express their Spanish thought process immediately without losing their place in the game. I grade the students on their vocabulary variety, correct verb conjugations, pronunciation, fluidity, and enthusiasm.

An American English teacher grounds his eleventh-grade boys' understanding of a lofty and elusive abstraction—"transcendentalism"—by inviting them to "sing of themselves":

My best and favorite classes to teach occur during the unit on transcendentalism in the form V American literature curriculum. Over the course of six weeks, we read Ralph Waldo Emerson, Walt Whitman, and Henry David Thoreau and attempt to define the slippery word *transcendentalism*.

Some of my favorite moments in the classroom always occur during this unit because I get to step back and watch my students teach each other. For example, while reading Whitman's opus, *Song of Myself*, each student is assigned two stanzas where they lead the class in discussion. Students must read the stanza out loud, relate it to the transcendental themes of the unit, speak to specific lines from the poem, and then offer a discussion question.

I find this to be one of my "best practices" because I watch the boys discover a confidence in their ability that they perhaps did not realize they possessed. When I watch boys arguing confidently and knowledgeably about the existence of the Oversoul, I know that they understand transcendentalism. This lesson works because it allows my students to learn from the text, from me as I contribute to the class discussion, and, most important, from each other.

The unit culminates with a project in which students create their own *Song of Myself*. Students can present this song using any media they wish. The wide range of talents of our boys always impresses me, as I see presentations revolving around art, music, poetry, theater, and pottery, to name only a few. This assignment gives the boys an opportunity to focus on what truly represents them, and they always put their best effort into the assignment.

I enjoy teaching this unit because I believe Thoreau, Whitman, and Emerson put into words some thoughts that have been percolating in the outer reaches of their minds. A high school boy can easily relate to the concept of following his inner ''genius,'' and that helps lead to the success of the unit.

An American teacher of engineering puts his boys to active work on a problem he believes lies very close to their hearts: designing the "perfect car" for an eighteen-year-old boy:

A truism for boys is, ''Tell me and I will forget it; show me and I will remember it; involve me and I will understand it.''

After a lifetime in the engineering business, I learned that the core essence of good engineering is teamwork and the ability to make good decisions. Therefore, this lesson is designed to involve the boys in creativity in a group process. It also introduces them to how a formal process may be applied to make complex decisions and how, if they understand how their future customer may make their decisions, then they will make smarter choices.

My lesson is where the senior engineering class, in teams of two, is asked to design the perfect car for the eighteen-year-old male. Once the groups have designed their car, the entire class then participates in the process where we agree on six important criteria that we would use to compare each team's car. These criteria may be safety, performance, fuel economy, style, initial cost, tricked out, storage, comfort, and so on. The entire class of boys and teacher decide what these criteria are to be. The class then divides 100 points among the chosen six criteria, with more points being assigned to those attributes that are deemed more important. I do the same, but as a parent, I obviously assign the points differently.

Each team then presents its design to the class, and the rest of the class debates and assigns a number of points to the car for each criterion. Through the assignation of these, the class begins to see what customers might value and how their earlier deign choices affected their success.

In this American English teacher's "best lesson," his seventh-grade students are asked to make the case for admitting a decidedly unscholastic character, Mark Twain's Tom Sawyer, to their school. In attempting to explain and endorse Tom's irrepressible boyishness, students are encouraged to evaluate their own:

At the conclusion of reading *The Adventures of Tom Sawyer*, I have the students write a letter of recommendation to our school on behalf of Tom Sawyer. Students may choose to recommend or not recommend Tom for acceptance. The letter they compose will consist of an essay that states the student's reasons for or against accepting Tom Sawyer. Students must use details and examples from the novel to support their opinion. They will focus on Tom's character and his growth in maturity as a means of justifying their decision. Students will be given an actual recommendation form used by our school.

Prior to starting the novel, I tell the students that they will be writing a letter of recommendation for Tom to attend the school just as they had asked teachers, alumni, or other significant people to write letters of recommendation for them. In this way, it makes a real-world connection.

I explain that normally, one would not write a letter against a student attending a school and that if they were ever in the situation where they felt that they could not write the type of letter the applicant was looking for, then they should politely decline and explain that in a gentle manner.

However, for the purposes of our assignment, the students were allowed to write a letter cautioning the school against Tom's acceptance if they felt that was in the school's best interest. I felt this would engage the students more since they had a choice, and it would make them have to weigh the pros and cons of accepting Tom.

Additionally, I provided the students with a T-chart on which they could cite incidents from the story that would support either recommending or not recommending Tom. The purpose of this was not only to choose a side and support it, but also to encourage the students to take notes as they read.

In class, I created a chart that included such topics as mature–immature, responsible–irresponsible, self-centered–others-centered, and honest–dishonest. Periodically (three or four times) during the reading and discussion of the novel, we rated where we thought Tom stood on each topic. What the students noted was that Tom was gradually growing or improving in each category. It was not always a smooth growth, as sometimes it was two steps forward, one step back. However, we were all in agreement that there was growth.

On completion of the novel and beginning the recommendation letter, the question then turned to evaluating Tom's character and determining whether he could or would be successful at our school. Students then had to determine whether Tom's growth in maturity, responsibility, and other characteristics outweighed his earlier "sins" in the book.

As a means of honoring scholastic excellence, an American mathematics teacher devised a classroom ritual intended to recognize high achievement as something comfortably within masculine norms—and even romantically heroic:

In my third year back in the classroom following an eighteen-year hiatus, I was looking for a practice in my all-male school that would be rewarding for the stronger students.

It seemed many teachers adhere to the 90/10 rule: spending 90 percent of their discretionary efforts directed at 10 percent of their students. I wanted to generate positive student energy by "rewarding" those who were performing well.

The practice I adopted is called "Last Man Standing." After grading a chapter test, all tests that are not in the "A" range are returned first. Then all students who have NOT received a paper are asked to stand. Papers in the "A" range are then returned in increasing grade order, the student with the highest grade being Last Man Standing.

My goal of generating positive student energy has been aided by this practice. The stronger students want to be the Last Man Standing. The weaker students have invested more preparation energies because they want to join classmates who are publicly asked to stand. The repartee between students during the practice is, to me, priceless (boys being boys).

Incidentally, each student standing receives a sincere congratulations and thanks, a handshake, and eye-to-eye contact . . . intended to provide closure to a positive event and encouragement to continue making the preparation investment.

THE BOYS RESPOND

The student responses emphatically corroborated the teacher claims for the effectiveness of lessons in which some personal element in a boy's experience was addressed in class. Like their teachers, the boys reported responding with special enthusiasm to lessons in which they felt that either the subject matter or its method of delivery was pitched especially to them.

The boys reported responding with special enthusiasm to lessons in which they felt that either the subject matter or its method of delivery was pitched especially to them.

For this U.S. twelfth grader, the opportunity to make a personal connection was provided him by a history class assignment to interview his father, which served to open up a more expansive reflection on generational continuity:

For my senior exam in my History class, we were assigned a project to interview a member of the school's community and get some of their thoughts and opinions about the school. Many students in the class chose to interview teachers, advisors, athletic coaches and alumni. I chose my father. My father graduated from this school and is now still active in the community as a member on the board. For the actual interview, we sat in his office and I had the opportunity to ask him questions, such as: "What values did the school instill in you?"; "Do you think you would have had the same experience at a different school?"; "Has the school changed since you were there and has it been a different type of experience watching the school from a parent's view?"; "What's your opinion around the Honor Code?" I got the opportunity to ask my father questions that would have never come up in other every day situations. It was very interesting for me to have this conversation with my dad, especially with this being my senior year, because it gave me some insight into what I would be thinking back on about the school when I am his age. I had to record the whole interview, which lasted around 45 minutes. Then we had to write a transcript of the whole interview. We also had to take the 45 minutes and cut it down to the most important 15 minutes and then report it to the class. We got to put pictures with the interview. It was really interesting to hear everyone else's interview and all the different opinions of the school from people in our community. This project made a lasting impression on me and will be something that I will think back on as I think of my school.

Another U.S. senior recalls discovering and identifying his life's purpose in response to a particular assignment: Ralph Waldo Emerson's essay "Self-Reliance":

The most memorable moment in my scholastic career came in my junior year English class. I was learning about Ralph Waldo Emerson and in particular his essay, *Self Reliance*. I realized what I wanted to do with my life after learning about Emerson. His message was that the thing that makes you happiest in life is the thing that you are meant to do with your life. That message, coupled with the way that my teacher taught it, resonated with me and I then knew that I was meant to be a video game designer. Because of that English class I was then able to focus both my college search and my life in general. If it wasn't for my teacher, Emerson, or the school,

I would have most likely not known what I wanted to do with my life. But because I was able to find out what makes me happiest in life, I am now able to live my new life as joyously as I can; I certainly owe this new life to my experiences at the school.

This Canadian seventh grader valued his opportunity to activate a strongly held personal conviction in the course of executing an imaginative English class assignment to document the effects of bullying:

I recall the time, in English class, when we had to make a bullying movie. I was paired up with four of my friends. Our goal was to make a movie to show to the class about how bullying is bad. We made a sheet that had all of the screen shots and scenes. After we were done, we were allowed to take out a camera from the computer lab. I got really excited because I was always against bullying and this was the time to show to my classmates how bullying was bad. We started filming and it was great. Our movie was about how bystanding was almost as bad as bullying. A student was getting bullied by two people in the hallway while his friend was watching the fight but never stood up for him. An example of this is that if you are watching your friend getting hurt and not standing up for your friend you're also hurting him. Like I said, I was always against bullying and so I thought this movie might change the way my classmates thought about bullying. Weeks after the movie, I still saw bullying in the hallways, but in my mind I knew that our movie touched some of the bullies' hearts.

A Canadian eleventh grader expressed similar appreciation for being challenged by his art teacher to reveal his true identity in an acrylic portrait:

I remember one project in my grade 11 visual arts course that completely motivated me to do my best. The subject matter dealt with a self-portrait that defined who we were as individuals. There were no guidelines that we had to follow. We had complete freedom to express ourselves using acrylic paint as a medium. This project really allowed myself to see who I was as an individual under all the layers of pain and oppression. It allowed me to freely channel all my anger and problems into one visual image that defined who I was. Though the end product was great to witness, the process was as well enjoyable. I enjoyed all the feedback and suggestions my art teacher gave me to enhance and strengthen my message. She gave me inspiration, advice, and sources where I could see techniques that could help portray my intended image. That is what I remembered. That was a memorable moment to me because it allowed me to connect to my teacher in a manner that was not based on grades but instead based on who we were as individuals. It was great to relate and be able to express myself openly to a professional who had gone through the exact same stress I was under.

This U.S. senior appreciated the challenge posed in his economics class to project himself financially fifteen years into the future:

In twelfth grade Microeconomics, I did a project in which I projected where I would be in life in 15 years. I gave myself an occupation, a residence, and a lifestyle which I could see myself living at that time. I then mapped out my complete financial status using a Microsoft Excel spreadsheet. I accounted for nearly all of the expenses that I could face as a 30 year old man living on his own. I accounted for salary, taxes, among other things and really set up a financial picture of what my life could look like in 15 years. This project helped me to understand the real world financially, and how much things have to be taken into consideration when spending money and living a certain lifestyle. I got a great grasp of income and expense and the project gave me insight as to what to expect in the future.

This U.S. eleventh grader expanded on the importance of a past lesson: an assignment four years prior that had required him to write his "autobiography."

Reading it from his older perspective alternately fascinated him and made him cringe, yet he celebrates the value of the earlier exercise in helping him to appreciate his capacity to change and grow:

> In the eighth grade, we had to write an autobiography for English. Truth be told, we had been writing it for the entire year; our teacher had us make "journal entries" about our lives as much as we could. When I finally got around to writing the actual autobiography I found that I couldn't stop. I wrote and wrote, I poured my soul out, my immature, sophomoric eighth grade soul. When the autobiography was completed, it was over thirty pages, thirty pages of garbage, of genius, of me. I hate that paper now, at the time I liked it, now I hate it. When I wrote it, it was good, most certainly, it was good. It showed who I was and what I thought and felt, it was excellent; but now, a few short years later, I hate it, maybe I don't hate it, but hate the person I was when I wrote it, but regardless of my feelings towards it or me, I was passionate about writing it. I had fun writing it, I laughed about what I've done, I cried about what I've done, it was passion incarnate. So, in summation, I find that passion brings certain creatures to light, and that we change with the years more than we like to admit. And to think that these epiphanies came from an eighth grade English project.

Asked what kind of student response to a particular lesson they would most like to see, few teachers would not be heartened by a student's testimony that the lesson in question had "fascinated" him to the extent that his imagination was inflamed for the rest of the school day, so that he couldn't wait to get home to his computer and begin indulging his "craving for more"—which was precisely this (non-Christian) South African tenth grader's response to a divinity lesson on biblical revelations:

> Divinity, Grade 10. I have found at the start of this year, a new appreciation for the divinity lessons at my school. This is known as a lazy subject to some of the less-appreciating groups of the school and at a certain stage, to

myself as well. We tended to shut down before class; the idea of focused religious study doesn't usually spark too much interest. In my case I found the one-sided opinion particularly annoying, not so much the material covered. I am not a Christian, but I have large interest in the beliefs of other people and enjoy learning about them. So in the lesson in question, our school priest decided to cover the prophecies and end-of-the-world visions seen by the writers of the books in the bible. This immediately struck my interest. As we went through various scripture stories, I found myself fascinated and the craving for more came over me. After class I strolled over to my next lesson, lost in thought, my imagination running wild. As I got home that day, I went straight to my computer and followed my interest further.

CHAPTER

NOVELTY, DRAMA, AND SURPRISE

Over the past quarter-century, findings from neurological science have converged with long-held observations in experimental and clinical psychology to the effect that memory attaches to strong feeling. And because memory is a crucial component of every student's capacity to master, replicate, and use what is offered in instruction, the implications of teachers' arousing strong feeling, and thus stored memory, are profound. Many of the reporting teachers noted the transitive efficacy of surprising students in some way, perhaps by conducting usual class work in an especially dramatic or unexpected manner.

In some instances, presenting unlikely material for analytical consideration appeared to arouse an especially receptive climate for learning. There were, in fact, two separate accounts from geographically distant and otherwise quite different schools about the positive results of lessons on flatulence. Extreme theatricality, pushing limits, taking students temporarily out of their comfort zones, or simply delighting them in unexpected ways were highly endorsed as effective practices for boys.

A HINT OF DANGER

Perhaps unsurprisingly, teachers in all disciplines noted—and to an extent were willing to indulge—their boys' fascination with (sometimes literally) volatile material. The following account from a veteran New Zealand chemistry teacher suggests the transitivity of providing students with a safe brush with danger:

Sometimes chemical reactions are too violent, unpredictable, and indeed forbidden in a school laboratory. Boys are fascinated by things with an

Boys are fascinated by things with an element of danger.

element of danger. An example is the reaction of the alkali metals with water. With care, some reactions can be demonstrated in a school laboratory (lithium, sodium, potassium), but others cannot. YouTube has some wonderful videos, particularly the Brainiac series, that boys can and certainly do follow on their computers at home. Bathtubs have the elements placed in them, and the bathtubs are blown to pieces with the most reactive metals. It is important, though, to show the part that can be safely demonstrated for the lesson to have the same impact. Once the reactivity of alkali metals is viewed, it is always remembered. Nobody would ever repeat the Brainiac experiments, but the clips are available. I think boys also become very conscious of laboratory safety and appreciate the limits of what can be done.

A New Zealand colleague found it effective to take such demonstrations to a more theatrical level:

One of the most effective ways to reach boys when teaching chemistry is the theatrical demonstration. This method is employed best by "mad professor" types with lab coats and strange glasses, combined with color, gases that envelop the floor of the lab, and explosions to match. This can be achieved in the school laboratory with a little organization and imagination. The lab coat must not be new, should have many stains on it, and may well be colored by construction or tie-dying. The teacher needs to adopt a thespian approach and get the boys to believe they are on the set of a Harry Potter movie or something similar. It is essential to act out the demonstration as you do it and elicit the help of one or more of the boys in attendance.

Probably the most effective level for stimulating an interest in chemistry is the first year of "pure chemistry," which for us is grade 10. At this level, you are generally getting boys who want to study chemistry because they see it as a tool to go further in science and a form of entertainment if there are lots of exciting, practical things. Some of the better demonstrations I have used are:

- A large stick of sodium in the school swimming pool

- Balloons filled with hydrogen/oxygen in a two-to-one mix lighted with a long taper outside

- Smaller-scale explosions of sodium and consequent spattering of sodium hydroxide in a fume cupboard

- Anything with dry ice

The transitive benefits of stimulating students by exposing them to dangerous and even tragic mishaps were affirmed in this English teacher's use of the *Challenger* space disaster to stimulate his students to identify the elements of effective rhetoric:

This was a class introducing rhetorical devices of speeches to advanced-level tenth-grade boys. The lesson began with a short clip of the *Challenger* disaster streamed from YouTube. It was then explained that prior to 9/11, this was probably the most public postwar disaster in America. It was particularly hard felt since a lot of time had been spent on a PR campaign to reignite interest in the space race with the inclusion of a teacher on board. The explosion had been watched live by millions, including school children.

Students were then asked to comment on what the expected and appropriate reaction would be from the U.S. president. The results from this brainstorm were put on the board.

The class then watched a clip of Ronald Reagan's famous speech made that same day, in which he declared that "the future doesn't belong to the faint-hearted." Boys were asked to comment on what his main message had been and any particularly effective phrases that stood out.

A transcript of the speech was then handed out, and we listened to the whole speech again. On the other side of the handout, students were now asked to respond to a list of rhetorical devices—some of which were known to them. Students had to either find an example of a particular device or explain which device was being employed in a particular sentence or phrase. In each case, students were also required to identify the reason for the use of the device. Final questions concerned the main aims of the speech.

Students were then called on to give their answers, and corrections were written into students' books. At the same time, a list of rhetorical devices with a simple definition for each was written on the board, and students were asked to write it down in their books.

The lesson ended with a brief overview of what made this particular speech effective, with comments being elicited from students and written on the board.

A New Zealand teacher introduced his mixed-year high school students to Newton's law of cooling by assigning them to approximate the time of death of a murder victim:

During the interval of our double-period class, I set up the classroom as a murder crime scene. With a taped outline of a body on the floor and a thermos of warm water placed on the body, the scene is set. Upon entering the room, the boys are subjected to the situation of walking around the body. The instructions are given. Armed with a thermometer, they are required to find the approximate time of death. Given a temperature of the body an hour before, they must measure the temperature of the body and room temperature. Doing the calculations using Newton's law of cooling, it always amazes the students that they are all within ten minutes of each other. This is a good practical demonstration of the uses of differential equations. The model creates a lot of debate about methods and interest in the mathematics side of science.

An American classics teacher of seventh-grade boys engaged his class actively in the assassination of Julius Caesar by having them take turns as assassins and victim:

As I approached teaching *Julius Caesar* to seventh-grade all-male English students, I planned to focus on the plotting of the conspirators and the actual murder of Caesar. At the beginning of the unit, I asked all the students to bring a bed sheet from home (a double/full size worked the best). They would leave the sheet at the school, and each day they entered my class, they would put on their "toga" and wear it for the duration of the class. This helped them get the feeling they were in Rome as they actually read aloud the play.

We focused on each conspirator by identifying his connection with Caesar, and then we tried to understand his motives for assassination. As the boys dressed the part, read the part, and then acted out the part, Shakespeare seemed to come alive. I had them act out "bathing their arms in Caesar's blood" and take turns being Caesar or a conspirator. We watched part of the movie to gain a visual perspective; then we made it our own.

We went outside to the steps of our school (the Capitol, if you will), and Caesar stood on the steps as the conspirators boldly and publicly assassinated him, reveling in his fatally wounded body, dripping with blood from all the stab wounds. The boys would ask to reenact it over and over, each wanting to have a turn at being Caesar and Brutus.

VISCERAL EXPERIENCES

Although exposure to visceral experiences initially can be off-putting to some students, several teachers found the drama of such exposure to be transitive to sustained and long-remembered engagement in the material under consideration. This New Zealand biology teacher noted the transitivity of the dissection process:

> Every year I demonstrate a lung dissection with my senior biology (year 12/13) class. It comes as a heart/lung set—a pluck—and I concentrate on the lungs since the students do a heart dissection themselves at a later date. In these times, dissections are not as accepted as they once were, and it is a rare occasion. The students are fascinated by the real thing, and, to me, this is real biology. Along with the actual cutting up of the lung (boys are usually very interested in cutting things up), I have a large repertoire of stories about lung cancer, pulmonary embolism, and diseases, which accentuate the event. The students are delighted when I inflate the lungs with a Bunsen burner hose and always encourage me to blow it until it bursts (which it never does). The students poke and prod the lungs and are often surprised at the pink and spongy nature of the tissue. Once, many years ago, a student fainted. From time to time, I meet ex-students who have gone into medicine, and they tell me that they remember the dissection and that the human biology part of the course prepared them really well for the university course.

An American teacher of health and physical education reports that his most successful lesson was the introduction to his tenth-grade students of what was for them a dreadful reality—testicular cancer:

> In a unit on cancer, I bring in a group of people to discuss testicular cancer with our boys. The group involves a cancer survivor, who explains his journey through diagnosis and treatment; a medical doctor who works with cancer patients, to answer questions the boys have about cancer in general; and a hospital staff person, who describes the patients' experience

through their eyes. The combination of these professionals being present in the classroom lends a feeling of importance to the lesson. A short film is also shown that chronicles the life of a college athlete who is diagnosed with and eventually succumbs to testicular cancer.

It is a vivid and moving lesson that has really resonated with the boys in the past. The lesson is taught to tenth-grade boys in the health portion of our health and physical education curriculum. This is generally a sensitive issue for boys to discuss, but with the help of the group, they are able to bring the boys face to face with a disease that affects millions.

While some kinds of exposure to visceral or repellent subject matter might be considered exploitative or potentially emotionally overwhelming, even the most unthinkable and unviewable material can serve to deepen boys' empathy and understanding under the guidance of a thoughtful and sensitive instructor. This South African English teacher recounted a lesson in which he brought the realities of the 9/11 World Trade Center attacks very close to home for his senior boys:

We were to discuss a poem entitled "Man Falling," dealing with the 9/11 attacks [and drawing on] the by now iconic photo taken of Jonathan Briley as he plummeted to earth. I chose to use a PowerPoint presentation and prefaced the lesson with a slide show of pictures taken at school of an old boy who had perished in the attack, without telling the boys why I was showing them this. They had a lot of fun laughing at this little boy with socks around his ankles, missing teeth, wet from being thrown into the swimming pool on the last day of his senior year. The next slide was of the impact on the northern tower. I could point to the 106th floor where Nick would have been preparing a business demonstration. I knew it would get their attention, but was unprepared for the shock they experienced as evidenced by their absolute silence, stillness, and (to my horror) several teary eyes. In attempting to make the poem real and relevant to us, I had succeeded—possibly too well. After a read-through of the poem and a few YouTube clips showing the impacts, pictures of jumpers, and the aftermath, we could discuss the poem itself with great understanding.

CROSSING BOUNDARIES, BREAKING EXPECTATIONS

Teachers participating in this study submitted a wide variety of lessons in which the principal, and most transitive, element was surprising the students, often to their delight. This New Zealand English teacher enthusiastically departs from standard classroom decorum as he introduces his students to some of the more expansive characters in Shakespeare's plays:

The main idea of this lesson was to introduce the class to a larger-than-life Shakespearean character—in this case, Sir Toby Belch from *Twelfth Night* (I have adopted a similar approach with other characters from other plays, with similar success). All students, boys and girls, need a context in which to study—in this case, Shakespeare. I am trying to provide that here-and-now historical, Falstaffian figure, if you will. A man of his time. A man given to great gouts of excess—food, drink, and so on—Henry VIII style. To complete the picture, I own full Elizabethan nobleman's regalia, and I wear it in class while delivering the lesson. Initially, when I add to the effect by burping, farting, and so forth in a very loud manner, this creates a degree of mirth among the student body, but when I explain the significance of Sir Toby's surname, they invariably settle down and start to get the picture. If they are a bit slow on the uptake, I can always introduce the notion of sex. Sir Toby was infatuated with his niece's (Lady Olivia) chambermaid, Maria. This infatuation leads to an examination of a particular form of love in the play. Eventually Sir Toby "boarded and woo'd her."

Drunken carousing, dancing, capering, and stoops of wine plus the "gulling" of Malvolio (one of the two major subplots in the play) all add to the over-the-top character of Sir Toby. I always act the part myself (and usually end up very hoarse for my pains). This ALWAYS works. I find that a clinical dissection of Shakespeare's language is a waste of time—far better to let the part (and the character) "flow." I usually follow my own performance with a screening of the excellent BBC television production of the play, starring Robert Hardy as Sir Toby.

In summary, the main idea here is to engage all five senses of one's students. I believe that my approach is successful, and I also believe that my students' understanding of this character, this play and the language therein is improved.

In the following account, a New Zealand English teacher outlines a series of experiences that intentionally shatter boys' expectations about what constitutes "school"—to help them to understand the work and intentions of a great modern writer:

To introduce the class to the notion of the absurd, it is important to break them out of their normal routine so they can appreciate what Beckett was trying to do in the theater.

Tactics used during units on *Waiting for Godot* and *Endgame* over the years include:

- Class and teacher allowed to speak only in questions.

- Teacher remains silent throughout the lesson.

- Teacher doesn't turn up for class but sends a messenger near the end of the lesson: "He or she will be there tomorrow."

- Class spends lesson sitting underneath desks.

- Teacher confines himself or herself inside a large dustbin at the front of the classroom.

- Class are blindfolded.

- Class watches the projected time countdown of the lesson on a large screen:

    40:00

    39:59

    39:58

    39:57

    39:56

    39:55

    And so on until the bell rings.

- Perform the 1969 play *Breath* (running time: 30 seconds):

I can't go on. I go on. I can't go on. I go on. I can't go on. I go on.
I can't go on. I go on. I can't go on. I go on. I can't go on. I go on.
I can't go on. I go on. I can't go on. I go on. I can't go on. I go on.
I can't go on. I go on. I can't go on. I go on. I can't go on. I go on.
I can't go on. I go on. I can't go on. I go on. I can't go on. I go on.
I can't go on. I go on. I can't go on. I go on. I can't go on.
I go on. I can't go on. I go on.

These devices need to be employed sparingly . . .

Breaking student expectations so that they can gain a fresh perspective does not necessarily imply abandoning or negating scholarship. In the experience of this American football coach (and English teacher), expectations are sometimes usefully shattered by the reverse process: introducing scholastic material into the extrascholastic world—in this case, the rough and tumble of contact sports:

I teach two sections of eighth-grade English—about thirty students of the sixty in that grade—and I also am one of the coaches of eighth-grade football, basketball, and middle school track teams. The practice I use almost every day in the classroom and on the athletic field is to use the vocabulary and quotations from our poetry and Shakespeare lessons. For instance, the offensive line in football must leave the huddle with "panache" (a word essential when teaching *Cyrano de Bergerac*), or using "we band of brothers" from *Henry V*, or quoting from Tennyson's "Ulysses": "To strive, to seek, to find, but not to yield." Vocabulary words like *ubiquitous, truculent, umbrage,* and *alacrity* work well in context when talking about sports.

School lore and literature, both fact and fiction, is full of appreciative accounts of memorable eccentrics. This Australian mathematics teacher builds eccentricity quite intentionally into his instruction:

Changing the "state" of a student or class by using unusual language or gestures—for example, "the equation $y = 2$ is independent of x"—so staring at the whiteboard or interactive whiteboard from a few centimeters away for several seconds and saying I can't find any x here usually does the trick. Kids remember the unusual, that which is different, that which is eccentric. In math, I use or make up words or phrases few have ever heard of—the funnier, the better. In getting them to remember algorithms like the quotient rule in calculus, instead of the dry algebra format, saying, "Do me leave me minus do me leave me over me squared," and pointing to the relevant terms seems to aid learning considerably.

Keep the kids on the hop so they seldom know what you are going to do next. I've seen one teacher lying down at the back of the classroom talking to twenty-five boys, and they were enraptured! Put on some music in the classroom—baroque is allegedly the best for learning. Boys soon get the idea of it and bring CD's in for a listen. No heavy metal, of course! Burning incense also adds variety to a class—something different. It seems unlikely that the smell per se has any effect on their learning, but they feel special because they are treated differently. On occasions use a red or green or blue paper for a worksheet or handout . . . they'll wonder why it's different. Keep them guessing about what is happening next. Boredom bedevils learning.

Keep them guessing about what is happening next. Boredom bedevils learning. Few veteran teachers are unaware of the high stimulation that results when clearly "inappropriate" material makes it way into a lesson. This Canadian English teacher was able to channel what could easily have been an anarchic response on the part of his students—to a consideration of flatulence—into productive inquiry and analysis:

The genesis of this class was a newspaper article on farting—a natural draw for grade 9 boys. The article was an amusing overview of the science involved, with demographic surveys, sidebars of slang terms, and so on.

The immediate application was analysis of a general interest piece of journalism: What was the headline? How were the first paragraphs slanted to draw the reader into the piece? How were statistics and scientific research woven into anecdotal and amusing cultural references to make it an interesting read?

But the real payoff was in the planned discussion. The lead question was derived from the cold statistics: men and women, old and young, cultured and crude—we all fart, on average, fourteen times a day. So the question that arises is, "How come we are so embarrassed or offended by a perfectly necessary, universal, and natural body function?"

A few boys zeroed in on results, not cause: social disapproval, parental admonishments, and so forth. Then one boy weighed in with: "It's one more mask we put on to pretend that we aren't an animal like every other species on our planet." The floodgates opened. We had a discussion that ranged from vivisection to animal testing to factory farms to all the other horrors we visit on the rest of the animal kingdom—all from an amusing little article on the social improprieties of farting!

In their responses to their favorite lessons, students made many appreciative references to the enlivening effects of their teachers' good humor and jokes. Some jokes are durable enough to become "classics"—as might be said of the American comedy team Abbott and Costello's famous routine, "Who's on First?" [a famous comedy dialogue between the American comedians Bud Abbott and Lou Costello confusing the names of baseball players whose names are pronouns, that is, "Who" and "What" and so on] which for this American English teacher became a "best lesson" on the uses of pronouns:

Objective: To introduce students to the various functions of pronouns and the importance of their proper use.

Materials: "The Perils of Pronouns: 'Who's on First?'" A recording of Abbott and Costello's comedy routine "Who's on First?"

Time required: One forty-minute class period

Procedure: I ask the class what the word *pronoun* means. Most respond with examples and explanations such as, "It's like a noun, but it's not."

I guide them to break the word down into its parts: *pro-* (for) and *noun.* With a working definition of *pronoun* as a word that stands in for a noun, I distribute the packet "The Perils of Pronouns: 'Who's on First?'" I direct them to page 25 and say, "Now we're going to listen and read along as pronoun confusion creates havoc at the ballpark."

After listening to the recording of "Who's on First?" (during which most of the boys progress from being perplexed to being convulsed with laughter and, finally, to remarks such as, "He thinks the pronoun's a name!"), I ask, "So what was the problem in this dialogue?"

After brief discussion of the many types and misuses of pronouns in the routine, we begin studying and practicing personal pronouns.

I believe this lesson is particularly effective with boys for a number of reasons. First, it appeals to their love of the great American pastime. When we act it out at the end of the pronoun unit, there is much competition for coveted roles "based" on players' positions. Because the boys already understand the story, as it were, they can focus on the wordplay. And that is the second way the lesson seems to draw them in.

By the time we reach the exchange where Costello asks, "When you pay off the first baseman every month, who gets the money?" and Abbott responds, "Every dollar of it," the boys have picked up on the word confusion and start to anticipate and even try to guess the next example. Many actually read ahead to find it.

Finally, most students have been so conditioned to think of grammar and groan that it's a pleasant surprise when they get the chance to have some fun with it.

An American teacher of mathematics recounted the transitive effectiveness of surprising his students by one day, without warning, presenting his lesson in mime:

To mime a geometry class, certain parameters have to be set, and a certain system of classroom management and style must be in place.

On rare occasions, I present a lesson in mime. I give no indication to the students prior to the class but merely walk into the room, take attendance in silence, and then present the day's lesson. I begin by writing the words "practice problems" on the board. This is the accepted cue that they are to open their notebooks to section 1. When I start a typical class this way, I begin with easy review problems and begin to introduce some new concepts as the problems increase in difficulty.

I might begin by drawing a trapezoid, labeling the parts, and writing "Area = ?" Typically someone will volunteer an answer, and I will write it on the board if it is correct. Facial features and body language are part of the feedback to coax, encourage, or redirect thought. Though some students are not quick to participate in the class, there are always plenty of students who will ask questions and explain steps to others. If the class is stumped, I may give a nonverbal clue such as writing a formula or pointing to a certain part of the drawing or equation to attract their attention to a specific point they may be overlooking. I may write the first step in setting up an equation. In my typical class, students are encouraged to work together as a class or in small groups to solve problems, so there is usually no hesitation for at least one student to volunteer an answer and for others to either support him or add their own solution. There will often be a great deal of student-to-student exchanges. Because there is no auditory queue, the students must be more visually focused on the lesson. Students are very engaged as problem solvers, sharers of strategies, or seekers of strategies.

When we finish, I move to the next part of the board, and, again with body language, I will rock between problem 1 and problem 2 indicating that I am about to move on but can return to the first problem if there are still questions. The class continues through the practice problems, at which time I write the homework assignment on the board. With time about to expire, I attract attention with dramatic body language, wait until there is silence, look at them, and say, "Have a nice day." Many will quickly ask questions about the process of the day, but we usually wait until the next day to debrief.

The following day when we debrief, students are asked why I ran class that way and what the advantages were. Every time the consensus by the students is "to get us to think for ourselves." Students speak positively about the entertainment factor, the amusement of my movements, the change in routine, and the opportunity to work together. Occasionally a student will have difficulty with the efficiency of the class because he felt that I should have taught the material directly rather than allowing the students to try strategies that led to dead ends. Typically this is the concern by the conscientious student who is very concrete in his approach to math and sees the assignments as disconnected rules that must be memorized with little emphasis on logical thinking.

An Australian teacher of art and design found that inviting her students to consider the absurd proved to be a stimulating prod to better work, especially for impatient or resistant boys:

This unit of work is for year 11 visual communication and design students. It is based on the Japanese design philosophy of Chindogu (weird tool), or useless design. Chindogu are design solutions to the everyday problems of life. Chindogu designs must spectacularly miss the mark in solving a problem. For example, the problem of eating hot noodles was solved by attaching an electric fan to chopsticks. In another Chindogu, weary subway travelers wear a helmet suction-cupped to the train window so that they can doze upright, and a sign on the helmet indicates what station they should be woken up for. This absurdist approach to problem solving is useful in order to focus on the purpose rather than the appearance of a design. . . .

By asking the students to produce a Chindogu as a design task, they must define and focus on the specific nature of the problem. Because they have been given permission to be absurdist in their approach, students are free from restrictions of logic, ambiguity, and practicality. They focus not on appearance but on problem solving. The results are usually extremely humorous, and students enjoy themselves immensely. Students who stick to "safe," practical solutions are encouraged to raise the stakes and to design for greater impracticality until they see the humor in what they are doing. Importantly, they realize that the design problem is central to the design process and that there can be multiple design solutions.

Introducing an anomalous element into familiar classroom business has been a feature of a number of best lessons. For this South African geography teacher, the catalytic ingredient was also delicious:

> The teaching of contours has always been a challenge because it is an extremely difficult concept to grasp from diagrams. Added to this, my experience has taught me that the use of as many senses in the teaching situation is what acts as a reminder of the information that is being taught. In discussion with other geography teachers, I came upon a tried-and-tested method.
>
> I arrived in class with small individual chocolate cakes and knives. The smell of the cake and the thought of what it must taste like immediately drew the attention of my class, but not before I had assured them that they would be eating it at the end of the lesson. They broke up into groups of three and four. I gave each group a sheet of overhead projector transparency that was divided into sections that were numbered and labeled. I then slowly guided them through the process of carving these patterns into the cake. Making use of images on the screen in front of them, the group was divided into the person who was carving the cake landscape, a person who was making sketches of the cake, and a person who kept a careful eye on the screen and on the sketches and held the group task together. Finally, the group tidied up the sketches and added the relevant labels.
>
> Each group displayed their completed task to the class and was advised by the other class members if anything had been omitted or needed adjustment. Each pattern was discussed, and photos of each were projected onto the board. The spirit of competition came alive, and the boys selected the best set of diagrams and the group was rewarded. Finally, we arrived at what they had all been waiting for: to eat the cake.

THE BOYS RESPOND

The student narratives were in clear alignment with the teachers who reported the special effectiveness of introducing dramatic novelties and surprises into the classroom. Among the other transitive effects of such novelties is their capacity, as revealed in this British twelfth grader's account, to draw students out of a purely conceptual, distanced understanding of classroom material to a vividly immediate one:

> The best lesson I've ever had was a Physics lesson. One day we did an amazing experiment. The experiment itself was quite simple and it didn't take a long time to prepare it. However, the Physics (and also Chemistry) behind it is very interesting. What's more, almost the whole class managed to participate in it. Basically, the whole experiment is about an amazing, very "light" and safe fire effect. First you need to prepare some chemical bubbles (I think it might have been soap bubbles, but I'm not sure. It might have been dish washing liquid or some other substance). Then you take a small pipe with gas (you must be able to change the amount of gas flowing through it and be able to cut it off, otherwise it will not work). You should put this pipe into the liquid and produce the bubbles. Then you wet your hands (both sides!), turn off the gas and take some bubbles into your hands. Finally another person lights the bubbles (with matches). For a second or two a very nice and even quite big fire burst appears. It doesn't hurt or burn hands at all. Since it doesn't last very long and the gas is turned off, the whole experiment is very safe to yourself. I only regret that no one had a camera at that time so I don't have a photo. However, what's more important is that even though I'm generally not interested in practical Physics (I prefer the theory), this experiment has really fascinated me. In my opinion it's one of those experiments after which you can say, "Wow, that's great, I want to be a physicist!"

That tacitly understood sense of wondrous—perhaps even faintly dangerous—volatility was expressed also by a New Zealand tenth grader, who retained his fascination for the demonstration in question more than a year after it occurred:

> Back in ninth we had a memorable lesson in science. We were learning about tectonic plates and volcanoes. We walked in to the room and there on the desk we saw a large pile of red solids in the shape of a large volcano.

> Mr. A. told us to stand back and then he lit the pile. All of sudden the pile started spiting fire out just like a volcano. It seemed like a volcano was on his desk. This lesson was memorable as I never saw this before, and it was really cool to see.

In reviewing such responses, we felt a growing conviction (untested) that had we asked the boys to recount their grossest classroom experiences, we would have received fifteen hundred similar accounts—for example, this U.S. eighth grader's year-old evocation of a dissection:

> In seventh grade, in Mr. G's class, we dissected squids. We did all of this by hand. Once we took out various parts of the squid, some people ate the eyeballs, played with the esophagus, and drew with the ink. We later on cooked the squid into breaded calamari. It was both fun and tasty.

Or this seventh grader's similarly absorbing exploration into the innards of a chicken:

> Seventh grade Life Science class was probably the most enjoyable science class I have been enrolled in. The whole semester was based on how things move: muscles, ligaments and tendons. So, on this day we had a chicken dissection. I paired up with my partner, and we suited up, I put on Latex gloves and we acquired all the instruments we would need. I held the scalpel in my hand and cut an opening down the length of the chicken's wing. Then, slowly, we peeled off the skin and were greeted by a maze of muscles, ligaments, tendons, and veins. Then our teacher said that we could have some fun; she said pull on the tendons and ligaments. I did this and the chicken wing moved. I was amazed that we could make a dead chicken move. Then the bell rang and my partner, who was cleaning up, waved goodbye via a chicken wing.

In addition to such visceral engagements in life sciences, boys were also inclined to celebrate impressive pyrotechnics. This South African tenth grader's physics lesson was brought memorably home by "deafening noise" and "powerful shock waves":

> Close to the end of last term, we did an experiment with hydrogen. We filled a balloon with hydrogen and then lit it with a match. When the balloon popped, the hydrogen inside reacted with the oxygen and created an enormous explosion. The noise was deafening and the shockwaves were very powerful. The class was very interesting and I learnt a lot. I think it was a very effective lesson because everyone was more focused and interested.

The boys' appreciation of engaging novelties and surprises was by no means limited to the sciences. This Australian ninth grader feels his appreciation of the reliability of historical narrative was heightened by his teacher's staging of an impromptu stabbing:

> Early in the year, our teacher was demonstrating how history can be wrong because people mainly write about their experiences. To prove his theory he got a student and "stabbed him." Our teacher then got others in the class to run through everything they had seen. Almost everyone's story was different in some way. I found this interesting, not because of the idea, but the way he explained his idea through example.

Two Australian seventh graders agreed that their "best class" was the English lesson in which the richness of Shakespearean vocabulary was illustrated by guiding them into altogether new realms of insulting one another:

> The best subject I have ever participated in was a class at the beginning of term two. In this English class taught by Mr. A. we were studying a unit of Shakespeare and to help us understand language from Elizabethan times

we read some sheets and then we hurled insults at each other. I found this very engaging because I really enjoyed the unit and the whole idea of insulting people in my class in Shakespearean language was so fun and out there. My best insult was when I called E. a "surly rumpfeed strumpet." This was my most engaging lesson so far this year.

My favorite lesson was when in English we were hurling Shakespeare insults at each other. This lesson took place near the beginning of term two in the English department. Since in this topic, we were looking at Shakespeare, our English teacher gave us a sheet with many insults made up by Shakespeare. We were instructed to try and memorize as many as we could in five minutes. He told us that we would be trying to insult each other with as many insults as possible. The person with the best insult for that round would get a point. The first person to reach 4 points won the duel. But the trick was that we could not look at the sheet of paper with the insults in the duel. It was all based on memory. Our teacher was to decide who won the round. The class had great fun ridiculing each other with insults such as "puttock" and "ratsbane." I enjoyed this lesson because the topic was funny and interesting and because it put a different view on learning, other than just writing on the board and trying to remember impossible facts. The setup was good as well because the desks were in a big square because in the duel, we had to stand up and face each other. We were not allowed to break eye contact with the other person. This lesson was one of the most fun lessons so far, along with a few others. Again, I really enjoyed this lesson because it was one that put a different and better view on learning.

PART

Two

Effective Relationships

Boys experience their teachers before they experience the lessons they teach. Classroom teachers are in fact more focal than actors on a stage, but their theaters are smaller and more intimate and they are typically the only members of the cast. Over the course of a school year, they deliver to each of their classes about 180 consecutive performances. Before a single unit of instruction is completed, teachers have registered critical information through their physical presence, youth or age, ease or tension, posture, tone of voice, and distinctive mannerisms. In minutes, if not seconds, students will sense a decidedly welcoming presence, or not.

As the boys we surveyed reflect on school experiences that worked for them, they tell stories of being uplifted by a teacher's warmth, humor, passion, or care. They relate seeking, finding, and submitting themselves to the inspiration of trusted mentors. Many talk about responding to a highly structured, demanding, no-nonsense teacher, especially when they find that teacher to be fair; others praise the teacher who is warm, easygoing, and kind—a "friend." Certain teachers have a gift for bridging their life experiences to those of their students. They tell personal stories and show clear interest in the stories their students tell them. Some teachers have a comic gift and are receptive to such gifts in their charges.

Whatever the particular style of transmission, the fundamental element in the successful transmission of classroom business from teachers to students is the establishment of trust. Coming to trust the teacher personally eases—indeed, makes possible—boys into the learning relationship. In this regard, boys' experiences confirm what Carol Gilligan (2005) has asserted about learning in general: "trust, the core of relationship, and truth, which is at the core of education, are inseparable" (p. xi).

The boys in our study who experienced this enabling trust describe their school experience in a way that bears no relation to the way contemporary schoolboys are portrayed in commercial media. Their stories are overall positive and expansive: they appear grateful, excited, and confident. In their best-selling book, *Raising Cain* (1999), Dan Kindlon and Michael Thompson write of "destructive boy archetypes, including the 'wild animal' and the 'entitled prince'" (p. 36); neither was in evidence in the stories we reviewed. In his phenomenology of boyhood, sociologist Miles Groth (2007) surveyed contemporary cultural representations of boys and concluded that the image of boys as wild and resistant to civil society has taken deep hold: "Boys both attract our interest and scare us. This should not surprise us, since boys embody human being in its original disorganized, imaginatively luxuriant wildness before the advent of settled civility, society, and culture" (p. 8). Against a background of such assumptions and stereotypes, our finding that boys respond constructively and with great feeling to teachers they like, admire, and trust represents an important corrective.

We have seen in previous chapters the kinds of care that committed teachers invest in preparing and presenting their lessons. As important as it is for teachers, often through arduous trial and error, to determine the transitive elements that will make a lesson work, no amount of pedagogical tinkering will ensure successful transmission and reception until the right kind of teacher-student relationship is achieved. In the words of educational psychologist Robert Pianta (1999), relationships are simply the "developmental infrastructure" for the successful engagement of boys in learning (p. 67).

In other research, Miriam Raider-Roth (2005) has proposed the "relational learner" as the most apt model for how students acquire knowledge in general: "Just as the theory of the relational self postulates that the self is born and develops in the cradle and life of relationships, so the notion of the relational learner postulates that the learning self is constructed and developed within the relationships of school" (p. 21). This model grows out of research documenting the critical role of relationships generally between caregivers and developing children. The quality of children's early attachments has consistently been found to contribute to children's overall developmental success. Simply put, securely attached children fare best. What such research tells us, in effect, is that relational connections are not merely a matter of mutual gratification to the caregivers and children involved; those connections serve essential developmental purposes. They are, in the words of psychologist Ann Masten (2001), the "ordinary magic" of human flourishing.

The critical importance of relationship in the learning process has been addressed in a number of Australian studies. Andrew Martin (2003), whose work explores differences in boys' and girls' motivation to achieve in school, asked boys: "Please describe the teacher that brings out your best work or keeps you most interested and motivated in school and schoolwork." The responses were clear: "Particularly critical to students' engagement and motivation in a particular subject was their *relationship with their teacher*" (p. 54). When engagement and motivation break down, the causal factor is once again relational. Another Australian research team found that boys' alienation from school was directly linked to relational factors: "The boys think . . . the adult world is 'not listening' and not generally interested in their view, their well-being, their educational needs and outcomes" (Slade, 2002, p. 1). As yet another Australian writer puts it, "The formal curriculum may tend to be the 'main game' in the teaching of girls. For boys . . . that is but one narrative in the classroom; running parallel or in conflict is the relational narrative" (Merry, 2009, p. 30).

What do teachers do to build relationships that enable them to succeed with boys? That answer may lie in what Carol Rodgers and Miriam Raider-Roth (2006) have termed *presence*: the "state of alert awareness, receptivity and connectedness to the mental, emotional, and physical workings of both the individual and the group" (p. 267). When a teacher is fully present, they write, "the moment is one of recognition, of feeling seen and understood, not just emotionally but cognitively, physically, and even spiritually. It is a feeling of being safe, where one is drawn to risk because of the discoveries it might reveal; it is the excitement of discovering one's self in the context of the larger world, rather than the worry of losing one's self in the process" (p. 267).

More than a century ago John Dewey called for the same quality, which he termed "heightened vitality," and what the contemporary educational philosopher

Maxine Greene (1973) calls "a state of wide-awakeness." Nel Noddings (2003), a practicing teacher as well as a theorist, sees the impact of her presence this way: "I do not need to establish a lasting, time-consuming personal relationship with every student. What I must do is to be totally and non-selectively present to the student—to each student—as he addresses me" (p. 180).

Chapters Ten and Eleven explore in more detail how teachers establish a personal presence with the boys they teach. In these chapters, we shuttle between the perspectives of boys and those of teachers in order to illuminate the strategies teachers adopt to reach boys. Chapter Ten identifies strategies that promote teacher-student connection. Chapter Eleven examines more closely the part teachers' knowledge—of their subjects, of boys, and of teaching—plays in establishing productive student relationships.

CHAPTER

10

A TEACHER'S PRESENCE

To enter the teaching profession is to enter a complex of relationships, most of them with students. For those relationships to become substantial enough to generate student motivation, new understanding, appreciation, and mastery, the teacher must project what we are calling *presence*.

A teacher's authentic presence is essential in overcoming whatever standing resistance a student carries with him into the classroom. Before a boy accepts an invitation to engage in scholastic activity, he takes a measure of the person extending the invitation. To engage, to attend closely, to work hard, to try—these commitments are not easily won, especially if a boy is being asked to engage in an activity that may be far from his personal strengths and interests. To enter into such an engagement could expose a boy's most dreaded limitations. Moreover, to engage in any particular bit of scholastic business is to disengage from pre-occupations perhaps closer to a boy's heart. Why would a boy—or anyone else, for that matter—do that? More to the point here, for whom would a boy do that?

INVITING ENGAGEMENT

Appreciating what they are asking of their students, many teachers, like this American teacher of high school juniors, make themselves personally available, perhaps expanding the boundaries of standard instruction to a diner or a living room:

To reassure my students that I will support them 100 percent on a daily basis, I often "do lunch" with them to get in a little extra help. The week after spring break, we meet two nights a week and Sunday afternoons to review for the Advanced Placement exam. We often have a bite to eat during the evening sessions. It means a lot to them to know that I am willing to take time away from my personal time to give them all the help and support I can. There are some nights that we discuss strategies in test taking, some nights we solve problem after problem, and some nights we just chat about how they can calm themselves down during the test. I tell them that I know I wouldn't get all the answers correct, so they can feel a bit more confident that they will face questions, not only in chemistry but in life also, where the answer isn't going to come that easily. We teach our boys to be the best in whatever they do. While I support that idea, I feel we must teach them that they will not always be the winner. The fact that they played the game at all is what makes them the true winner.

> *A teacher's presence does not by any means imply pandering.*

A teacher's presence does not by any means imply pandering. There is no formula for the transformative, generous gesture. And, in fact, exceptional gestures are not necessary. The establishment of presence refers simply to whatever teachers can do to convince a student to cross the threshold into engaged learning. Many students surveyed noted being drawn into otherwise daunting scholastic work because of a teacher's willingness to disclose something of their lives outside school:

One day in Chinese class, our teacher decided to tell us the story of her childhood in China. It was possibly the most interesting class I have ever had. Since she grew up in China during the Cultural Revolution, she had many stories to tell us and I probably learned more in that class than I did over the entire course of a history class. Later I did realize how much she had left out of the story, mostly the terrible toll it took on her family, but it did not detract from how informative it was one bit.

A teacher's authentic presence is not a pose. It is not conveyed in any willed or acquired "technique" of pleasing or amusing students. As the following boy's reminiscence makes clear, an effective teacher may well be demanding and rigorous—even an apparent "grump":

> The September of my freshman year I began Biology. Being a very information-oriented class with much memorization required, the homework load was hefty, with nightly assignments involving reading and making note cards, including Latin roots and their definitions. Biology was a challenging class for me and required a great deal of my time, leading to many late nights. However, when the bell for first period rang, I never dreaded the beginning of Bio. Though the class was designed to teach us Biology, science was only half of the material. We learned about so much more than plants and animals. I believe our teacher tried to come off as a grump so that his students would not joke around with him, but in reality he was one of the most good-humored individuals I have ever met, and took quite a bit of flack. We learned some history of the capital of Virginia, Richmond. We learned about electro fishing and how our teacher had a license to electrocute fish so that they were stunned and floated to the surface for ten minutes so that they could be analyzed. We learned a little about his experiences as a firefighter, and we even learned why Frosties [a cereal] don't melt and what happens to them when left in a hot car over the course of a week or more. We even learned about his involvement in the Model T Ford club of which he was a member and on which he served as a board member. Amazingly, our teacher somehow managed to either take up an entire class period talking about the like, or he was able to tie the stories into something we were learning. Biology was a wonderful experience despite the difficulty of the course, and the life lessons and interesting facts that I learned, accompanied with the science aspect of biology, helped me to better understand life and its meaning.

Teachers frequently establish their presence through an inspired gesture, a comment, or an unexpected shift in the tone or substance of a presentation. Students learn from such gestures that their teachers are more dimensional than they thought—and so is the subject they are studying. Chapter Nine reviewed successes teachers attributed to introducing dramatic novelties and surprises into the class. For the boys we studied, these gestures—often seemingly lighthearted—go a long way in reassuring them that their school lives can be continuous with "real life." This Australian tenth grader fondly recalls such a gesture that occurred two years prior:

> My most memorable school moment was in 8th grade Math. Math was a memorable class for me because I was in a very friendly class and I had a good teacher. The moment which stands out in my memory is the Arm Wrestle between my teacher and another student. Leading up to the Arm Wrestle our class was being very loud and not working. The teacher noticed this and set a reward for working hard and quietly. The reward was that he would arm wrestle the strongest member of our class. As our class put our heads down and got to work I felt very motivated because of the reward. I worked very hard that lesson and learned a lot of new skills. The arm wrestle between the teacher and the student was a very entertaining event and I can still remember it vividly today.

A memorable, authentic gesture, however slight or quiet, can go a long way in establishing a teacher's presence, as this U.S. philosophy student recalls:

> My experience took place in philosophy and religion class during senior year. It was raining that day and the sound was drifting in through the window. My teacher paused in the middle of a sentence and waited as the rain fell outside. She told us all to close our eyes and sit there just breathing and listening to the rain. For ten minutes [she] showed me her harmony of nature and the peace of just being.

Because they find themselves the objects of students' careful study, teachers have the potential to stand for something important—transitive—to their lessons. What they convey about their actual presence in their students' lives can lead boys to a deeper learning.

ANSWERING, "WHAT'S THE POINT?"

School curricula do not typically address the most important question boys ask of their teachers and of the subjects they teach: How does this material bear on my life, and why does it matter? In fairness, it is a profound and difficult question. If they are honest, teachers will confess to having asked such questions themselves, perhaps even acknowledging that their own personal answers are provisional, because they are still asking. The boys in our study responded touchingly and gratefully to teachers who were willing to address the "why" question, especially when the teacher shared personal experiences of seeking meaning and purpose.

This American student of senior year English was personally transformed by his teacher's willingness to share a formative personal experience:

> The story that stands out most in my mind does not have to do with a specific lesson out of a book or a certain project. The moment that stands out most for me occurred this year in my English 4 [senior year] class. New to the school, not much was known about this teacher who transferred from a rival school in our athletic conference. The first few weeks went by cautiously as the students tried to feel out who this person really was. At the start of class one day, the discussion turned to the issue of applying to college and taking a streamlined path of life. The teacher proceeded to tell us his story, which has inspired me to think outside the box and shy away from conformity. Finishing high school in three years, our teacher lived what should have been his senior year in Alaska. The following years, he went on to play collegiate football at the University of Washington. From college, his path took him to such opportunities as coaching football in Japan, studying at Harvard and Columbia, fly fishing in the clear streams of Idaho and now on to our school. Moving forward, I fear that I will go to college, get a job and settle down without experiencing life like this teacher has. I look at his story to tell myself that there is more than one route to take.

The line between teachers' sharing their search for answers to ultimate questions and imposing those answers on students is sometimes difficult to determine—yet that line must be drawn. A charismatic teacher is worryingly well positioned to lead students to embrace any number of dubious value positions. For the sake of boys' emotional and intellectual development, however, it is probably best that concern about "imposing" values stops short of forbidding teachers to hold and express them. A teacher's educative presence often depends on the clarity and passion of his or her particular convictions. To hold such convictions is not necessarily to proselytize; it may instead be an appealing invitation to students to set about finding out where they stand and what they stand for. This eighth grader, for example, reveals the energizing effect of his teacher's outspoken resistance to accepting assertions "on authority":

> It was in grade 8 in English class that I experienced my favorite learning experience. It just so happens that the teacher of that class was also my favorite teacher. He was my favorite teacher because he was real. He always said what was on his mind and never held anything back because it might be insulting or inappropriate. The thing that I loved the most about what that teacher offered to the class was the discussions. In class we would talk about anything that came up in the world, wars, politics, behavior, cultures, life, etc. Anyways, back to my favorite English class. . . . The thing that I remember the most about that class was when the teacher brought up the topic about killer bees coming to Northern America. He told us that in the early 2000s, the government warned the population that there was going to be a killer bee infestation. He then said that he had never seen a killer bee in his whole life and that just because the government says something, it doesn't mean that it's always the truth. I found this really awakening and truthful. I never had any other teachers like him that were so open and straightforward.

Teachers who enter the profession primarily because of their fascination with their subject often achieve a valued presence with their students. Although the boys in this study reported appreciation and respect for a variety of qualities in their teachers, no single attribute was noted more admiringly than teachers' infectious enthusiasm for what they teach. Such enthusiasm tends to be reciprocal, as a number of teachers, including this teacher of middle school science, reported with obvious satisfaction:

I take special care to pick out current events that I feel will be most interesting to middle school–aged boys. My enthusiasm for their learning about science in the "real world" and how to use their developing personal problem-solving skills further promotes my strategy of hooking boys into how wonderful science in the real world can be. My enthusiasm often overflows into my participants, and it is an amazing thing to observe a group of boys generate memorable discussions with current events and problem-solving skills serving as a vehicle for blooming conversation.

Boys take a shrewd measure of not only their teachers' mastery of their subjects but also of their enthusiasm for what they are doing.

This U.S. teacher of classical languages concludes, after nearly fifty years of teaching boys, that boys take a shrewd measure of not only their teachers' mastery of their subjects but also of their enthusiasm for what they are doing:

Perhaps the effectiveness of any activity is more determined by the teacher's enthusiasm and expertise than by the activity itself. Students learn better when the presentation not only clarifies the point being made but also derives from an individual in whom they have great confidence as an educator and as a teacher who is knowledgeable in the discipline. Of course, it does not hurt if the methodology employed provides the student with some enjoyment. I have found over my many years in this occupation that imparting knowledge (at the high school level) cannot of itself promote the desire of the student to excel in your discipline (particularly if that area of study is Latin or ancient Greek). More is required, and the "more" takes the form of a genuine interest in the subject matter that the student can readily observe.

A popular, if unexamined, assumption about school-aged boys is that they are school resistant and anti-intellectual generally. This stereotype is especially pervasive in commercial television and movie portrayals of boys. Our study, however, revealed little, if anything, of this stereotype. To the contrary, boys responded with a respect bordering on reverence to intellectual attainment—whether their own or that of others. Their accounts of being transported by especially accomplished teachers include this tenth-grade science student's experience in the classroom of "the smartest man on campus":

> The name of the class was Energy. My teacher is easily the smartest man on campus. Sometimes in class it was hard for him to get points across because he was so smart. Towards the end of the year everyone in the class was so intrigued with what he was teaching. I have never seen so many students in one class that were actually excited to come to class everyday. Late in the spring our entire class period was fun. Everyone in the room became great friends because the class size was so small. Earlier in the year, the experiments and tests were so hard that our entire class (8) got together every night in the library to work on Energy homework. Although the information in the class was still difficult, the whole class grew a liking for the material. If the class were co-ed or any larger, there would have been a completely different atmosphere but instead everything came together to form a perfect class and class size.

ELEVATING THE SUBJECT

Teachers tend to be aware of the relative success or failure of a given lesson. Moreover, effective teachers, if somehow made to put modesty aside, are able to identify the personal qualities, choices, and methods responsible for their effectiveness. It is less clear that practicing teachers are aware of the depth of the impression their best efforts make. The late Frank Ashburn, founding headmaster of the Brooks School in North Andover, Massachusetts, and a poet, called well-taught students "unseen harvests," because the real fruits of good teaching are often realized long after students leave school. Nevertheless, the boys we asked to share their best classroom experiences celebrated with considerable energy the experience of being awakened to stimulating new learning.

This tenth-grade history student is unable to name just what his teacher did to ignite his interest. It happened, he writes, "the moment I walked into the classroom," and he is quick and eager to appreciate it. One suspects his teacher would be pleased—and perhaps surprised—to know the impact of her presence:

> The particular class experience that is most memorable for me is the moment that I walked into [the classroom] where my first year 10 American History lesson took place. From the moment I walked into that classroom I was filled with excitement and passion for History. It was like nothing I had ever experienced. My teacher loves History and is so enthusiastic about it. Her love of History instantly transferred over to me. I was fascinated and captivated by it. It was the first time I put a genuine effort into anything academic. From this point on I learned to put work into everything especially History. This was definitely the changing point in my schooling.

This twelfth-grade U.S. history student recounts a similarly transformative experience, this one retracing events on a historic battlefield. Here he experienced the presence of his teacher in a new and evocative context, allowing him a deepened appreciation:

> Each year, there is a junior class field trip to Gettysburg, Pa. This trip was particularly engaging because of my fifth form American History teacher. He always brought an unmatchable enthusiasm to the classroom, and the possibility to see and interact with him "in his element" at a place of monumental importance in American History was a very exciting event. Although we had a guide, our teacher constantly chipped in his remarks about the battle (and many times took lead of the group). He showed us how the Union won the battle, and brought the textbook and the summer reading (*The Killer Angels*) alive with an in-depth analysis. He was an expert on the subject, and students paid attention to him because he knew every detail about the battle and the war. I remember vividly the history, stories, and places I learned about the battle because of the passion and attention to detail my teacher brought to the battlefield. Through my teacher's class, I learned a tremendous amount about U.S. history and it has helped me define who I am.

ESTABLISHING PARTNERSHIP

Effective student-teacher relationships are not composed entirely of deft, intuitive, and unconscious touches. Teachers and students alike indicate the positive effects of intentionally offering relationship, in one way or another building an aspect of partnership. This senior remembers the elevated feeling he experienced when given a chance to enter into partnership with his biology teacher:

In junior year Honors Biology class last year, I stayed after class to help my teacher prepare the electrophoresis gel for the next day's laboratory experiment. I explained to her that I had the ability to stay because of a free period immediately after the class, allowing ample time for me to aid her in any way. The lab took place the next day, and the transition into the lab for my classmates was noticeably eased by my added effort the day before, since the equipment was already in place, ready for use. Because of the time required for the staining process to occur, I decided to stay further and help my teacher stain the DNA samples in the gel. The process took less than half the time required if she alone was to stain all of the samples. After taking a cursory glance at the samples, we deemed together that the lab had been a success for each lab group. Smiling at each other because of this resounding success, she congratulated me for our lab success and thanked me for my assistance. I had spent the extra time in the lab room because I enjoyed biology, this experiment in particular, but my explanation was met only with further thanks. I did not feel that I had done anything extraordinary or worthy of her lauds because I was merely acting on my own principles. The experience has stuck with me through the months since then, and I feel that it is one of the best student-teacher relationships that I have ever had due to further references to that morning several weeks later when discussing college recommendations. I continued to excel in the class because of my devotion to the course and my teacher. I was proud to nominate her for a teacher award and was the first to rise for a standing ovation when she earned the school's student appreciation award. These awards exemplify the personal achievements that she guided us through, making me give her the title "class mom" because of her efforts in purveying her knowledge to each student in the grade, regardless whether or not they were in her class. My personal experience was just one of many such instances.

Relationship begins in mutual recognition; each party must "take in" the other. For a teacher to take in the distinctive presence of the ten, twenty, or thirty individual students composing a class, it may help, as this teacher reported, to acknowledge and greet each student by name as they meet each day:

> By greeting each boy as he enters, I get a strong impression as to where they are focus-wise on any given day. In addition, each boy understands he is important, known by me, and that his participation in the class is valued and important.

These intentional gestures are not lost on students, as this U.S. eleventh-grade boy writes:

> When I first walked into English class my junior year I was greeted by my new teacher with the correct way to handshake. I knew that this class would better me and build my character. To this day, every discussion and class is uplifting and offers many ways for the mind to think. I am grateful that I was able to know [teacher] and will take many of his lessons to heart.

A formal daily greeting and a handshake serve to announce and acknowledge that ensuing class business will be carried out in this relationship. Teachers can be even more intentional in establishing partnership in the learning process. A U.S. student of American literature recalls the inspiration he felt at being called by his teacher to look at his schooling in a new way:

> The teacher walked in, and I had only seen him in passing in the hallways before; he'd always seemed uptight, yet very serene looking at the same time. After introducing himself, he told us his expectations for the course. He didn't want us to "play the game of school," where the student tries his hardest to do what's necessary to earn a certain grade. Instead, he

suggested that we each strive to come up with creative thoughts and push the boundaries of our writing skills—the grades would be a bonus. He explained that the class would be run in a seminar setting, with each student contributing to the discussion of the assigned reading and talking not just responding to the teacher's questions, but also to the thoughts of our peers. Something clicked on that first day because ever since, I have been able to go into class not expecting to earn a grade, but rather to learn. Not only has it made each day more enjoyable, but I find that I am much more engaged in my classes. While it wasn't a lesson in the traditional sense of the word, something about the way he told us his expectations unlocked my mind.

OFFERING CARE AND COACHING

In his intriguing book *The Talent Code* (2009), Dan Coyle documents extraordinary gains in performance of all kinds—scholastic, athletic, and artistic—when individuals are able to sustain effortful engagement in tasks just beyond the margin of their existing competence. Working to master skills that are almost, but not quite yet, in our grasp requires us to maintain a state of arousal and concentration that can feel aversive. Yet the ability to stay in this effortful zone accounts for our greatest advances in learning and accomplishment. It would follow that teachers and coaches of the right disposition and presence are positioned to play a crucial part in seeing their charges through various trials of confusion and uncertainty to ultimate mastery. The boys in our study recognized and were especially appreciative of this kind of support from their teachers, as this tenth-grade Canadian boy relates:

This took place in Computer Studies in 10th grade with the teacher. When we began programming, I had difficulty understanding how it worked and how to do it. However the teacher was very understanding towards me and helped me through the whole way. She never gave up on me even though I kept on having difficulty, and finally, after many morning and lunch extra help sessions, a light finally turned on in my mind and I understood everything. I was able to get a really good score on the big test of that unit, but that is not the point of the story. The thing that is memorable is that she never gave up on me and always believed that I could do it. There is no way that I could've understood this confusing and complex unit without her extensive aid. She went the extra mile to help me, and that's what makes this school so great.

A ninth-grade Australian boy mired discouragingly in the transition from arithmetic to algebraic understanding might well have never made the cognitive leap forward without the guidance of a timely—and, one suspects, gifted— "extra Math helper":

I was constantly having trouble in Math in middle school. The topic was Algebra. I couldn't get my head around it. The more I tried, the more I just couldn't get it. After a couple of lessons an extra Math helper for our class came in and I asked her how to work out these equations. She went through it slowly and I started to understand it a bit better. She wrote in my book her working out and I started to understand it even better. Then with the next couple of problems I did the same working out she did and I started to get them right. I felt extra motivated to continue with my work as I felt great about understanding what we were doing. It made me continue on and I finished with 48 out of 50 in the test. It was from that lesson that I stopped having problems with Algebra.

As we reported at the start of this book, one of the central findings of this study was that boys tend to elicit the pedagogy they need. For this to occur, teachers must perceive and evaluate the behavior and attitudes their students present, including resistant behavior and attitudes. Such behavior, far from being a "problem," can provide the very information teachers need to adjust their approach and material to their students. Teachers who make such adjustments may not necessarily be aware of the underlying relational dynamic at work—only that "that didn't work, but this seems to." Some teachers, however, are highly conscious of the need to adjust their pedagogy to their students' responses, as this U.S. math teacher reports:

I have never felt that mathematics is best taught by a particular approach or method. I do not usually follow any specific approach for a particular course. The type of students in the class determines the style I use to teach. In my advanced courses, I have been more of a guide than a teacher. I have found that the boys are challenged more the less I speak. I lead a lesson or ask a question and allow the boys to come to their own conclusions. I believe that part of motivating the boys is being successful at reaching the boys at their level. I'm not always successful at it, and there are times when I get lucky. One particular time I just happened to fall on dumb luck. When I thought about how much information these boys collected on a daily basis and I looked at all the music that is literally at their fingertips, I should not have been surprised when they were easily able to remember a crucial step by singing. I was just fortunate to stumble on this through my own frustration.

I have found that the boys are challenged more the less I speak.

It has always been fulfilling for me to hear boys talk about this particular class years later. I had the chance to teach a handful of the same boys a year later in geometry. It was fun to hear them singing to themselves whenever they had to solve quadratic equations with factoring as an option. I simply used a tool in the math class that they had been using for the majority of their lives, from learning nursery rhymes to whatever is playing in the Top 40. I have no problem admitting when I am lucky, but I stumbled onto something that has been effective for me.

CHAPTER

11

A TEACHER'S KNOWLEDGE

Few teachers of long tenure have not experienced moments when they felt personally challenged by a particularly oppositional student or a difficult class. Reflexively, if not helpfully, teachers in such circumstances are likely to fall back on their "authority" as teachers: the assumption that as older, accomplished, credential-bearing figures, they are entitled to determine both the substance of classroom business and the behavioral atmosphere in which it is carried out. Teachers experiencing such difficulties hope that the disciplinary apparatus of their school's administration will support their authority and that, ultimately, the school authority is grounded in the law of the land. Although these assumptions are reasonable enough and indeed true at a certain level of generality, they are not likely to advance anybody in the direction of better teaching and more engaged learning. This is because teachers' real authority does not lie primarily in their title or role but rather in the presence they convey through the mastery of their craft—in their knowledge.

KNOWING THEIR SUBJECTS

Teachers at their thoughtful best know there is no substitute for their own subject mastery. We were struck by many such acknowledgments made by teachers in their responses to being asked why they thought a particular lesson or approach succeeded—for example:

First of all, I think a most significant factor that allows me to be a successful and effective teacher is my confidence in the classroom. I am a native speaker of Japanese; I was born and raised in Japan and attended public school in Japan; and I did extensive research on Japanese history during my college years. Therefore, I have a good command of the language and a rich understanding of the history of the language.

Boys are quick to sense this kind of "confidence" in their teachers and the mastery on which it is based. While many boys, especially younger and less sophisticated ones, are not yet capable of explicitly naming the invigorating element of mastery in their teachers' daily work, they are nevertheless quick to sense it and, like this eighth-grade student of German, to appreciate it:

In 8th grade, I had a teacher for German. He was very young, but is the teacher that I remember most. He taught me this language for the year of 2006, and was extremely enthusiastic about his subject. His eagerness for us to learn was infectious, and actually made the class, which was full of kids who didn't really like learning languages, interested and engaged. He was always willing to answer any peculiar questions we had about the language, and because he was always in the mood for a long talk about the finer points of German, he really motivated me to study it further. He really kick-started my language learning, and has made me want to continue my languages after I leave school. This teacher is especially memorable for me because he was able to switch between having detailed conversations with the more interested students, and then switching to a subject that would interest the other boys, while still managing to relate this to the subject in some way. He gained the trust of our class through this, which is probably why the class was so willing to learn from him.

The deep engagement good teachers generate in their best lessons grows out of their facility with the material they are teaching, not some kind of gift for enthusiasm. Teachers who have achieved such mastery are able to convey transformative lessons even on Friday afternoons, as in this account offered by a tenth-year British boy:

It was a Friday afternoon when all I could think about was the weekend. With important exams around the corner we had to complete the syllabus by the end of the lesson. The rest of the class were in an impatient mood and I believed that it would be very difficult for the teacher to control them. However my history teacher inspired the class with a passionate speech about a major battle in the First World War. The students, including myself, changed from an unruly rabble into a class impassioned by historical events. My teacher taught us about the immense loss of life at the Battle of the Somme and we also discussed the problems with General Haig's tactics at the Battle and whether Haig deserved the epithet the "Butcher of the Somme." I believe that my teacher kick-started my passion for history, which since that lesson has been my favorite lesson. In my opinion, in lessons it is vital for teachers to show excitement and a true passion for their subject. This is what my teacher did and if a group of teenagers can be motivated through this method it shows that this is the only way that teaching should be carried out, with a passion for the subject being integral to good teaching.

In an educational climate devoted to producing and comparing the results of standardized tests measuring students' "basic proficiency" at each grade level and the expectations that teachers will coach their students to pass these tests, little time or attention has been given to what is perhaps the most generative aspect of a successful teacher's work: expertise in one's chosen field. A New Zealand tenth grader recounts how an "expert" English teacher left his class with an understanding and enthusiasm that went beyond "basic proficiency":

Every Tuesday our teacher takes [our combined classes] to the library and has a group discussion about the poems we are studying. A few weeks ago we were studying a poem by William Wordsworth, and our teacher brought in an "expert" on the poet. This teacher spent the lesson talking to us about Romantic poets, and what they write about. He also spoke a lot about philosophy, which I found very intriguing. He spoke about how the poet related his ideas to nature, and how the Romantic poets saw Nature as almost holy. The entire class was in rapture and he explained all his ideas concisely and involved all the students, asking questions to those who were holding back a little. I found the lesson extremely helpful and gave me a good insight on the structure of Wordsworth's poems.

KNOWING BOYS

Even an encyclopedic mastery of subject matter does not ensure its successful transmission to others. A gifted poet may have little to say about poems generally or about how to write one. Savants capable of solving staggeringly complex analytical problems are sometimes utterly incapable of explaining what they have done; they just do it. Effective teachers, by contrast, combine mastery of the subject matter with the ability to convey it to others. Their own mastery, in a sense, is less central to them than enabling their students to attain similar mastery. At the heart of this dual accomplishment is a commitment to those they teach that impels them to devise, revise, and improvise pedagogy until they succeed in engaging their students.

Effective teachers combine mastery of the subject matter with the ability to convey it to others.

This U.S. twelfth grader's physics teacher had more than sufficient knowledge to convey the basic principles of velocity; he had an empathic knack for making what could have been routine instruction memorable—and thus bringing it home to the boys' understanding:

When I think back to my sophomore year, this class always sticks out the most in my mind. My teacher took every chance to make the class as interesting as possible. If I had to choose one instance of this that was truly memorable, I'd have to say it was when he taught us about velocity. Instead of using some boring problem like a ball on a ramp, our teacher had us figure out if a short bus's brakes gave out at something like 50 mph and it went off a cliff at a 64 degree angles, where would the Boppo the Physics Clown have to be standing in order to make the impact a whole lot funnier? While it was still a physics problem, and it still required all the same math, our teacher always seemed to find a way of presenting the material that made it engrossing and entertaining.

A teacher's empathic capacity to engage—to jostle, joke, surprise, to do whatever is necessary to drive a lesson home—was highly valued in the boys' accounts of their best school experiences. Boys who felt they were seen and known by their teachers expressed an eager willingness to throw themselves into the class, to try, to try harder, to exceed themselves, as did this U.S. twelfth grader when he was in the presence of a committed history teacher who, in addition to "terrifying" him also "knew [him] so well":

The most engaging activity that I have participated in my 13 years at my school has been my junior year advanced American History course, in particular, the preparation I went through as I approached the American History AP examination. Aside from the class being the most engaging and interesting class I have ever encountered in my school, it was so memorable because of the experience I had with my teacher. I was terrified of the man, but at the same time he was one of my favorite teachers because he knew me so well. He knew my limits and he knew when I was or was not trying, and did not hesitate to point it out, often in front of the class. What set this class apart also was the relationship that not only I, but everyone forged with him. It's the only class that I have had a Friday night study session for (until nine o'clock, I must mention), and yet I was not upset in anyway, because the time with him in the classroom was so engaging and interesting. He would shout at the top of his lungs and make heartfelt exclamations about George Washington, while never hesitating to pull out a picture or two and slam it on the front desk. He would even grab your tie (I have had at least one ripped apart by him) and throw it behind your back or slam your binder into the ground if he thought you were slacking, or sometimes just to get a point across. Overall, the experience was so memorable because of the person behind it.

Accounts like these have a clear subtext: teachers who forge productive relationships with the boys in their classes do so by observing and then responding to whatever may be particular, or gendered, in their approach to learning. Such teachers, whatever their views on the biological or social construction of gender, shape their instruction to what they find boys require at one stage of development or another. And while teachers may be reluctant to designate themselves as such, over extended practice they become experts at teaching boys. This expertise, along with the mastery of their subject and their relational gifts, is an integral part of their authoritative presence.

In their views on the masculine dimension of their students' lives, the teachers in this study tended to be pragmatic. While on balance most believed that their lessons had been honed to fit boys' tendencies and interests in particular ways, they were also reluctant to be narrowly formulaic about "the way boys learn" or "what works with boys." This Canadian teacher, for example, prefers to let the "evidence" boys present in the classroom determine his responses to them, rather than to be guided by prevailing assumptions about the nature of gender:

I acknowledge that boys have different learning styles to girls, for example, but I don't tailor my lessons to cater specifically for gender differences; I tailor them to meet the specific student's needs from a cultural, linguistic, and academic perspective. This may very well inadvertently include strategies that are associated with teaching and learning of boys, but this is not something that I consciously set out to do. I look at the individual as having more learning variables than just those relating to gender.

Many of our teachers participating have taught in both boys' schools and coed schools. Some of them noted pointed differences in the way they found that boys and girls to respond to particular challenges. Others noted differences in degree, not of kind.

This South African English teacher finds that certain instructional strategies are "especially suited to boys," resulting in both superior understanding of the material and more productive classroom behavior:

> I feel that the war poems activity is especially suited to boys as they learn better when they are not passive observers. They need to be actively engaged in lessons as they are often restless in class, and the negative energy can therefore be channeled in a positive direction. This has a positive effect as far as class behavior is concerned.

A New Zealand science teacher finds "an element of danger" appeals to boys, a finding consistent with the lessons set out in Chapter Nine. About a laboratory demonstration that resulted in an impressive explosion, he writes:

> Boys are not afraid of things that have an element of danger. They want to see it for themselves, not just be told about it. They like things big and dramatic. They always want to assist or do the demonstration for themselves and experience the moment for themselves . . .

A Canadian teacher concurs about the special appeal to boys of certain kinds of classroom business—in this case, a seemingly inappropriate but in fact highly productive lesson—on flatulence. The lesson, fully narrated in Chapter Eight, reportedly generated serious and penetrating discussion about the nature of self-consciousness and the origins of social conventions. The teacher writes that the lesson not only engaged his boys; it made a durable impression:

> Ninth-grade boys find the whole topic of farting hilarious. Both of my classes were delighted/shocked, and more important (no pun intended) moved to see what examining a common social faux pas could lead to. In end-of-year interviews, half a dozen boys referred to that discussion as being particularly memorable—and not because of the subject matter but what it revealed about us naked apes.

Again, most teachers were reluctant to claim to have a definitive theory about how boys learn at any stage of their lives, but this young teacher observed that teachers of boys soon acquire a sure sense of "what works":

> Although I have no expertise in knowing how to teach boys, I can conclude, based on class discussions, student comments, and reactions to various practices, what works and what does not. I have continuously observed that when new learning involves activities where the boys can stand, move around, and share ideas, they produce work of better quality and enjoy demonstrating what they know.

WHERE TEACHING MEETS BOY

Boys are quick to sense their teachers' willingness to extend themselves, at times even to risk appearing foolish in the service of driving home a point.

Successful teachers are often willing to make an extra, even unconventional, effort to connect to their students. Boys are quick to sense their teachers' willingness to extend themselves, at times even to risk appearing foolish in the service of driving home a point. Two years after the fact, a British eleventh grader recalls warmly a Latin vocabulary lesson his teacher decided to render in song:

> Two years ago in Latin at the time the teacher made a song up to describe what the Latin translations for the English words were. It would have been a boring lesson otherwise but the song made it fun and interesting. It was the way that the teacher sang the song that made it funny and memorable. He was only saying ten different Latin words but he put on a funny voice and did a little dance which made it really funny and interesting. Even though this lesson was over two years ago I can still remember it really well and still remember it as a fun and effective learning period. I have since dropped Latin but I can still remember that particular lesson and what we were being taught even though I don't remember anything else about Latin. This fun style of teaching was used by this teacher quite a lot and I learned a lot that year and got good exam marks.

Improvising pedagogy to better reach boys need not involve theatricality of any kind. The successful adjustment may entail no more than placing the instruction in the context of boys' daily lives. This U.S. English teacher could, with reason, have despaired of the decline in his students' command of standard written English due to their constant, subliterate "texting" of one another, but he decided instead to conduct his writing instruction in the context of electronic messaging:

> Each of these assignments has a distinct feel to it. In the first one, boys are working independently at first, and then they come together at the end of the unit for a group discussion. The process of typing instant responses to each other in real time while sitting next to each other is a new one for many of the boys. It feels awkward at first, but then it becomes very natural. In fact, it feeds off their tendency to text-message each other constantly. We take that and make it academically oriented. This exercise allows each boy to be heard, even the slow thinkers and typists. Shyness goes away, and the boys learn how to conduct a conversation or argument without resorting to childish retorts.

In Chapter One, teachers from a variety of academic disciplines recounted the heightened level of engagement boys reveal in the process of designing and making things. To recognize the facility and deep satisfaction boys gain from creating products in school serves to honor the process—and the boys engaged in it. Boys fully engaged in making things report feeling elevated and energized. Schools and teachers seeking to "get it right," especially those hoping to reach otherwise unreachable boys, would do well to reconsider the curriculum-wide potential that designing and creating products holds for boys. As this Canadian teacher of technology writes, the act of building things—in this case, models—dissolves the boundary between boys' inner lives and school:

> Students have autonomy in selecting the model and have a vested interest in making their project look good. This is something with tangible results and available for display either at home or in the class. Boys are asked if they would like to donate their model to the class. Such models are hung from the ceiling and serve as reminders of times spent in the environment. It is not unusual to have boys come back years later, look for their model, and reminisce. Through model building, relationships and bonds develop that are relevant for the students. Observation of the class in action consistently would show twenty-two students working at their construction; the bell goes, and when they look up, almost ninety minutes have gone by in the blink of an eye. This is flow theory in practice and is a characteristic of this unit.

CONCLUSION

The boys who participated in this study could not have been more responsive and appreciative to the teachers who took pains to reach them. The submissions we received were collected in a fairly perfunctory manner. Given the unmonitored freedom to write what they pleased and given the certainty that among any sample of fifteen hundred schoolboys, some will be seriously troubled and others preoccupied with personal concerns, we were immediately struck by the generosity and richness of what the boys conveyed to us.

Impressed as we were by what the boys reported, we believe their teachers would be even more pleased. As so many of the boys reported, the efforts of their teachers resulted in more than absorbing lessons. Those efforts resulted in boys' reconsidering their place in the larger world and with a new determination to learn more and succeed personally. A number of boys reported nothing less than "finding themselves" in consequence of dedicated teaching, as in the case of this Canadian senior's experience in history class:

> My previous history teacher used simulations for history which definitely keeps you involved and is of course a lot of fun. I thought senior history would be a drag after this. I was mistaken—never been so happy to be mistaken either. I got a teacher who taught history the way it should be taught: like a storyteller. That's how history has been passed on for years—why it stopped, I don't know. He would speak like a true storyteller—as if around a campfire—taking notes would be like discussions, and you would leave with a practical understanding of history; nothing glorified or undervalued either. It was a pleasure, and the class would moan every time it was time to go, eager to hear the next thing.

Three

Lessons for Educators

As we have presented our findings at schools and conferences since completing the study, audiences composed of teachers and other educators have asked the inevitable question: What does all this mean we should do? Those who work with boys in classrooms, after-school programs, and other educative contexts may find in the examples of effective practices in this book promising new approaches or perhaps a positive affirmation of their own best work. But behind these narratives there may also be broader implications for teachers and schools. How did teachers come to compose these lessons? What did their schools do to nurture such relationships and practices in their classrooms?

CHAPTER

12

ENHANCING
TEACHER-STUDENT
RELATIONSHIPS

Whatever the degree of satisfaction or concern teachers may feel about their effectiveness in reaching and teaching boys, few would assert that there is no room for improvement. Teachers who find that too many boys in their classes are unengaged, resistant to instruction, or chronically disruptive have special reason to reconsider their practices. Teachers in coed schools who are concerned about boys' underrepresentation in honor societies and on honor rolls and their overrepresentation in remedial programs and disciplinary proceedings stand to benefit considerably from exposure to practices that have been found to engage and motivate boys. Teachers who are concerned about the underengagement and underachievement of certain types of boys may also discover promising alternatives in the work of a body of international colleagues who have succeeded with such boys.

We found that boys sustain their engagement in classroom business when they feel held in a positive, trusting relationship to their teacher. The establishment of this relationship precedes their engagement and subsequent achievement. The critical factor in establishing such relationships is the kind of presence boys perceive in their teachers. The boys who participated in this study readily acknowledged their responsiveness to teachers who appealed to them as welcoming, aware of them as individuals, personally distinctive—*real*—and in authoritative command of their subject matter.

Teachers hoping to form productive relationships with boys cannot merely imitate or approximate presence; they must actually have it. Taking the measure of this essential feature of one's work as a teacher thus requires considerable self-awareness. Each teacher standing before a classroom of students projects a presence, but not every teacher's presence invites a boy's trust and relationship. Teachers cannot command their likability and acceptance; if they could, the boys in their charge would forfeit their autonomous choice to engage with the teacher in a learning relationship. But if teachers cannot command the relational partnership, they can determine the kind of welcome and the warmth they extend. They can also determine the depth and quality of their lessons.

Taking measure of one's actual classroom presence can be a humbling and even threatening prospect, and it is especially difficult at the very moment it is probably most necessary: when certain students or perhaps whole classes are unresponsive and oppositional. No teacher wants to entertain the notion that he or she is disliked—even when, at least circumstantially, it is actually true. To acknowledge being resisted, disliked, or merely endured by students is to open up a still more dreadful possibility: that one is inherently uncompelling and unlikable. No one wants to acknowledge such perceptions. The idea that one may be a forbidding, unwelcoming, or perhaps incompetent presence is simply not admitted to consciousness; it is categorically denied, not considered. Instead the "problem" is projected outward to the students, whom the teacher considers to be ill mannered and ill prepared—in effect, unreachable and unteachable. Teachers may blame the school's woeful administration and declining scholastic standards, which reflect declining standards generally; faulty parenting; loss of civility; a youth culture preoccupied with commercial and electronic distractions; and drugs. Teachers harboring these denials and projections are likely to consider themselves martyrs to high standards presumed to have been upheld in an idealized past. They may well succeed in insulating teachers from any dreaded hint of their own failure to engage their students, but they will not solve the problem. Such teachers will continue to be resistible presences in their schools, and their students will disengage from them.

The fact of the matter is that when a teacher's presence is insufficient to forge relationships with students, opportunities to learn are lost. That is without question a problem—but it is not an unsolvable one. Teachers committed to succeeding with students, including difficult students, including difficult boys, must be willing to undertake an honest self-appraisal. This may entail acknowledging that they may be to some degree responsible for the relational difficulties with a resistant student or a problematic class. This may include a frank realization that they are indeed disliked—but that the situation is correctible. Teachers genuinely committed to reaching their students and facilitating their progress and mastery will be willing to reconsider all manner of prior practice in the interest of improvement, including the presence they offer students.

The boys and teachers participating in this study noted a number of qualities that characterized productive student-teacher relationships. Merely listed, these foundational qualities may seem obvious, yet many teachers, even experienced teachers, do not incorporate them into their daily practice. To see if you do, consider whether you can answer the following questions affirmatively:

> *Teachers committed to succeeding with students, including difficult students, must be willing to undertake an honest self-appraisal.*

- Do I greet each of my students individually every day?

- Do I exchange words with each of my students every day?

- Am I readily available for individual help and counsel?

- Am I a person a student might want to seek out for help or counsel?

- Am I a person a boy would want to seek out for help or counsel?

- Do I actually pay attention to my students?

- Do I notice how my lessons are received by students as I teach?

- Do I modify how I am presenting lessons in response to the effects I observe in my students?

- Do I have a clear picture of each student's incremental progress or decline from day to day, week to week?

- Do I take the initiative to seek out and confront students whose scholastic progress or personal behavior concerns me?

- Am I comfortable sharing with my students personal experiences relating to my own learning and growth?

- Do I communicate to my students how I came to know and love my subject? (Do *I* love, or still love, my subject?)

- Do I ever acknowledge to my students inspiring teachers and other figures who exemplified or taught me the things I value most?

Finally, can teachers honestly and affirmatively answer two even more basic student questions:

- Do you know me?

- Are you interested in me?

The findings of our study strongly suggest that teachers' answers to these questions provide some indication of their relational presence.

In addition to honest introspection, there are a number of straightforward ways for teachers to assess the kind of presence their students perceive in them. The most direct of these is to ask, and dedicated teachers do this readily. It is neither uncommon nor inappropriate for teachers at the outset of a course, or anywhere along its path, to ask, "Am I [or is this material] boring you?" "Does this seem [or am I being] too hard?" "Am I being clear?" "Am I giving you enough time?" "Am I being fair?" When students perceive that such questions are asked not because a teacher is desperate for their approval, but because she or he really wants to know, they have entered the threshold of receptive relationship. As that relationship develops and deepens, teachers come to rely on regular corrective feedback as they solicit honest answers to honest questions. Teachers offering such relationship are also able to admit an occasional lapse of judgment or a mistaken utterance, admissions that instead of undermining student confidence and respect actually enhance them. Such teachers, to use the language of the boys and teachers in our study, are willing to risk being "real," acquiring presence as they do so.

There are of course other resources to draw from in taking measure of one's teaching presence. Periodic or end-of-course student surveys can, besides providing useful student responses to texts, materials, and instructional methods, convey helpful impressions of the relational climate the teacher has established. Anonymously submitted surveys may include pointed criticism, some of it potentially hurtful. Some complaints may be grounded in students' personal troubles unrelated to the teacher, and these can be identified by including in the survey questions designed to take the measure of students' overall satisfaction with the school year, other teachers, and peer relations.

In addition to surveying students, teachers may get helpful impressions of their relational dynamics with students by inviting teaching peers or specialists to observe their classes. Often such visitations are part of a school's standard process for faculty evaluation. Whether initiated by the teacher or mandated by the school, a close, objective observation of a teacher's interaction with students can provide a perspective impossible for a teacher to achieve alone. Videotaping classes has the added advantage of allowing teachers to revisit selected moments as often as is necessary for them to shed new light on former practice.

Reviewing these approaches to self-assessment—introspection, student feedback, collegial observation and feedback—should not suggest that a teacher's capacity for generating productive student relationships can be achieved using some formula. Self-assessment, however teachers choose to carry it out, is an integral part of professional development. But the truth is that however much teachers study the effects of their efforts, they are ultimately limited to their personalities and interpersonal skills. Deepening their capacity to listen, extending themselves in care, expressing delight or interest, exhibiting patience when their lessons are thwarted by a recalcitrant or otherwise struggling student: these are the stuff of presence.

Detached, unhappy, or otherwise self-absorbed teachers are likely to receive clear messages from the boys in their classes about the impact of their personalities on their teaching. All sorts of professionals working with oth-

> *Boys are not likely to be quiet in their reactions to ineffective teaching.*

ers face similar occupational demands, of course. But for teachers of boys, the requirement may be altogether make-or-break because of the intimacy of daily classroom relationships and because boys are not likely to be quiet in their reactions to ineffective teaching.

The establishment of a teacher's presence rests on each individual's personal inclination to relate. That inclination is itself based on the pleasure and satisfaction the teacher has experienced in mastering his or her subject—and the anticipated pleasure of sharing that mastery with others. If there has been no such pleasure or if the challenge of sharing it with the actual students filling the chairs of one's classroom is not itself a pleasure, there is no basis for a learning relationship—which is no more than another way of saying that not everybody is cut out to be a teacher. But for those who are, the capacity to forge relationships, like other elements of a teacher's craft, can be developed and improved.

We have suggested that teachers' relational capacity depends on a positive inclination. That inclination has a source—usually the warm attention of their own teachers, their parents, and other nurturers. In this respect, the relational capacity is a kind of "paying it forward." For others, the lack of such mentors may motivate their interest in offering such attention. In these instances, teachers may sometimes feel that they struggle to invent the means and style for relating well, but their memories of life without such buoying assistance can itself point the way to what their students need most.

Both of us have had the good fortune to work closely for years with colleagues who have a gift for relating effectively to children. One memorable example is a consulting psychiatrist who had an extensive practice with troubled boys and as a consultant to a number of schools. He was the person teachers and staff would turn to when a boy would stop doing his school work altogether, or would sink into unreachable depression, or would act out so provocatively that he was no longer manageable at school. Especially memorable was this man's gift for transforming the way teachers and staff thought about their most difficult boys. Quite honestly, after repeated confrontations, admonishments, and stress resulting from a troubled boy's repeated delinquencies, teachers sometimes find themselves deeply disliking certain boys, dreading the next encounter with them, working and wanting to separate them from the school as soon as justifiably possible. Such boys were this professional's specialty.

His success with a previously unreachable boy, it seemed, always began with relationship: establishing trust, easy communication, and mutuality. To the astonishment of the boys' teachers, he seemed to be able to do it every time. After observing his success over some years, staff at the school would ask him what was the technique, his secret? To such questions he would invariably laugh and look the questioner dead in they eye. "Hard as it might be to believe," he would say, "I really *like* these kids."

CHAPTER

13

ACTIVATING THE ELICITING PROCESS

Teachers dedicated to reaching boys adjust their approaches until the boys are productively engaged. Some of these adjustments are relational; others involve selection of materials, allotting more or less time to specific tasks, or determining activities that might be better addressed cooperatively or competitively, in groups or in teams. A good number of the successful adjustments reported involved setting boys to physically active tasks. What we are calling "eliciting" consists of teachers' registering boys' responses to their instruction, including resistant responses, and modifying various elements until the resistance is overcome. This mutually reciprocal process should result in a cycle of continuous improvement unless something interferes with it.

We have outlined the basic forms such interference may take, including school and state-mandated requirements that do not allow the kinds of pedagogical flexibility necessary to make effective adjustments. For example, state, district, or school requirements for teachers to submit and adhere to a year-long sequence of lesson plans pose serious obstacles to flexible adjustment, as do highly programmatic textbook-driven courses in which daily lessons, homework, lab work, examinations, and supplementary activities are built into the design of the text. Preparing students for state-mandated proficiency tests necessarily limits teachers' flexibility in responding to distinctive student learning styles, as do large class sizes, heavy student loads, and structural limitations on students' and teachers' personal access to one another: lack of time or designated places for students and teachers to meet outside the classroom, inflexible student schedules, classroom periods too short to address each student meaningfully, school terms and school years too short to achieve desired outcomes.

Apart from these procedural or structural obstacles, teachers themselves may harbor any number of attitudes and value positions that do not recognize—or perhaps reject outright—any need to adjust their pedagogy to students' responses, resistant or otherwise. Such attitudes were nowhere evident in our study's examples of lessons that worked, which often contained admissions of former missteps in which their prior lessons failed to engage. Overt boredom, itchiness, disrespect, or defiance may be difficult feedback to assimilate, but teachers who reflexively attribute all off-task behavior to attention deficits or behavioral problems may miss important signals about the effectiveness of any given lesson.

Teachers who reflexively attribute all off-task behavior to attention deficits or behavioral problems may miss important signals about the effectiveness of any given lesson.

In pointing out the benefits of assessing student feedback of all kinds, we are not suggesting that students should never be reprimanded, corrected, or brought to order and attention. Standard disciplinary measures, including occasionally dire ones, are sometimes necessary—and they need not be obstacles to effective teaching or relationship building. Calling students to order and to appropriate conduct is an extension of a committed teacher's regard for them. Moreover—and there is more than another book on this subject!—a disciplinary encounter with a student can be and often is the first critical step in establishing a productive relationship. Teachers' disciplinary touches are an extension of their commitment to their subject matter and to seeing each student through to his best potential. With respect to the potentially wounding effects of outwardly negative transactions, including disciplinary ones, the late psychoanalyst Eric Berne, founder of Transactional Analysis, was fond of saying, "Negative strokes are not the worst outcome; *no* strokes is the worst outcome."

THE COED CLASSROOM: WHAT BOYS AND GIRLS ELICIT TOGETHER

In addition to exposing these concerns, the eliciting model invites a fresh consideration of how teachers in coed classrooms might better attend to boys' feedback as it bears on pedagogy and lesson content. This is an especially important consideration, as far more children are schooled coeducationally than in single-sex contexts. In the United States, despite a number of recent initiatives to establish single-sex public schools and single-sex classrooms in otherwise coeducational schools, coeducation is massively predominant, enrolling 99 percent of the nation's children. This is not to say that American single-sex schools may not continue to be invaluable laboratories for assessing gendered aspects of schooling, but for the foreseeable future, most boys and girls will attend school in coeducational settings.

Our findings suggest strongly that boys—in settings that are responsive to them—elicit teaching that reflects their interests, preferences, and needs. And we suspect that similar conclusions would be drawn from a parallel study of girls in girls' schools, which brings us back to the point at issue. If a teacher's best pedagogy is indeed elicited through a process of fluid, reciprocal exchanges with students, and if gender-specific behavior on the part of boys and girls in coed classes elicits different gender-specific responses from the teacher, might the resulting pedagogy be less clear, less appealing, and ultimately less effective than if pitched more particularly to boys or girls? If so, bringing out the best in boys and girls in coed settings would seem to be problematic.

But perhaps not. For one thing, it need not be assumed that teachers of mixed classes cannot devise ways to conduct their lessons in a manner that appeals to both boys and girls. Even the strongest advocates for instructing boys and girls separately must acknowledge that boys and girls at any specified age or stage of development do not present a uniform bundle of scholastic behaviors. The range in the kinds of student responses observable in single-sex classrooms is considerable, and although that range may be narrower than the behavioral range of boys and girls together, addressing multiple personality types and multiple learning styles simultaneously is clearly important to the effectiveness of teachers in single-sex schools. To respond effectively to the wider range of responses in coed settings may be an additional challenge—but a challenge ably met. Moreover, there are instructive clues to doing so in the practice of effective teachers in single-sex schools.

It need not be assumed that teachers of mixed classes cannot devise ways to conduct their lessons in a manner that appeals to both boys and girls.

Here it is instructive to revisit an American science teacher's "best lesson" that we reviewed earlier. His approach may point the way to accommodating a range of student responses to a given assignment, while at the same time engaging his students in the process of identifying their preferences and strengths. The resulting gains are dual: deeper engagement in the material under study and a deeper metacognitive awareness on the part of each student of how he—or she—best learns:

In my class, I spent a considerable amount of time describing the electron cloud model of the atom. This is very abstract for the boys and requires a number of different strategies. We first worked with drawing an atom on paper. Students found out what the atomic number was and filled in each orbital with the correct number of electrons. I have a marble board that resembles Chinese checkers and allows the boys to create an atom by placing each electron, neutron, and proton in different wells of the game board. For the last activity, I had the boys acting out the atom in the center of the room using color-coded index cards with N, E, or P written on them. On the last page of the atom quiz, I asked the boys for feedback about which model worked the best for them in the class. Here are some quotes:

Favorite Model: Drawing on Paper

"When you draw it you can see what an atom is and you can count the electrons easier and it is not as loud."

"I like drawing the electrons. They were easier to see."

Favorite Model: Marble Board

"The marble board has a few good things. First, it is to scale, unlike the drawing and acting. Second, unlike the drawing on paper, the marble diagram shows protons and neutrons. Finally, unlike drawing it with paper, the marble board is more hands-on. Overall, the marble board is the best model used in the science class."

"I like it because it is easier to correct mistakes and I think it is more fun."

> ### *Acting It Out: Favorite Model*
>
> "I like acting it out better because you get to have fun and stand up plus playing with the marbles distracts me. Also acting out helps you remember it better."
>
> "I really like acting it out, because it is active, fun, and shows the electrons moving which makes it a better model."
>
> Expressing opinions regarding each model, each boy in the class really helped me realize the different approaches each student has when learning the material.

Teachers of coed classes committed to developing the full potential of each student, including what might be gendered aspects of that potential, may simultaneously respond to the needs of both boys and girls. Doing so may not even be intentional; boys and girls may have successfully elicited what they need. But there is little question that teachers' awareness of and capacity to respond to whatever may be influenced by gender in their students' responses will improve their efforts to reach them.

Again, teachers are likely to find their students increasingly responsive to material presented from multiple perspectives, even stereotypically masculine and feminine perspectives. Even more effective are teacher invitations for students to demonstrate mastery in a variety of ways.

Depending on the subject matter, students may be divided into same-gender groups to meet challenges and solve problems. Such groups and the class as a whole might be invited to reflect on the difference in boys' and girls' group responses to the assigned challenge. Same-sex problem solving in a coed setting may, besides productively exercising gender-specific inclinations and energy, result in a fruitful consideration on the part of both boys and girls of how each child thinks and learns.

THE TRANSITIVE FACTOR IN EFFECTIVE LESSONS

If boys do indeed elicit distinctive and possibly boy-specific responses from their teachers, what are they? Can they be clearly identified? Are they generally applicable to boys in a variety of scholastic settings? We found that there were clear contours to the lessons teachers reported as especially effective, or best, with their boys. Moreover, the boys corroborated what the teachers reported, appreciatively noting the very elements of instruction that teachers themselves believed carried the lessons. Those elements composed what we have called the transitive factor in effective lessons.

We have illustrated and discussed these transitive factors—the elements of instruction that engage attention, sustain concentration, and result in superior performance—under eight categorical headings: creating products; lessons as games; motor activity; role play and performance; open inquiry; teamwork and competition; personal realization; and novelty, drama, and surprise. One or more of these elements were at work in each of the best lessons submitted. Running through nearly all of the teacher accounts was an emphasis on active, often on-your-feet engagement in the task at hand. Also, applications of up-to-date information technology were a feature in many successful lessons.

Teachers seeking to better engage the boys they teach, regardless of their academic disciplines, would do well to consider the implications of these transitive factors for the lessons they plan:

- What, for example, are the potential benefits of requiring the creation of a tangible product in a class that might otherwise be language driven or text driven?

- How might the repetitive exercises necessary to build basic skills, the memorization of facts and sequences, or the review of extensive sweeps of material prior to examinations be energized and lightened by incorporating those tasks into a diverting competitive game?

- In what ways might increased movement be built into the consideration of highly conceptual classroom business?

- How might students' engagement be deepened by inviting them out of their collective passivity into challenges to assume some other, perhaps historical, identity, to be persuasive on some critical issue before their classmates, to take responsibility for making challenging material clear to others?

- What are the opportunities in any given course to set students to solving problems and conducting research into questions and problems to which there are not yet definitive answers, where the challenge is not to discover "the answer" but to draw the clearest conclusions they can about new and unfamiliar data?

- To what extent can a teacher responsibly and productively dissolve the barrier between learning and play by organizing research and presentations into team efforts and imaginative competitions?

- How might classroom engagement be deepened by selecting texts, materials, and discussion topics designed to invite each boy to examine essential aspects of his past, his nature, and his character—including the purpose and direction of his life?

- In what ways might students be stimulated to bigger and better thinking by drawing them out of what is familiar and expected in the classroom by the introduction of genuine novelty or surprise?

Whether all children might respond to such adjustments to standard teaching is a good, and open, question. Do boys in particular respond to these transitive factors in their lessons? The findings of this study emphatically conclude that they do.

CHAPTER

14

WHAT SCHOOLS CAN DO

A teacher's disposition to create lessons that will engage and exercise boys' distinctive approaches to learning is likely to reflect the value commitments and overall ethos of his or her school. Dedicated teachers may reconsider and improve their pedagogy in any number of settings, but the process is more likely to succeed when it is institutionally encouraged, supported, and shared. It is therefore essential to ask not merely what teachers can do to understand boys better and teach them more effectively, but also what kind of school is likely to facilitate those outcomes.

FOSTERING LEARNING RELATIONSHIPS

The preceding chapters have stressed the importance of relationship building in engaging boys productively in classroom business: creating a respectful, reciprocal classroom climate in which boys feel they are seen, known, and valued. That kind of classroom is most likely to be created and maintained in a school committed to respectful, reciprocal transactions at every level of operations. The relational climate in classrooms to some extent will reflect the relational climate of the school. Concerned, respectful, and empathic transactions between teachers and students are reinforced and strengthened in schools where transactions between administration and faculty, school and parents, faculty and faculty, faculty and nonteaching staff—are mediated by the same values.

A positive, productive relational climate in a school cannot be authoritatively imposed. There is no clear set of steps to follow. No amount of studying it, reading about it, or discussing its merits will bring it into being. Educational observers from Aristotle to John Dewey to contemporary advocates of teaching values in schools have noted in strikingly similar terms that certain critical human behaviors—truth telling, keeping commitments, behaving respectfully, being fair, being kind—must be practiced in order to be learned. In his summary of effective moral instruction, Marvin Berkowitz (2002) concluded that "the primary influence on a child's character development is how people treat the child" (p. 58).

Instructive fables and stated precepts do not teach community-sustaining values, but if those values have been internalized through experience and practice, fable and precept may reinforce them. We are "habituated" to virtue, Aristotle maintained, before we can intellectually embrace the value of being virtuous. Intellectual understanding confirms the importance of virtue, but it cannot create it. Similarly, children are habituated to caring, reciprocal relationships before they are able to justify their value.

In good schools effective teaching is honored above all else.

Schools with warm, respectful relational climates are good bets to be responsive to the relational requirements of successful teaching, including the gendered aspects of those relationships. In such schools, beginning teachers are mentored and stimulated by patient, seasoned masters. Teachers share their practices and their classrooms with colleagues and other observers, sharing observations about relational as well as instructional practices that work. In good schools teachers are not reluctant to share their concerns about students or the effectiveness of their methods. In good schools preparing students for standardized tests, submitting lesson plans, and keeping pace with mandated curricula do not divert teachers from the higher-order business of creating lessons that result in students' positive engagement and ultimate achievement. In good schools effective teaching is honored above all else.

REACHING BOYS: A PROFESSIONAL DEVELOPMENT PRIORITY

In addition to the role of relationships in teaching boys more effectively, we have pointed out the need to reconsider ways boys—indeed all children—elicit what they need from their teachers. This finding should be widely reassuring to school leaders because it implies that as long as teachers are responsive to their students' reactions and feedback—to their voices—lessons will be refined until they work.

In order for faculties to determine just what it is that their students are eliciting, there must be both personal and professional development time to compare, demonstrate, and reformulate teaching approaches. Professional development time is limited in all schools, but one measure of a school's governing values is what it chooses to address when its faculty comes together. We believe that schools will succeed in improving classroom practice to the degree that they devote their professional development efforts to it—that is, to what their own teachers are doing with their students day-to-day.

An active forum for teachers to share their most gratifying successes and most persistent concerns will both reflect and create a climate for instructional innovation and improvement. Indeed we have little doubt that teachers in any school faculty set to the task of identifying the single most effective lesson in their current practice—or, perhaps, the most effective lesson for boys or girls—would bring to light approaches that would inform and stimulate their colleagues to better work.

Again, successful teachers exhibit a dual mastery. They have mastered their subject and the pedagogy to convey it to a variety of students. Schools succeed with boys to the extent that they honor and help teachers realize this dual mastery. Good schools explicitly make this their top priority.

National, state, or systemwide initiatives aimed at improving teaching and learning must avoid being so prescriptive as to prevent the flexibility necessary for teachers to relate effectively to each student and each class. It is hard to imagine a more well-intentioned educational goal than to leave no child behind—but it is equally hard to imagine realizing that aim if the principal means to achieve it are devising quick-scoring tests to document putative "competence" at each grade level and coaching students to pass such tests. Precisely measured aggregates of student progress tend to hold the greatest allure to legislatures and agencies well distanced from classrooms. Effective teachers direct their efforts to other ends: building relationships, refining pedagogy, promoting engagement and mastery, some forms of which are easily measured and some not.

We see encouraging signs of a renewed national attention to factors that actually improve teaching. In the United States, the newly appointed secretary of education, Arne Duncan, has made clear and repeated appeals for schools to embrace the "mentoring" dimension of teaching. Inspired by his own experience and what he subsequently observed in tutorial programs in Chicago's public schools, he has called for teachers and school leaders to develop the relational component of their work: to get to know students personally, take an interest in their lives beyond the classroom, and extend personal guidance to students in making choices about their subsequent schooling. He has noted the success of such mentoring in improving the performance and prospects of minority students in inner-city schools, notably boys.

The long and often beleaguered history of school reform efforts has been marked, understandably, by an impulse to "rescue" substandard schools. These efforts have alternated among investing new capital in staff and facilities, desegregating and otherwise recomposing student bodies, and devising instruments to measure student and teacher proficiency so that, presumably, the nonproficient can be made proficient. These rescue efforts, however well intentioned and otherwise laudable, divert attention from data more likely to improve schooling: existing classroom practices that *work* with all kinds of children in all kinds of settings.

DOING BETTER BY ALL CHILDREN INCLUDES DOING BETTER BY BOYS

The mission of schools worldwide is to realize the potential of all children. A critical factor in doing so is to acknowledge that "all children" does not mean "generic children," because children are not generic. Children are morally equivalent—equally valuable—but they are not otherwise equivalent. They bear distinctive histories, ethnicities, and cultural identities. With respect to any given proficiency, some are behind, and some are ahead. Within their cultural identities, they bear all manner of personal distinctiveness, including their passions and aversions, their distinctive ways of processing words and images. Moreover, "all children" are boys and girls. To realize the potential of boys and girls requires acknowledging the distinctive ways each may respond to instruction.

> *To realize the potential of boys and girls requires acknowledging the distinctive ways each may respond to instruction.*

In educational practice today, too little attention has been paid to what succeeds in engaging boys in the classroom, an observation that may go a long way to explain why boys from each major ethnic group—whites, blacks, Hispanics,

Asians, and Native Americans—perform less well than female counterparts in each group (Mead, 2006). To the extent teachers and educational policymakers continue to ignore differences in what boys and girls present in the classroom, these learning "gaps" between girls and boys and, more important, the full realization of both boys' and girls' learning potential will continue to be compromised. Evidence that some boys seem to be progressing satisfactorily or even thriving does not diminish the urgency of addressing whatever boy-specific—and girl-specific—responses students reveal in the course of their instruction.

An important—and potentially invigorating—first step in engaging teachers in a consideration of their students' gender-specific responses is simply to conduct open forums to share what they observe in their classes. These shared observations will inevitably reveal all kinds of stereotyped gender behavior on the part of students—as well as stereotyped gender attitudes on the part of teachers. Airing them is an essential step in exploring more effective approaches to engaging both boys and girls. We have led such forums in a variety of schools in the United States and abroad, and the participating faculties have without exception been eager to convey and hear about reported successes and frustrations in reaching boys and girls. Moreover, these discussions were clearly richer for including teachers of different grade levels and different subjects.

A REMEDY AT HAND

Our study was undertaken in a climate of concern that too many boys are failing to thrive in school. The remedy for this we believe is at hand and abundantly in evidence in a variety of school settings all over the world. The remedy lies in the successful practices teachers have devised to teach and reach boys. It lies in the kinds of relationships teachers forge with their male students and their responsiveness to the distinctive things boys say and do in their presence. It lies in teachers' devising subject matter and activities and methods of delivery that engage boys and sustain their attention as they master new operations.

Whatever dissonance, confusion, and conflict may hover in the air as stakeholders assert new and competing claims about the nature and needs of boys and girls and the essential or trivial differences between them with respect to how they learn and should be taught, few could reasonably argue with the proposition that many boys are not thriving in school. Nor could one possibly argue there is no room or reason to improve.

Albert Einstein famously defined insanity as "doing the same thing over and over and expecting different results." The effective instruction of boys does not require deep immersion in imponderables or tortured theorizing. Boys—some boys, in some settings—are effectively taught every day of the school year. The teachers responsible are easily located, seen, and heard from. That many of them are willing and eager to share their good work with their colleagues throughout the world is very good and welcome news.

APPENDIX

DESIGN AND RESEARCH METHODS FOR THE TEACHING BOYS STUDY

The Teaching Boys research project was undertaken by the Center for the Study of Boys' and Girls' Lives (CSBGL) on behalf of the International Boys' Schools Coalition (IBSC) to explore whether there are pedagogical practices that are especially effective for boys' scholastic engagement and achievement. A fuller report on the original study has been made public (Reichert & Hawley, 2009). The study was based on five assumptions:

1. Valuable evidence of effective practice can be determined from what teachers themselves say about their work.

2. The data reported by teachers will be rich and varied enough to sustain analysis.

3. Students can be asked in a simple and direct manner about school practices that have helped them to engage with their lessons and that these accounts will provide additional corroboration and dimension to teachers' reports.

4. Schools are repositories of pedagogical practices that have evolved and been refined over many years. Boys' schools are likely to be particularly valuable sites in this regard.

5. Across a variety of schools, from different geographical and cultural contexts, a set of themes may emerge that can illuminate broader conversations about boys' education.

In this research approach, we adopted an emic stance (Lett, 2007), trusting that from insiders in boys' schools, we might best capture the high art of effective pedagogy. This approach contrasts sharply with purely quantitative methods that attempt to correlate specific, replicable instructional practices with easily measured results, such as performance on standardized tests or countable instances of specified student behaviors. It is important to note that the methodology of this study is no less empirical for being qualitative. Indeed given the kinds of outcomes sought—descriptions of lessons and practices that participants regarded as effective—a qualitative approach is not only valid but especially promising. The scientific validity of a qualitative research project derives from several factors: the accuracy of description and interpretation, the theoretical understanding of the subject by the researchers, and, most important, the practical usefulness of the study's outcomes (Winter, 2007). Some methodologists regard "authenticity," a consideration of the degree to which the project and its findings "facilitate and stimulate" action (Manning, 1997, p. 108), as the most important criterion for validity.

Both of us have had a long-standing relationship with the IBSC, as well as with particular member schools in the coalition. Michael, founding director of the center, has been on staff at the Haverford School outside Philadelphia in the United States as a consulting psychologist for twenty-three years. Rick was a teacher and headmaster of the University School in Ohio for thirty-seven years and, in this capacity, served as founding president of the IBSC. In our work with CSBGL, we developed a methodology, the Boys' Audit, that has achieved promising results for deepening schools' understanding of their practices with boys. This research process uses both guided self-study and a mixed-methods assessment, including faculty and student surveys as well as focus groups and observations, and aims at making a school's curriculum for boys more visible and its outcomes more objective.

Working closely with the executive director and other staff of the IBSC, we developed a design for the project. Given the international scope of the sample desired and cost limitations, we determined that on-site visits would not be practical; the study therefore would rely solely on responses to an online survey. We gave considerable thought to recruiting a school sample that would be geographically and culturally diverse. Ultimately an invitation was communicated to the membership of the coalition, and interested schools were invited to apply to participate.

We worked closely with the coalition to select participating schools from those that expressed interest. From January to June 2008, a sample of eighteen member schools, representing a careful geographical and school type range, was selected. Although all of the participating schools were fee based, there was considerable variation, country to country, in the degree of government-funded support and the economic profiles of the student bodies. The following schools were chosen to participate in the study:

- Auckland Grammar School, Auckland, New Zealand

- Belmont Hill School, Belmont, United States

- Brisbane Grammar School, Brisbane, Australia

- Christ Church Grammar School, Perth, Australia

- Collegiate School, New York, United States

- Crescent School, Toronto, Canada

- Dulwich College, Dulwich, England

- Gilman School, Baltimore, United States

- The Haverford School, Philadelphia, United States

- Knox Grammar School, Sydney, Australia

- Lindisfarne College, Hastings, New Zealand

- McCallie School, Chattanooga, United States

- Salisbury School, Salisbury, United States

- Selwyn House School, Montreal, Canada

- Saint Alban's College, Pretoria, South Africa

- Saint Christopher's School, Richmond, United States

- Saint John's College, Johannesburg, South Africa

- Trinity Grammar School, Melbourne, Australia

Instructions for participating schools were produced by coalition staff, in close consultation with the research team, and were distributed in booklet form, which we reprint here. Careful attention was paid to anticipating questions and providing sufficient structure that some consistency across various schools could be achieved.

GUIDELINES AND INSTRUCTION

We look forward to our relationship with you during the course of this project. *Guidelines and Instructions*, we hope, will provide a foundation for our communication.

Stages of the Project

- *Announcement:* December, 2007

- *Selection and Confirmation:* Project Schools are selected, and confirm their participation (January-February, 2008)

- *Preparing for the Project:* The researchers connect with the Project Coordinator, by email and/or phone, to introduce the document *Guidelines and Instructions*. The requirements of the exercise are reviewed; and strategies and options for the organization and timing of the exercise are determined.

- *Carrying Out the Exercise in Project Schools:* Faculty and students are introduced to the project, and proceed to complete the on-line surveys. As required, the research team and the IBSC assistant liaise with the school project coordinator, and provide any status reports.

- *Debrief:* After the completion of the project, the school coordinator may request a data report for the school—the compendium of all submissions from the school, for distribution to, and possible discussion with, faculty.

- *Data Analysis and Report Writing:* After July 1, the research team begins the process of analyzing the data from all the project schools, and prepares a report by September, 2008.

- *Publication of Report:* The report is received by the IBSC, and is made available first to the Project Schools. The report will then be published in the IBSC community, and to the wider educational community.

When It's All Over, What Will "Success" Look Like?

Before we provide direction about the set-up of the exercise in a Project School, let's imagine "what success looks like."

At the end of the project, the researchers are able to say:

- "The teacher data from this school are rich and compelling. All—or nearly all!—teachers submitted. They found time to write thoughtful submissions, with lots of nuance and detail, thereby opening up paths for the researchers' analysis. There is a high quality in the submissions. No one 'blew this off.'"

- "The student data from this school are also rich and compelling. Boys submitted intriguing information, and seemed able to amplify and stretch their writing in response to the questions. This data look extremely helpful."

- "The process of coordination with the project school was smooth, and the set-up of the project was good."

At the end of the project, the coordinator in the school is able to say:

- "We had a good (to great) experience with the project. Teachers (and students) were interested in it, saw its relevance, and had some good discussions. It helped our ongoing staff development on effective teaching in relation to the 'boy focus' of our work."

- "The set-up for the project was positive and clear. Teachers (and students) knew exactly what they were being asked to do, and why the project was of value both to our school and the wider community of boys' schools."

- "It was relatively easy to get teachers to complete the task. The on-line survey process worked well."

- "The student survey process was well set up. Boys seemed interested in the project, and understood exactly what they were being asked to do."

- "The researchers followed up with any request for materials or data collection that were additionally useful and relevant to the school."

- "We are looking forward to the publication of the report, and to reviewing it with our teachers."

- "We are proud to have been associated with the project."

Prepping the Project

To achieve these outcomes and to be able to declare the project a success, the exercise requires:

Leadership

From the beginning, the project has the full backing of the Head, the project coordinator and other school leaders. Teachers need to understand that exercise is a professional obligation, one to be taken seriously. Some ways by which this leadership for the project can be asserted include the following:

- The Head and other school leaders complete and share their own submissions with faculty, to set a tone for thoughtfulness and thoroughness. These actions demonstrate that the project has the full backing and participation of school leaders.

- School leaders communicate the same message—are on the same page—about the importance and value of the project.

- Orientation to the project is clear and thorough, and teachers (and students) understand what they are being asked to do. Time has been allocated for the project.

- School leaders set and monitor a standard of accountability—to ensure that teachers complete the task and pay attention to the quality of their submissions.

Communication

From the onset, school leaders clearly explain what the project is, why it is important, how teachers (and students) are involved, and what they are being asked to do.

Accountability

School leaders need to set a standard of accountability. There is always the risk that other obligations and the business of the day will get in the way. Depending on the way the exercise is carried out (see below), school leaders might say, for example:

- "The researchers and the IBSC will be providing updates on the school's progress with submissions, and we will be in contact with those who have not yet submitted. Our expectation is for 100% participation."

- "We have asked the researchers and the IBSC to provide the school with a compilation of our school's submissions. We will be sharing it with our teachers, as a collection of professional discussions about our practices for and thoughts about teaching boys. Please note, therefore, that your submission will be read by others in the school, as a record of our participation in the project; it will, therefore, reflect on our school. In addition to the final report from the researchers, which is based on the wider global sampling, this record of our own submissions can stimulate our ongoing professional development.''

Setting Up the Exercise

It is important that the school ''creates time and space'' for the completion of the exercise. Each school will need to work out a process and a time-line that best suits their school culture and schedule.

While staff emails may help along the way, especially one that provides technical details and a link to the survey instrument, we strongly advise against the ''teeing up'' of the exercise by email communication alone. It is important to find real time with teachers, so that questions can be answered—and the expectation and process understood.

Options include:

- Clear time at a staff meeting or at a staff development day for the project. After orientation to the project, teachers would be given time to sit down and complete the on-line survey. The advantage here is that the exercise is condensed and completed in a highly focused way. A disadvantage is that some teachers may need time to ''process'' the exercise, and to think about what they might choose as an example, etc. One solution might be to prompt a short exercise in the meeting: ''turn to a neighbor and talk for 5 minutes''; or break into small groups—by department or some other criteria—to discuss. Because this is an on-line survey, an additional challenge may be access to computers for many teachers at the same time.

- Another option could be to introduce the project at a general staff meeting, but then defer the exercise to subsequent meetings of smaller units—such as a department meeting. Here, the department head would lead a discussion about the project, and teachers might help one another to unearth an activity and line of writing. Teachers would be given time in this scheduled department meeting to complete the exercise. An advantage in this model is that teachers are given time and space in a smaller format to be thoughtful and focused. Department heads would need to be conversant, and on-side, with the exercise.

- A third way is to introduce and explain the project and the survey process at a faculty meeting, and then give faculty a deadline to complete the exercise on school or personal time. This approach is the least demanding on school meeting time, and would give teachers an opportunity to ''get their heads around the project,'' and to complete the survey exercise when they are ready to do so. A disadvantage is that some teachers may delay or forget, requiring monitoring and prompts from school leaders.

Timing of the Exercise

While there is no perfect time in busy schools, the coordinator may want to select the "least inconvenient time" during the months available before the July 1 deadline. The researchers hope that many project schools will be able to carry out the project earlier, so that data analysis can start.

Student Survey

The student survey involves a different process. We measure success according to the degree to which students understand the task, and write well in answer to the questions prompted in the survey.

Selecting Student Groups

The first task is to select some student classes or groups, with a total number of approximately 100. The classes or groups should represent the range of age/grades targeted in the project, and should also be drawn from different departments, so that students are not inadvertently cued in the direction of a particular subject area:

- Young adolescents—ages 12–14

- Mid adolescents—ages 15/16

- Older adolescents—ages 17/18 (last two years of high school)

The classes or groups should reflect, as far as possible, the full ability range of boys in the school. Classes in core or compulsory subjects where boys are not "streamed" by academic ability would be a good place to start. An interesting, alternative approach is to use advising/house groupings, if these are mixed age levels and ranges of ability.

Setting Up the Student Exercise

A degree of careful planning needs to take place here, because boys, especially younger boys, will naturally not be able to relate to the project goals with any ease of understanding.

- The project coordinator will want to identify teachers who will be able to work easily with the boys, and who understand and support the goals of the project.

- The project coordinator and teachers will then need to orient students to the task, its relation to the teachers' role, and the importance of the project for the school.

- It is important to say that their submissions are confidential—teachers will not know the names of the submitters, and that it is not necessary to tie a story directly to the name of the teacher.

- Boys may ask for examples, or direction. They might be told that we are not looking for stories about "a favorite teacher"—this is not a competition—or just about "fun" times in class. Boys need to glimpse the link between their own learning and what the teacher was doing—a project they loved, an exercise that really got and held their attention, a lesson that clicked for them, a text or topic that was taught in a way that kept them going. Nor are we just looking for a mark or a result that was their best, although it could be that this stands out in some way.

- One strategy might be to ask a student to volunteer a story and to tease out with the boy and the class why this might be a good example. It may be an idea to hand out a hard copy of the survey instrument, so that they can understand what they are being asked to do.

- Some boys may not be able to come up with anything, or may feel negative about the task. While they can be helped and encouraged a little more, it is important to respect the integrity of the research, and not interfere or intervene too much.

- Once the exercise is introduced, the boys should complete the exercise in the school. They will therefore need access to a computer lab or classroom with a sufficient number of computers. Assigning it for completion at home or in spare time may lead to delay, and it will be harder to chase down those who have not completed the exercise. To foster attention and reflection, the project might be introduced one day, and the survey completed in the next scheduled class.

- Many younger boys may tend to write short responses. They should be encouraged to extend and stretch their writing. It may be helpful to remind them that this is not an exercise for evaluation, but that it will be scrutinized and deciphered by the researchers.

For each school, one member of the research team was designated as contact person and was in contact by phone or e-mail throughout data collection. Together with the school project coordinator, they considered the particulars of the individual school—schedules, grade and class configurations, faculty considerations—in order to position the study in a manner that would be most practical and most likely to secure faculty and student cooperation. Although the process varied from school to school, typically the study was introduced to faculty of middle and upper school boys (aged twelve to nineteen years) at a school meeting led by the head, and both the merits of the school's participation as well the benefits were described. Effort was made so that faculty could complete the survey within meeting times already established. In a similar manner, classes of adolescent boys were recruited by the coordinator, who explained the school's interests in participating in the study and arranged for boys to complete the survey during a class time.

After this orientation process, teachers were asked to identify and describe a lesson or unit, or teaching strategy or technique, they judged to have been notably successful in engaging boys and deepening their learning. The survey questions also asked them to reflect on whether and why they felt the lessons selected might be especially appropriate for boys and if they thought the learning outcomes could be measured in some way. Students, in a parallel survey, were asked to identify and describe what they considered to be meaningful, memorable, and successful teaching practices.

The survey was introduced to teachers with the following instructions:

The task: to narrate clearly and objectively an instructional activity that is especially, perhaps unusually, effective in advancing boys' learning.

You are not being asked to describe or discuss effective teaching generally, or to describe a whole term-long or year-long course of study. The teaching practices sought here are individual projects, assignments, or instances of classroom process in which boys rise to the material under study with heightened attention and energy, resulting—perhaps measurably, perhaps not—in superior work. This is of course a highly subjective appraisal. Nevertheless, teachers are clearly aware of activities and moments when boys rise to instructional business with heightened interest and energy. Teachers tend to register this awareness in the satisfaction of having had an exceptionally good class, series of classes, or perhaps an exceptional moment in class. Students register the experience in the quality of their attention and of their participation. Students carry their interest in a good learning experience outside of the classroom, continue to think and talk about the idea, text, or project with peers and family on their own time. Good practices generate student questions and researches beyond those required in the assigned exercise. What is effective in a practice may lie in the appeal of the subject or text under review. For example, teachers of preadolescent and adolescent boys report heightened responses to texts illuminating boyhood passages: *Lord of the Flies, Catcher in the Rye, Night.* Sometimes it is not the text, but an approach to discussing the text or to writing about it that elicits the heightened response. Often, good practices are characterized by an active challenge: to create or build something that must pass a test of performance. Physics students frequently report that their most memorable and satisfying experiences were having to construct, either collaboratively or independently, something that worked: a weight bearing bridge, a mousetrap-powered vehicle, a device that would enable an egg to be dropped from rooftop to pavement without breaking. Sometimes effective practices seem to derive from the social structure of the learning exercise: in competitive or non-competitive pairings or teams. Boys also frequently report good learning experiences occur when a scholastic activity has been structured as a game, perhaps with differential rewards and prizes.

Teachers were then asked to respond to these additional questions:

Please describe an effective practice you have employed. In narrating your observations, take care to avoid evaluative terms like "wonderful" or "inspired." Instead, show the qualities that evoke those feelings in you with clear narration of what is said and done in the course of the lesson. (Suggested length: 250–500 words, but do not feel limited to this length.)

1. To what do you attribute this lesson's special effectiveness? (There is no need to be authoritative or "scientific" in this appraisal.)

2. Is there something about this lesson that you believe is specially pitched to boys' learning?

3. Are there measurable outcomes—or outcomes that might conceivably be measured—that could objectively document the effectiveness of this practice?

In response to these survey questions, the project received an outpouring of detailed and obviously well-crafted lessons from teachers, totaling 942 responses. Forty-four percent of the responses were from schools in the United States, 22 percent from Australia, 18 percent from New Zealand, 7 percent from Canada, 7 percent from South Africa, and 2 percent from England. The study asked teacher respondents to report their gender and teaching experience to gauge the degree to which these factors might influence, in some way, the types of lessons they submitted or their rationale for the lessons. Three-quarters of the teachers were men and the remainder women. Respondents ranged rather evenly from one to forty-four years of teaching experience.

To provide an independent assessment of the lessons narrated by the teachers, we also surveyed a sample of approximately one hundred boys from each school with an equally simple questionnaire about memorable lessons. The project was introduced to the boys in the following way:

Thank you for participating in this survey! Your school is participating in a special project, Wisdom of Teaching in Boys' Schools, sponsored by the International Boys' Schools Coalition. In a separate survey, teachers in your school are being asked to talk about a lesson or an activity that they find especially memorable, and that they think is very effective in engaging boys in your school. The second component involves a survey of students. Your answers to the questions that follow are very important to the success of the project. It is important for you to know that your report is confidential. The project researchers will read and summarize survey answers, and their report may include comments and quotes, but student names will not be used.

The students were then asked several demographic questions, including their name, age, grade, school, a rating of their motivation and achievement levels, as well as their socioeconomic status and ethnicity. Then they were given the following instructions:

In the box below, tell us the story of a class experience that stands out as being especially memorable for you. By this, we mean that it was especially interesting, engaging or motivating for you. It might be a particular lesson, unit of study, a choice of text or subject matter, a class activity or exercise, or a project or assignment. It doesn't have to be an occasion when you achieved well in a subject, but simply one in which you found yourself especially engaged, interested or motivated. When you tell this story, please give as many details as you can in describing what took place. Avoid judging or praising with words like "terrific" or "best"; rather, show what occurred. You do not need to give the name of the teacher, but if it is easier for you to refer directly to the teacher by name, it will be removed later on.

In all, 1,547 boys responded, ranging from twelve to nineteen years old. Of the total, 31 percent of the boys attended school in the United States, 26 percent in Australia, 14 percent in South Africa, 13 percent in New Zealand, 11 percent in Canada, and 5 percent in England. The study also asked boys a few additional questions in order to assess whether motivational and achievement levels, or socioeconomic and ethnic variety, might be observed to differentiate responses. In the boys' own estimations, 22 percent were "highly motivated," 52 percent were "well-motivated," 19 percent were "average," 6 percent "somewhat less motivated," and 1 percent "not motivated at all." Again in the boys' estimations, 24 percent were "top achievers," 49 percent "above average," 25 percent average, and 2 percent "below average." In socioeconomic terms, 15 percent placed their families' economic positions in the top group, 52 percent "above average," 27 percent "average," and 7 percent "below average." Ethnically, 62 percent of the boys said they were in the majority ethnic group in their countries, 22 percent said they were minorities, and 16 percent said they would be harder to categorize.

Once responses were collected from participating schools, we set about to analyze the data using an iterative coding process, with the initial set of themes deduced separately and the second representing a synthesis of the previous two (see Henwood & Pidgeon, 2003). Interrater differences led to clarifying conversations and were fruitful for refining coding categories; the data were reviewed again and again with an ever-sharper coding eye. In addition, our themes and interpretations were explored in ongoing independent readings by coalition staff, particularly by Brad Adams, executive director, representing a school insider's perspective. This member check process helped us to refine our conclusions (Maxwell, 1992; Creswell & Miller, 2000). Coalition staff helped us describe and identify common themes.

A draft report was then written and was read by a team of member school leaders for initial feedback (Reichert & Hawley, 2009). Based on this feedback and conversations with the research team, we submitted a final report that has been distributed to participating schools and made generally available to coalition members. This report, which includes teacher and student narratives more comprehensively and contains less analysis and synthesis, is the basis for our book.

REFERENCES

Berkowitz, M. W. (2002). The science of character education. In W. Damon (Ed.), *Bringing in a new era in character education* (pp. 43–63). Palo Alto, CA: Hoover Institution Press.

Coyle, D. (2009). *The talent code.* New York: Bantam Dell.

Creswell, J. W., & Miller, D. L. (2000). Determining validity in qualitative inquiry. *Theory into Practice*, *39*(3), 124–130.

Dewey, J. (1938). *Experience and education.* New York: Collier Books.

Gilligan, C. (2005). Foreword. In M. Raider-Roth, *Trusting what you know: The high stakes of classroom relationships.* San Francisco: Jossey-Bass.

Greene, M. (1973). *Teacher as stranger.* Belmont, CA: Wadsworth.

Groth, M. (2007). "Has anyone seen the boy?'': The fate of the boy in becoming a man. *Thymos: Journal of Boyhood Studies, 1*(1), 6–42.

Henwood, K., & Pidgeon, N. (2003). Grounded theory in psychological research. In P. M. Camic, J. E. Rhodes, & L. Yardley (Eds.), *Qualitative research in psychology: Expanding perspectives in methodology and design* (pp. 131–156). Washington, DC: American Psychological Association Press.

Kindlon, D., & Thompson, M. (1999). *Raising Cain: Protecting the emotional life of boys.* New York: Ballantine Books.

Kohn, A. (1986). *No contested: The case against competition.* New York: Houghton-Mifflin.

Kohn, A. (1993). *Punished by rewards.* New York: Houghton-Mifflin.

Lett, J. (2007). *Emic/etic distinctions.* Accessed at http://faculty.ircc.edu/faculty/jlett/Article%20on%20Emics%20and%20Etics.htm.

Manning, K. (1997). Authenticity in constructivist inquiry: Methodological considerations without prescription. *Qualitative Inquiry, 3*(1), 93–115.

Martin, A. J. (2003). Boys and motivation. *Australian Educational Researcher, 30*(3), 43–65.

Marx, J. (2004). *Season of life. A football star, a boy, a journey to manhood.* New York: Simon & Schuster.

Masten, A. S. (2001). Ordinary magic. *American Psychologist, 56*(3), 227–238.

Maxwell, J. A. (1992). Understanding and validity in quantitative research. *Harvard Educational Review, 62*(3), 279–299.

Mead, S. (2006). *The evidence suggests otherwise: The truth about boys and girls.* Washington, DC: Education Sector.

Merry, M. (2009). *Building a boy friendly school: The educational needs of boys and the implications of school culture.* Unpublished doctoral dissertation, Latrobe University.

Noddings, N. (2003). *Caring: A feminine approach to ethics and moral education* (2nd ed.). Berkeley: University of California Press.

Pianta, R. C. (1999). *Enhancing relationships between children and teachers.* Washington, DC: American Psychological Association.

Raider-Roth, M. (2005). *Trusting what you know: The high stakes of classroom relationships.* San Francisco: Jossey-Bass.

Raider-Roth, M., Albert, M., Bircann-Barkley, I., Gidseg, E., & Murray, T. (2008). Teaching boys: A relational puzzle. *Teachers' College Record, 110*(2), 443–481.

Reichert, M. C., & Hawley, R. (2009). *Teaching boys: A global study of effective practices.* Pawling, NY: International Coalition of Boys' Schools.

Rodgers, C. B., & Raider-Roth, M. (2006). Presence in teaching. *Teachers and Teaching: Theory and Practice, 12*(3), 265–287.

Slade, M. (2002). Listening to the boys: Issues and problems influencing school achievement and retention. *International Educational Journal, 1,* 201–229.

Winter, G. (2000). A comparative discussion of the notions of "validity" in qualitative and quantitative research. *Qualitative Report, 4*(3–4).

INDEX